Implementing DirectAccess with Windows Server 2016

Richard M. Hicks

■■■

Apress®

Implementing DirectAccess with Windows Server 2016

Richard M. Hicks
Rancho Santa Margarita
California, USA

ISBN-13 (pbk): 978-1-4842-2058-0   ISBN-13 (electronic): 978-1-4842-2059-7
DOI 10.1007/978-1-4842-2059-7

Library of Congress Control Number: 2016952413

Managing Director: Welmoed Spahr
Acquisitions Editor: Susan McDermott
Developmental Editor: Laura Berendson
Technical Reviewers: Jason Jones, Martin Solis
Editorial Board: Steve Anglin, Pramila Balen, Laura Berendson, Aaron Black, Louise Corrigan,
     Jonathan Gennick, Robert Hutchinson, Celestin Suresh John, Nikhil Karkal, James Markham,
     Susan McDermott, Matthew Moodie, Natalie Pao, Gwenan Spearing
Coordinating Editor: Rita Fernando
Copy Editor: April Rondeau
Compositor: SPi Global
Indexer: SPi Global
Cover image: Selected by Freepik

Distributed to the book trade worldwide by Springer Science+Business Media New York, 233 Spring Street, 6th Floor, New York, NY 10013. Phone 1-800-SPRINGER, fax (201) 348-4505, e-mail orders-ny@springer-sbm.com, or visit www.springer.com. Apress Media, LLC is a California LLC and the sole member (owner) is Springer Science + Business Media Finance Inc (SSBM Finance Inc). SSBM Finance Inc is a Delaware corporation.

For information on translations, please e-mail rights@apress.com, or visit www.apress.com.

Apress and friends of ED books may be purchased in bulk for academic, corporate, or promotional use. eBook versions and licenses are also available for most titles. For more information, reference our Special Bulk Sales–eBook Licensing web page at www.apress.com/bulk-sales.

Any source code or other supplementary materials referenced by the author in this text is available to readers at www.apress.com. For detailed information about how to locate your book's source code, go to www.apress.com/source-code/.

Printed on acid-free paper

To Anne, the love of my life and my best friend.

Contents at a Glance

Contents

About the Author

Richard M. Hicks (MCP, MCSE, MCTS, MCITP:EA, MCSA, MVP) is a network and information security expert specializing in Microsoft technologies. As a Microsoft Cloud and Datacenter/Enterprise Security MVP, he has traveled around the world speaking to network engineers, security administrators, and IT professionals about Microsoft networking and security. Richard has nearly 20 years of experience working in large-scale corporate computing environments and has designed and deployed perimeter defense and secure remote access solutions for some of the largest companies in the world. Richard is Founder and Principal Consultant of Richard M. Hicks Consulting and focuses on helping organizations both large and small implement DirectAccess, VPN, and Cloud networking solutions on Microsoft platforms. Richard is a contributing author for TechGenix (WindowSecurity.com, WindowsNetworking.com, CloudComputingAdmin.com) and the Petri IT Knowledgebase. He has also produced video training courses for Pluralsight. Richard is an avid fan of Major League Baseball and in particular the Los Angeles Angels (of Anaheim!). He also enjoys fish tacos, craft beer, and single malt Scotch whisky. He lives and works in beautiful, sunny Southern California. Keep up to date on all things DirectAccess by visiting his website at https://directaccess.richardhicks.com or follow him on Twitter @richardhicks.

About the Technical Reviewers

Martin J. Solis has worked at Microsoft for 21 years in various support teams and has been in the computer industry for over 30 years. As a PFE (Premier Field Engineer) at Microsoft, Martin supports large enterprise customers in the areas of DirectAccess, Active Directory, PKI, IPSec, ISA/TMG, and networking.

Jason Jones is a Principal Security Consultant for Microsoft Consulting Services (MCS) in the United Kingdom. He provides design, architectural, and technical consulting to Microsoft's customers and partners. His specialties include Microsoft Security, Identity and Access solutions with in-depth knowledge of Active Directory Certificate Services, DirectAccess, and Forefront edge security (TMG and UAG). Jason is a former Microsoft Most Valuable Professional (MVP).

Acknowledgments

On a technical note, this book would not have been possible without the contributions of the following individuals.

Jason Jones, my good friend and one of the technical reviewers of this book, has been an invaluable resource for me for DirectAccess. His deep technical expertise and broad deployment experience have been incredibly helpful for me over the years. We've had countless conversations and many late-night (for him!) email threads discussing the finer details of DirectAccess, and he's always made think more critically about the security aspects of the solution. Much of the content in this book is the direct or indirect result of my interactions with Jason. His contribution as technical reviewer has also served to make this a better book. I can't thank him enough for agreeing to work with me on this project. I hope we get the chance to work together again soon.

Ed Horley and Joe Davies each had a tremendous impact on the information in this book. Ed's book *Practical IPv6 for Windows Administrators* taught me a great deal about the intricacies of IPv6 in Windows, which is vital to the operation of DirectAccess. Ed has an immense working knowledge of and experience with the IPv6 protocol, and having the opportunity to work closely with Ed as one of the technical reviewers for his book was an invaluable learning experience. I consider Joe's book, *Understanding IPv6*, the bible for IPv6 in Windows. In addition, Joe's work on the *TCP/IP Protocols and Services* books for past releases of the Windows operating systems were foundational to my becoming closely involved with Windows networking and remote access. Thank you both for your continued commitment to IPv6 education and information sharing.

Martin Solis, another technical reviewer for this title, has been deeply influential on the outcome of this book. Martin is incredibly adept with DirectAccess troubleshooting, a topic that could fill an entire book of its own. His valuable insight and unique experience gained from implementing and supporting one of the largest DirectAccess deployments in the world has been enormously beneficial. Thank you so much for jumping into the middle of this project and agreeing to take on such a heavy workload, in spite of all your existing commitments. I am truly grateful for your efforts.

Michelle Lawson has had a profound influence on my technology writing. If any of this book is even remotely coherent, it is due in large part to her generosity and kindness in offering to review my work, often at a moment's notice. Without her efforts and mentoring, the outcome of this book might have been 300 pages of unintelligible drivel. Thank you for always being available to offer guidance and suggestions. They are always helpful and informative, and I appreciate it more than you know.

To my fellow MVPs, Shannon Fritz, Jordan Krause, and Benoit Sautiere, thanks for always engaging on the mailing list and making me consider new and different aspects of DirectAccess. To Benoit especially, your advocacy of DirectAccess and OTP, along with your documentation of OTP integration and troubleshooting, has been essential. And thanks also to Fredrik Johnsson, who has been exceedingly helpful with regard to all aspects of certificate authentication and Public Key Infrastructure (PKI).

Special thanks to current and former Microsoft product managers Scott Roberts, Bala Natarajan, Daniel Havey, and Mihai Peicu for always being open to engaging with me and answering my deep and sometimes unusual technical questions about DirectAccess.

On a personal note, there are some important people close to me without whose contributions this book would not have been possible.

To my mom and dad, thank you for all the years of support and unconditional love. I would not be where I am today without you.

To my mother-in-law, Judy Pearce, thank you for believing in me and investing in me nearly 20 years ago. You are single-handedly responsible for launching my career as an IT professional. I am deeply indebted to you, always.

To Anne, my amazing wife and best friend of more than 30 years, thank you for your unending love and support. I am nothing without you. There are no words to describe how truly blessed I am to have you in my life. If I am successful in the least, it is because of you.

And finally, to my Lord and Savior Jesus Christ, thank you for the amazing gift of life.

Introduction

In today's world, organizations that support telecommuting for their employees have a distinct competitive advantage in the marketplace. The available talent pool they have to draw on is not restricted to a limited radius around physical office locations. This enables them to hire the best people and ensure they are always productive regardless of their location.

The security and management of field-based assets have always been a challenge for IT administrators. Ensuring that remote devices remain updated and secure is difficult when corporate network access is sporadic.

DirectAccess, a remote access technology included as part of the Unified Remote Access role in Windows Server 2016, provides seamless and transparent always-on remote network connectivity for managed (domain-joined) Windows clients.

It provides ubiquitous connectivity and access to internal applications and data, and does so without requiring any user interaction. The solution allows remote workers to access internal resources in the same familiar way, regardless of their physical location, resulting in a superior remote access experience and increased productivity.

DirectAccess client computers have consistent remote network access, enabling them to update group policy and check in with systems-management servers more consistently than traditional client-based VPN allows. DirectAccess connections are also bidirectional, allowing IT administrators to proactively manage their field-based assets just as they do their on-premise systems. The end result is having fully managed and secure mobile computers.

DirectAccess is built using commonly deployed Windows platform technologies like Active Directory Domain Services (AD DS) and Group Policy, Active Directory Certificate Services (AD CS), and IPsec. DirectAccess also relies heavily on IPv6. While it is true that there are a lot of moving parts with DirectAccess, many of these technologies are likely to be familiar to Windows administrators. Technologies such as PKI and IPv6 will be required skills in the near future, so implementing DirectAccess is an excellent opportunity to get some exposure and practical deployment experience with these technologies.

This book is not written to be a comprehensive technical reference for DirectAccess. The technologies that support DirectAccess are already well documented, so the goal for this book is to create a clear, concise, and applicable installation and configuration guide to help you install, configure, troubleshoot, and support DirectAccess itself. It provides practical, real-world guidance for implementing DirectAccess in the most reliable and secure way possible. It also includes valuable tips and tricks that I've learned from deploying DirectAccess on a daily basis for the last five years.

I sincerely hope you find this book helpful and informative. Enjoy!

CHAPTER 1

■ ■ ■

DirectAccess Overview

The Unified Remote Access Role in Windows Server 2016 includes several remote access technologies. This book will focus on one of them—DirectAccess. For many years, Virtual Private Networking (VPN) has been the de facto standard for providing secure remote access, and is likely familiar to most system administrators today. VPN use in Windows networks has been around for quite some time, with roots dating back to Windows NT 4.0. By comparison, DirectAccess is a relative newcomer. It was first introduced with Windows Server 2008 R2, and has since undergone subtle but vitally important changes in architecture and infrastructure. DirectAccess is a unique and compelling way to provide secure remote access for Windows devices managed by the IT department. It provides a superior user experience when compared to traditional, client-based VPN, and it allows IT administrators to better manage their remote Windows systems.

DirectAccess

In 2007, Microsoft chairman and software visionary Bill Gates outlined his vision for something he called "anywhere access." Mr. Gates envisioned a world where data and information, applications, resources, and content would be available instantly and easily, no matter where in the world the user happened to be. DirectAccess is the realization of that dream for businesses. Many IT professionals mistakenly believe that DirectAccess is just another VPN solution. While there are some similarities between the two technologies, both in terms of the underlying technology and the functionality, DirectAccess brings some significant improvements over its predecessor.

Seamless and Transparent

DirectAccess is a paradigm shift in the way corporate IT provides secure remote access. Unlike traditional VPN, which is user initiated, DirectAccess works at the machine level to provide seamless and transparent, always-on secure remote corporate network connectivity any time the computer has an active Internet connection. Because it requires no user interaction,[1] it streamlines and simplifies the remote access experience for the end user.

Bi-directional

DirectAccess is also bi-directional, which is a key differentiator between it and VPN. The bi-directional nature of DirectAccess enables some interesting new use cases for secure remote access. For example, an administrator on the corporate network can initiate a remote desktop connection to a remotely connected DirectAccess client for the purposes of troubleshooting or providing assistance. Configuration and software can be deployed to DirectAccess clients using System Center Configuration Manager (SCCM), and vulnerability scans can be performed remotely.

---

[1]Unless strong user authentication is enabled

© Richard M. Hicks 2016

R. M. Hicks, *Implementing DirectAccess with Windows Server 2016*, DOI 10.1007/978-1-4842-2059-7_1

Not a Protocol

DirectAccess is not a protocol. It is a collection of Windows platform technologies that are assembled to provide secure remote access to on-premise data and applications for users who are located outside of the corporate network. DirectAccess relies on IPv6 for transport, IPsec for security, and Active Directory, Kerberos, and digital certificates for authentication. On the client side, DirectAccess leverages the Windows Firewall with Advanced Security (WFAS) and the Name Resolution Policy Table (NRPT).

IPv6

IPv6 is an integral part of the DirectAccess solution. In fact, DirectAccess communication takes place exclusively over IPv6. IPv6 was not commonly deployed, which was a significant challenge to the adoption of the DirectAccess technology. Early on, however, Microsoft introduced some new features to address this challenge, which included adding support for IPv6 transition technologies and translation components to enable DirectAccess clients to communicate with intranet hosts configured only with IPv4.

IPv6 Transition Technologies

Most commonly, the DirectAccess server and clients will be connected to the IPv4 public Internet. Since DirectAccess uses IPv6 exclusively for client-to-server communication, DirectAccess leverages IPv6 transition technologies to tunnel IPv6 packets over the IPv4 Internet. When the DirectAccess client is outside of the corporate network, it will choose one of three IPv6 transition technologies. They are:

- **6to4** - the client chooses 6to4 when it has a public IPv4 address assigned to its network interface. 6to4 tunnels IPv6 packets over IPv4 using IP protocol 41. 6to4 does not work when the DirectAccess server or client are located behind a network device performing Network Address Translation (NAT).

- **Teredo** - the client chooses Teredo when it has a private IPv4 address assigned to its network interface, or when 6to4 is not available for use. Teredo is designed to work when the client (but not the server) is behind a NAT device. Teredo tunnels IPv6 packets over IPv4 using UDP port 3544. To support Teredo, the DirectAccess server must have two *consecutive* public IPv4 addresses assigned to its external network interface. In addition, Teredo requires that ICMPv4 and ICMPv6 echo requests be allowed to all Intranet hosts.

- **IP-HTTPS** - the client chooses IP-HTTPS when it has a private IPv4 address assigned to its network interface and 6to4 or Teredo are not available. IP-HTTPS is supported when the DirectAccess client and/or the DirectAccess server is behind a NAT device. IP-HTTPS tunnels IPv6 packets over IPv4 using HTTP with SSL/TLS over TCP port 443. When supporting Windows 7 clients, performance and scalability can suffer because IPsec-encrypted traffic is encrypted again with SSL/TLS. This double encryption adds significant protocol overhead and places high demands on the CPU. Microsoft introduced support for null encryption beginning with Windows 8, which eliminates the double encryption and provides comparable performance to that of 6to4 and Teredo.

Outbound Management

The Intrasite Automatic Tunnel Addressing Protocol (ISATAP) is an IPv6 transition technology that is used for initiating outbound communication from the internal network to connected DirectAccess clients. It is recommended that if outbound management to DirectAccess clients is required then native IPv6 be deployed. Deploying IPv6 is not trivial though, so ISATAP can provide a simple and effective alternative to a full IPv6 deployment. The use of ISATAP for outbound management is only supported for single-server DirectAccess deployments.

Network Topology and IPv6 Transition Technologies

The DirectAccess server must have two network interfaces with a public IPv4 address assigned to the external network adapter to support the 6to4 protocol. Two *consecutive* public IPv4 addresses are required to support Teredo. If the DirectAccess server is configured with private IPv4 addresses in a perimeter or DMZ deployment with one or two network adapters, only the IP-HTTPS protocol is supported.

IPv6 Translation Components

IPv6 transition technologies allow the DirectAccess client to communicate with the DirectAccess server over the public IPv4 Internet. IPv6 *translation* components enable the client (which uses IPv6 exclusively) to communicate with intranet hosts that are only configured with IPv4. The following IPv6 translation technologies are automatically installed when DirectAccess is configured.

- **DNS64** - The DNS64 service (pronounced "DNS six-to-four") runs on the DirectAccess server that is functioning as a DNS proxy and translator for DirectAccess clients. DirectAccess clients send all name-resolution requests for the internal corporate namespace to this service. The DNS64 service receives DNS AAAA (quad-a) name-resolution requests from DirectAccess clients for internal hostnames. The DNS64 service makes another request to internal corporate DNS servers for the same name, usually receiving an A resources record back with an IPv4 address. It then converts this IPv4 address into an IPv6 address for the DirectAccess client to use.

- **NAT64** - The NAT64 service (pronounced "NAT six-to-four") runs on the DirectAccess server that is functioning as an IPv6-to-IPv4 translator for DirectAccess clients. NAT64 receives inbound IPv6 packets from DirectAccess clients, translates them to IPv4, and forwards them to the IPv4 address on the internal network.

While it is not necessary to understand IPv6 to implement DirectAccess, a working knowledge of IPv6 will most certainly be required to perform any troubleshooting should the need arise.

■ **Note**   I realize that the reliance on IPv6 for DirectAccess can strike fear in the heart of an IT administrator. Don't let that prevent you from taking advantage of this amazing technology! There was a time when we all had to learn IPv4, and so it is with IPv6. The world is moving to IPv6, so having this important skill in your tool belt will only help in the future. DirectAccess provides a practical application for the use of IPv6 and is an excellent way to begin developing a working knowledge of this important protocol. To learn more about IPv6, I encourage you to read Ed Horley's excellent book *Practical IPv6 for Windows Administrators* (Apress, 2013; ISBN: 978-1-4302-6370-8).

Evolution of DirectAccess

DirectAccess was first introduced as a feature of the Microsoft Windows network operating system in Windows Server 2008 R2. The original release required that IPv6 be deployed on the corporate intranet, which was a significant barrier to adoption. The deployment of IPv6 in general has been slow, and the adoption of IPv6 on private corporate networks is still in its infancy.

Implementing IPv6 is non-trivial, and takes a substantial investment of time and effort to effectively deploy it. Many organizations were unwilling to deploy IPv6 just to support DirectAccess. As such, DirectAccess in Windows Server 2008 R2 was not widely deployed.

Forefront Unified Access Gateway

Microsoft introduced Forefront Unified Access Gateway (UAG) 2010 in December of 2009. Forefront UAG was a remote access gateway that included support for SSL VPN, traditional client-based VPN, web application publishing, and much more. It also included new technologies designed to ease the transition to DirectAccess. Forefront UAG added the DNS64 and NAT64 services that translate IPv6 communications from DirectAccess clients to IPv4. Together, these two technologies eliminated the need to deploy IPv6 on the corporate network just to support DirectAccess, thus improving adoption rates.

Forefront UAG Challenges

While Forefront UAG 2010 eased some of the challenges of deploying DirectAccess, it also introduced its own unique set of challenges. Forefront UAG was itself difficult to implement and support, as it had steep hardware requirements, limited local redundancy, and no native support for geographic redundancy. In addition, Forefront UAG had its own licensing requirements, making the solution more expensive. Furthermore, it had only one supported network deployment model—edge facing. The Forefront UAG 2010 server had to be deployed with public IPv4 addresses to enable the DirectAccess role. The prospect of placing a domain-joined Windows server directly on the public Internet didn't sit well with many, even though Forefront UAG 2010 was capably protected by the Forefront Threat Management Gateway (TMG) enterprise-class firewall that was included.

Windows Server 2012

To address the shortcomings and limitations associated with both Windows Server 2008 R2 and Forefront UAG 2010 DirectAccess, Microsoft integrated the DNS64 and NAT64 IPv6 translation technologies into the core operating system in Windows Server 2012 enabling the deployment of DirectAccess without the need to deploy additional software. In addition, Microsoft added much-needed scalability and performance improvements, including native support for load balancing (integrated and external), geographic redundancy (multisite), and improvements to key IPv6 transition technologies. More important, Microsoft introduced flexible network placement with support for deploying the DirectAccess server in a perimeter or DMZ network behind a NAT device, and even support for a single Network Interface Card (NIC) deployment. Additionally, Microsoft added support for multiple domains and removed the requirement to deploy a Public Key Infrastructure (PKI) in some scenarios.

Windows Server 2012 R2

With the introduction of Windows Server 2012 R2, Microsoft did not make any significant changes to the core functionality of DirectAccess. However, they did make many subtle enhancements aimed toward improving security, reliability, and performance. This release mostly included updates that were available as hotfixes in Windows Server 2012 to address a variety of issues, including problems with one-time password (OTP) authentication, load-balancing configuration, and more.

Windows Server 2016

Once again, DirectAccess in Windows Server 2016 remains essentially unchanged from the version in Windows Server 2012 R2. The only significant change is the removal of support for Microsoft Windows Network Access Protection (NAP) integration, as this feature was formally deprecated in Windows Server 2012 R2 and has been removed with Windows 10 and Windows Server 2016.

There are no new features or functionality in this latest release. From a technology perspective, DirectAccess is mature, and since the release of the Windows 10 client operating system, it is now being deployed rapidly. Organizations large and small have adopted the technology, and those early adopters who deployed DirectAccess with Windows Server 2008 R2 and Forefront UAG 2010 are now migrating to DirectAccess with Windows Server 2016.

How DirectAccess Works

When a client provisioned for DirectAccess is outside of the corporate network, it will automatically attempt to establish a secure remote connection to the DirectAccess server over the Internet. The DirectAccess connection takes place at the machine level and requires no user interaction.[2] Most commonly, the DirectAccess client will be on the IPv4 Internet, so an IPv6 transition technology will be selected and a tunnel will be established with the DirectAccess server. Inside the IPv6 transition tunnel, authenticated and encrypted IPsec tunnels are established between the client and the server. It is over these tunnels that communication to resources on the corporate network takes place. The DirectAccess IPsec tunnels are defined as Connection Security Rules (CSR) in the Windows Firewall with Advanced Security on both the DirectAccess client and the server.

DirectAccess Supported Clients

DirectAccess is designed specifically for managed (domain-joined) Windows clients. It is primarily aimed at large enterprise organizations, as it requires the Enterprise edition of the Windows desktop client operating system. However, small and mid-sized organizations can still take advantage of DirectAccess as long as they meet the implementation requirements. The following is a list of supported Windows desktop client operating systems:

- Windows 10 Enterprise
- Windows 10 Education
- Windows 8.x Enterprise
- Windows 7 Enterprise
- Windows 7 Ultimate

Additionally, the following Windows Server operating systems are also supported as DirectAccess clients:

- Windows Server 2016
- Windows Server 2012 R2
- Windows Server 2012
- Windows Server 2008 R2

Any non-Enterprise editions (other than Windows 10 Education and Windows 7 Ultimate) or any other previous Windows desktop client or server operating systems (for example, Windows 10 Professional, Windows 7 Home Edition, or Windows Server 2008) are not supported.

---

[2]Unless strong user authentication is enabled

DirectAccess Security

DirectAccess IPsec tunnels use Authenticated IP (AuthIP[3]) and are authenticated using a combination of digital certificates, NTLM, and Kerberos. Both the computer and the user are authenticated separately. DirectAccess provides a high level of assurance that remotely connected devices and users are indeed legitimate.

In a typical configuration, two distinct IPsec tunnels are established—an infrastructure tunnel and an intranet tunnel.

- **Infrastructure tunnel** - Provides secure remote network access to limited internal resources. Specifically, only infrastructure services such as domain controllers and systems-management servers are available over this first tunnel. The infrastructure tunnel requires two forms of authentication. First, the client machine is authenticated using a computer certificate issued by the corporate PKI. Second, the client machine's computer account is authenticated against Active Directory using NTLM. If the client successfully passes both authentication steps, the infrastructure tunnel is established and the client can access infrastructure resources defined by the remote access policy. This tunnel uses 192-bit AES encryption and SHA-1 for integrity.

- **Intranet tunnel** - Provides the end user with full access to the corporate network. It is initiated when the user logs on to the DirectAccess client. The intranet tunnel also requires two forms of authentication. First, the computer is authenticated once again using the computer certificate issued by the corporate PKI. Second, the user account is authenticated against Active Directory using Kerberos. If the client successfully passes both authentication steps, the intranet IPsec tunnel is established. Like the infrastructure tunnel, this IPsec tunnel uses 192-bit AES encryption and SHA-1 for integrity.

The supporting infrastructure requirements make DirectAccess inherently more resistant to unauthorized access. For attackers to compromise a DirectAccess connection, they would require a computer that is a member of the organization's Active Directory domain, and the computer account would need to belong to the defined DirectAccess security group. In addition, a computer certificate issued by the company's internal PKI is required. The attacker would also need valid user credentials to access corporate resources.

An unauthorized user cannot gain full access to internal resources from just any machine. For an attacker to successfully spoof both an AD computer account and a computer certificate is extremely difficult. If successful, the attacker has likely already compromised the target organization.

■ **Note**   The default configuration of the IP-HTTPS IPv6 transition technology in DirectAccess may allow an unauthorized user to obtain an IPv6 address on the DirectAccess client network. Once this happens, the attacker can launch IPv6-related Denial-of-Service (DoS) attacks and potentially perform network reconnaissance. It is possible to mitigate these challenges using a custom configuration. More details can be found here: `https://directaccess.richardhicks.com/2016/05/10/directaccess-ip-https-preauthentication-using-citrix-netscaler/`.

---

[3]`https://technet.microsoft.com/en-us/magazine/2007.10.cableguy.aspx`

Why DirectAccess?

DirectAccess was designed to meet two very common and specific needs of many organizations. The first was to provide an easy-to-use, secure remote access solution. The second was to provide a better way to manage field-based Windows devices.

The DirectAccess user experience is incredibly simple. Compared to VPN, it is infinitely easier to use. From the user's perspective, resources on the corporate network are accessed in the same way, regardless of where they themselves are located. Mapped drives and shortcuts to files and applications work the same outside of the network as they do inside.

DirectAccess clients are always managed too. Because DirectAccess clients are securely connected to the corporate network whenever they have an active Internet connection, IT administrators can more effectively manage and monitor their remote Windows devices. DirectAccess clients update group policy on a regular basis and report to systems management servers much more frequently. The client's configuration and security posture are maintained, and compliance can be verified with existing management platforms.

DirectAccess connectivity is bi-directional, enabling administrators who are on-premise to initiate outbound communication to remote-connected clients. This enables help desk administrators to use Remote Desktop or Remote Assistance to provide assistance for users. In addition, security auditors can perform vulnerability scans on clients, and any software deployment mechanisms that use push technology will also continue to work when Windows devices are out of the office.

DirectAccess vs. VPN

VPN connections are user initiated and therefore optional. It is up to the user to decide when they want to connect to the corporate network. By comparison, DirectAccess is seamless and transparent in nature, is completely automatic, and requires no user interaction to establish a connection.

Many VPN protocols aren't firewall friendly, which can impede the successful establishment of a VPN connection. DirectAccess can establish its secure remote connection using HTTPS, which is commonly allowed through most firewalls.

VPNs often require investments in proprietary hardware and per-user licensing. DirectAccess can be deployed on existing virtual infrastructure and does not require additional user licensing.

Proprietary software is commonly required to leverage all of the features provided by VPN solutions. This software must be deployed and managed by IT administrators. DirectAccess requires no additional third-party software to be installed. All settings for DirectAccess are managed through Group Policy Objects (GPOs) in Active Directory.

A VPN connection can be established from any client machine with the VPN client software installed. This makes integration with a multifactor authentication solution an essential requirement, which makes the solution more complex and difficult to support. A DirectAccess connection can only be established from a client computer that has been provisioned for DirectAccess by IT, reducing the need to employ strong authentication for DirectAccess connections.

DirectAccess Limitations and Drawbacks

As capable as DirectAccess is, it is not a comprehensive remote access solution. It is designed for managed (domain-joined) Windows clients *only*. DirectAccess does not work with non-Enterprise versions of Windows (with the exception of Windows 10 Education and Windows 7 Ultimate), Windows RT, or Windows Phone mobile operating systems. It also does not work with any non-Microsoft operating systems.

As DirectAccess relies exclusively on IPv6 for client-to-server communication, there are some instances in which certain applications may not be compatible with DirectAccess. For example, applications that use protocols that have IPv4 addresses embedded in them (such as SIP and FTP) or applications that make calls directly to IPv4 addresses will not work with DirectAccess.

Choosing Between DirectAccess and VPN

You might be asking yourself, "Should I implement DirectAccess or VPN?" Actually, you can implement both. After all, DirectAccess and VPN aren't mutually exclusive. They are, in fact, quite complementary. DirectAccess can be used to provide secure remote access and enhanced management for Windows laptops managed by IT, while VPN can be deployed for non-managed devices. While you may not be able to entirely eliminate VPN with DirectAccess, it will certainly allow you to decrease the number of VPN licenses required and reduce your investment in proprietary hardware, management tools, and dedicated administrators, all of which translates into reduced capital investment and operational costs.

Summary

DirectAccess is a paradigm shift in the way secure remote access is provided for computers managed by the IT department. Unlike traditional client-based VPN, DirectAccess is seamless and transparent, always on, and bi-directional. It leverages existing, commonly deployed Windows platform technologies that are mature and well understood. DirectAccess essentially works by establishing secure, authenticated IPsec tunnels between the DirectAccess client and DirectAccess server. DirectAccess works with all Enterprise editions of Windows 7, 8, and 10, in addition to a few other selected SKUs. It provides a secure remote corporate network connection with a high level of assurance for provisioned clients. DirectAccess can be used to address the unique challenges of IT administrators tasked with managing field-based assets. DirectAccess isn't a comprehensive remote access technology, and may not completely eliminate the need for VPN, but it has the potential to significantly reduce an organization's dependence on it. Ultimately, the choice between DirectAccess and VPN isn't an either/or one. In fact, the two technologies are complementary and serve to address the unique and specific remote access needs of different users and device types.

CHAPTER 2

■ ■ ■

Plan for DirectAccess

Planning is by far the most important aspect of a DirectAccess deployment project. DirectAccess can be deployed in many different configurations to meet a variety of implementation requirements. Many design decisions and deployment options have implications for security, scalability, performance, client support, and general supportability. There are scenarios in which features are mutually exclusive. Some implementation models may limit future deployment flexibility or prevent additional security features from being enabled. A clear understanding of the implementation goals will help the architect design a solution that is reliable, secure, flexible, and supportable.

DirectAccess Server

DirectAccess can be installed and configured on Windows Server 2016 Datacenter, Standard, and Essentials SKUs. DirectAccess should be configured on a server dedicated to this workload. It should not be collocated with other workloads, such as Active Directory Domain Services (AD DS), Active Directory Certificate Services (AD CS), SQL, Exchange, and so forth. Although remote access roles such as VPN and Web Application Proxy (WAP) can be collocated with DirectAccess in some scenarios,[1] implementation best practices dictate that they be installed on separate servers. Crucially, collocating VPN or WAP on the DirectAccess server will also result in the loss of support for IP-HTTPS null encryption, which reduces performance and scalability for Windows 8.x and Windows 10 clients.

System Requirements

Windows Server 2016 and DirectAccess should be installed on a dedicated physical server for optimum performance. However, Windows Server 2016 and DirectAccess can be installed on a virtual machine hosted on any Microsoft Server Virtualization Validation Program (SVVP) validated hypervisor, including Microsoft Hyper-V, VMware, and many others. It is recommended that the server (physical or virtual) be provisioned with a minimum of four processor cores, 8GB of RAM, and 60GB of hard disk space.

Domain Membership

The DirectAccess server must be joined to an Active Directory Domain Services (AD DS) domain.[2] The DirectAccess server receives configuration settings from Active Directory group policies. In addition, IPsec tunnels used by DirectAccess are authenticated via Active Directory.

---

[1]The Web Application Proxy (WAP) is only supported on the DirectAccess server in single-server deployments. Additional information can be found here: https://technet.microsoft.com/en-us/library/dn451298.aspx
[2]Azure Active Directory (AAD) is not supported for use with DirectAccess.

© Richard M. Hicks 2016
R. M. Hicks, *Implementing DirectAccess with Windows Server 2016*, DOI 10.1007/978-1-4842-2059-7_2

The DirectAccess server can be joined to any domain in the forest. There is no requirement for the DirectAccess server to be joined to the same domain as the DirectAccess clients. If DirectAccess servers or clients are members of different forests, there must exist a full two-way transitive trust between the forests.

Windows Firewall

The Windows Firewall with Advanced Security (WFAS) is a critical component for DirectAccess. Fundamentally, DirectAccess IPsec tunnels are defined as Connection Security Rules (CSRs) in the Windows Firewall. Therefore, proper DirectAccess operation requires the Windows Firewall to be enabled for all profiles. The Windows Firewall must not be disabled on the DirectAccess server.

Third-party firewalls can be installed on the DirectAccess server, but they are not recommended. Many third-party firewalls interfere with DirectAccess operation. If a third-party firewall is required on the DirectAccess server, the Windows Firewall must remain enabled. Also, it is a good idea to consult the third-party vendor for specific configuration guidance for DirectAccess.[3]

IPv6

Communication between the DirectAccess client and server takes place exclusively over IPv6. IPv6 transition technologies included with DirectAccess eliminate the need to place the DirectAccess server on the IPv6 Internet or to deploy IPv6 on the corporate LAN.

Occasionally IPv6 is disabled via the Windows registry.[4] Although IPv6 does not have to be explicitly configured and deployed, it must not be proactively disabled in the registry on DirectAccess servers and clients. Doing so will break DirectAccess functionality.

Redundancy

Eliminating critical single points of failure in the DirectAccess architecture is essential to ensuring reliable connectivity. High availability can be configured with DirectAccess, both locally and geographically. The following topics describe load-balancing requirements and redundancy considerations.

Load Balancing

DirectAccess supports two types of local load balancing: integrated Windows Network Load Balancing (NLB) and external load balancers (ELB). For optimum performance, a physical external load balancing appliance is preferred. For small to mid-size deployments, a virtual external load balancer or NLB can be implemented.

Virtual IP Addressing

A virtual IP address (VIP) is assigned to the DirectAccess cluster when load balancing is enabled. VIP addressing requirements differ depending on the type of load balancer used. The following describes the VIP requirements for NLB and ELB:

- NLB
  - Each DirectAccess cluster requires a VIP.

---

[3]https://technet.microsoft.com/en-us/library/ee382257(v=ws.10).aspx
[4]Disabling IPv6 via the registry will prevent DirectAccess from working. More information about enabling and disabling IPv6 in Windows can be found here: https://support.microsoft.com/en-us/kb/929852

- The VIP must be on the same IP subnet as the dedicated IP addresses of the DirectAccess servers.

- DirectAccess servers with two Network Interface Cards (NICs) must be configured with a VIP for each interface.

- The dedicated IP address of the first cluster member becomes the VIP. A new dedicated IP address must be assigned to the DirectAccess server.

- If consecutive dedicated IP address assignments for DirectAccess servers are desired, plan to assign the IP address for the VIP to the first DirectAccess server during initial configuration.

- ELB

  - The VIP does not have to be on the same IP subnet as the DirectAccess servers.

  - The dedicated IP address of the first cluster member becomes the VIP. A new dedicated IP address must be assigned to the DirectAccess server.

  - If consecutive dedicated IP address assignments for DirectAccess servers are desired, plan to assign the IP address for the VIP to the first DirectAccess server during initial configuration.

■ **Note**   When an external load balancer is configured, it is recommended that the 6to4 and Teredo IPv6 transition technologies be disabled for DirectAccess clients and the load balancer be configured for IP-HTTPS exclusively.

Geographic Redundancy

Only Windows 8.x and later clients provide full support for geographic redundancy with automatic site selection and transparent failover. Windows 7 clients are supported in multisite deployments, but must be assigned to a single entry point. They always connect to their assigned entry point regardless of physical location and do not automatically fail over. To further enhance geographic redundancy for Windows 8.x and later clients, a Global Server Load Balancing (GSLB) solution can be used.

Network Topology

DirectAccess supports flexible network configuration and can be deployed in one of three topologies: Edge facing, Perimeter/DMZ, or LAN.

Edge Facing

The DirectAccess server must be configured with two Network Interface Cards (NICs). In addition, the following requirements must be met:

- External NIC

  - Requires at least one public IPv4 address

  - Two consecutive public IPv4 addresses are required for Teredo support

- Internal NIC

    - Requires one private IPv4 address

    - Can be located in a perimeter/DMZ network or on the LAN

    - If configured in perimeter/DMZ, it is recommended that all protocols/ports from the DirectAccess server(s) to the LAN be allowed

    - Static routes must be configured for all remote internal IP subnets

Perimeter/DMZ

The DirectAccess server can be configured with one or two NICs. In addition, the following requirements must be met:

- External NIC (behind transparent firewall)

    - Requires at least one public IPv4 address

    - Teredo support requires two consecutive public IPv4 addresses

- External NIC (behind edge firewall performing Network Address Translation [NAT])

    - Requires one private IPv4 address

- Internal NIC

    - Can be located in a perimeter/DMZ network or on the LAN

    - If configured in perimeter/DMZ, all protocols/ports from the DirectAccess server(s) to the LAN should be allowed

    - Static routes must be configured for all remote internal IP subnets

- Single NIC

    - Requires one private IPv4 address

    - All protocols/ports from the DirectAccess server(s) to the LAN should be allowed

LAN

The DirectAccess server only requires a single NIC configured with one private IPv4 address.

Edge Firewall Configuration

The topics covered in the following sections describe the firewall requirements for deployment topologies.

Edge Facing

Edge firewall rules are not applicable if the DirectAccess server is connected directly to the IPv4 public Internet. If the DirectAccess server is located behind a transparent (layer 2) firewall, it should be configured to allow the following protocols and ports inbound and outbound:

- IP protocol 41

- UDP port 3544

- TCP port 443

If the DirectAccess server is configured with a globally routable IPv6 address, it should be configured to allow the following protocols and ports inbound and outbound as well:

- IP protocol 41

- UDP port 500

Perimeter/DMZ

If the perimeter/DMZ network is publicly routable, the edge firewall should be configured to allow the following protocols and ports inbound and outbound:

- IP protocol 41

- UDP port 3544

- TCP port 443

If the DirectAccess server is configured with a globally routable IPv6 address, it should be configured to allow the following protocols and ports inbound and outbound as well:

- IP protocol 41

- UDP port 500

Perimeter/DMZ (NAT)

If the perimeter/DMZ network is located behind an edge firewall performing NAT, the edge firewall should be configured to allow the following protocols and ports inbound and outbound:

- TCP port 443

- NAT rule translating traffic from the public IPv4 address to the IPv4 address assigned to the external interface of the DirectAccess server

LAN

If the DirectAccess server is located on the LAN, the edge firewall should be configured to allow the following protocols and ports inbound and outbound:

- TCP port 443

- NAT rule translating traffic from the public IPv4 address to the DirectAccess server

Network Topology Considerations

Choosing which network topology to deploy DirectAccess with is based primarily on the existing network infrastructure. However, there are important security considerations to be made. An edge-facing deployment provides the greatest flexibility and widest IPv6 transition technology support. However, unless the DirectAccess server is protected with another firewall, this introduces some potential risk. The DirectAccess server must be joined to the domain, and having a domain-joined Windows server connected directly to an untrusted network (the public Internet) presents some risks. Here, the DirectAccess server is protected only with the Windows

Firewall. The Windows Firewall is a very capable host-based firewall, but it provides only a single layer of defense. Security best practices dictate that security should be performed in layers, making the deployment of the DirectAccess server behind an edge firewall an inherently more secure configuration.

Placing the DirectAccess server behind an edge firewall in transparent mode, or placing it in a publicly routable perimeter/DMZ network, is the preferred network topology. However, it is most common that perimeter/DMZ networks are not routable and use private, RFC1918[5] IPv4-based addressing. In these scenarios, the edge firewall also performs NAT. IP-HTTPS is the only IPv6 transition technology supported in this scenario. When supporting Windows 7 clients, scalability and performance are sacrificed at the expense of additional security. Windows 8.x and Windows 10 clients do not suffer from this limitation, as they support null encryption for IP-HTTPS.

DirectAccess Clients

DirectAccess clients must be joined to a domain. Ideally, they should be joined to the same domain as the DirectAccess server, but they can be joined to any domain in any forest that has a full two-way trust with the domain where the DirectAccess server(s) are joined.

Supported Clients

DirectAccess clients must be provisioned using one of the following Windows desktop client operating systems SKUs:

- Windows 10 Enterprise Edition

- Windows 10 Education Edition

- Windows 8.x Enterprise Edition

- Windows 7 Enterprise Edition

- Windows 7 Ultimate Edition

Additionally, the following Windows Server operating systems are also supported as DirectAccess clients:

- Windows Server 2016

- Windows Server 2012 R2

- Windows Server 2012

- Windows Server 2008 R2

Windows Firewall

The Windows Firewall must be enabled for the Public and Private profiles. Third-party firewalls are supported, but the Windows Firewall must still be enabled. In addition, third-party firewalls must not interfere with DirectAccess operation. Consult with the vendor for guidance on proper configuration for DirectAccess.

IPv6

IPv6 must be enabled on all DirectAccess clients. The IP-HTTPS IPv6 transition technology must also be enabled. Other IPv6 transition technologies (6to4, Teredo, and ISATAP) can be enabled or disabled per individual deployment requirements.

---

[5]`https://tools.ietf.org/html/rfc1918`

Connectivity Validation

The Network Connectivity Assistant (NCA), included in the Windows 8.x and Windows 10 client operating systems, validates remote corporate network connectivity via the DirectAccess connection. Windows 7 clients can be configured with the optional DirectAccess Connectivity Assistant (DCA) v2.0, which provides similar functionality to the NCA. DCA 2.0 deployment can be automated with settings managed through Group Policy. DCA 2.0 must be installed on Windows 7 clients when the deployment is configured to use One-Time Password (OTP) authentication.

Active Directory

The topics in the following sections describe Active Directory requirements and configuration for DirectAccess.

Forest and Domain Functional Levels

Any supported forest or domain functional level is acceptable as long as DFS-R is used for the distribution of Group Policy objects (SYSVOL replication). If SYSVOL replication uses the File Replication Service (FRS), DirectAccess is not supported.[6]

Read-Only Domain Controllers (RODC)

RODCs are not supported. DirectAccess servers must have access to a writeable domain controller.[7]

Administrative Rights

Deployments are most functional when the DirectAccess administrator is a member of the Domain Admins security group in Active Directory. If not feasible, then the minimum requirement is to grant the DirectAccess administrator full access to DirectAccess Group Policy Objects (GPOs). The DirectAccess administrator must have local administrator rights on any DirectAccess server(s).

Security Groups

DirectAccess requires at least one Active Directory security group. To support Windows 7 clients in a multisite deployment, each entry point in the organization requires an additional security group.

Group Policy Objects

GPOs are created in Active Directory during initial DirectAccess configuration. If the DirectAccess administrator is not a member of the Domain Admins group or does not have permission to create GPOs, GPOs must be preconfigured with full control permissions delegated to the DirectAccess administrator. For single-domain, single-site DirectAccess deployments, two GPOs will be required—one for DirectAccess Server Settings and another for DirectAccess Client Settings. For multisite deployments where Windows 7 support is required, an additional GPO per entry point for Windows 7 DirectAccess clients will be required. Multidomain deployments will require additional GPOs.

---

[6]https://technet.microsoft.com/en-us/library/dn464274.aspx#bkmk_frs
[7]https://technet.microsoft.com/en-us/library/dn464274.aspx#bkmk_rodc

Additional GPOs

Additional GPOs may be required to deploy the Windows 7 DirectAccess Connectivity Assistant (DCA), optional client configuration settings, optimizations, and automated client provisioning.

Certificates

The DirectAccess server requires two different types of certificates. A computer (machine) certificate is required for IPsec authentication (in some scenarios), and an SSL certificate is required for the IP-HTTPS IPv6 transition technology. The following topics describe certificate requirements and configuration for DirectAccess.

Computer Certificates

While computer certificate authentication is optional for some DirectAccess deployment scenarios, enabling any of the following features will require computer certificate authentication for DirectAccess clients:

- Windows 7 client support
- Load balancing (integrated or external)
- Multisite deployment
- Strong user authentication (OTP, smart card)
- Force tunneling

Certification Authority

Computer certificate authentication should be enabled for all implementations so as to provide the best security and greatest configuration flexibility. Computer certificates must be issued to the DirectAccess server(s) and each DirectAccess client by an internal private certificate authority (CA). The DirectAccess server(s) and clients must trust the internal CA. For best results, a Microsoft Enterprise CA is recommended.

Certificate Requirements

Computer certificates issued to the DirectAccess server and clients must include a subject name that matches the hostname of the computer they are being issued to. The certificate must also include the Client Authentication (1.3.6.1.5.5.7.3.2) Enhanced Key Usage (EKU) Object Identifier (OID).

SSL Certificates

The IP-HTTPS IPv6 transition technology requires an SSL certificate for authentication and encryption. Best practice is to obtain the SSL certificate from a publicly trusted third-party CA. However, an SSL certificate can be issued from the internal PKI. If Windows 7 clients are supported, the Certificate Revocation List (CRL) must be externally accessible.

For multisite deployments, a wildcard certificate may be used. If a wildcard certificate is not feasible, a unique certificate for each entry point is required. Multi-SAN certificates are not supported.[8]

---

[8]https://directaccess.richardhicks.com/2016/03/28/directaccess-and-multi-san-ssl-certificates-for-ip-https/

Network Location Server

The Network Location Server (NLS) is a critical infrastructure component in a DirectAccess deployment that allows clients to determine whether they are inside or outside of the corporate network. The following topics describe the requirements for the NLS.

Web Server

Any web server can be used for the NLS, including IIS, Apache, Nginx, and others. An Application Delivery Controller (ADC) can also be configured to serve as the NLS. Ideally, the server should be dedicated to the NLS role and should be made highly available. For large deployments where the internal network spans many physical locations and geographies, additional steps should be taken to ensure NLS availability in all locations.[9] Existing web application servers like Exchange OWA, SharePoint, and so on should not be used as the NLS.

SSL Certificate

The NLS requires an SSL certificate issued by a CA trusted by DirectAccess clients and servers. It is not necessary to use a public SSL certificate on the NLS; the certificate can be issued by the internal private PKI. The certificate requires a subject name that matches the NLS fully-qualified domain name (FQDN) defined in the DirectAccess configuration (for example, nls.corp.example.com). In addition, the certificate must also include the Server Authentication (1.3.6.1.5.5.7.3.1) Enhanced Key Usage (EKU) Object Identifier (OID), and the CRL must be available. Also, the NLS must be configured to allow inbound ICMPv4 echo requests from the DirectAccess server(s).

DNS

The following topics describe Domain Name System (DNS) requirements and configuration for DirectAccess.

Internal

Entries in DNS are made during the initial configuration of DirectAccess.[10] The DirectAccess administrator must have the ability to create new DNS entries. If that is not possible, the following DNS entries must be preconfigured by a DNS administrator.

Name	Record Type	Data
DirectAccess-CorpConnectivityHost	A	127.0.0.1
DirectAccess-CorpConnectivityHost	AAAA	<Client IPv6 Prefix>:0:0:7f00:1
DirectAccess-WebProbeHost	A	<IPv4 Address of DirectAccess Server Internal Network Interface>

---

[9]More information about NLS considerations for large enterprises read http://directaccess.richardhicks.com/2015/04/06/directaccess-nls-deployment-considerations-for-large-enterprises/.
[10]https://directaccess.richardhicks.com/2015/07/06/directaccess-dns-records-explained/

External

A DNS entry must be configured that resolves the DirectAccess public hostname to the external public IPv4 address of the DirectAccess server (or edge firewall, in a perimeter/DMZ deployment). For multisite deployments, each entry point will require a unique public hostname and corresponding DNS entry. An additional DNS entry must be configured when GSLB is implemented.

Strong User Authentication

The enforcement of strong user authentication is optional, but does have some drawbacks. OTP solutions negatively impact the seamless and transparent nature of DirectAccess, resulting in a degraded end-user experience. However, DirectAccess supports integration with a variety of multifactor authentication solutions, including RSA SecurID, OTP, and physical or virtual smart cards.

Certificate Server

To enforce strong user authentication, a Microsoft Enterprise CA must be deployed to issue certificates. This can be the same CA used for DirectAccess computer authentication and IPsec encryption.

RSA SecurID

RSA SecurID OTP authentication using physical or soft tokens is supported.

One-Time Passwords (OTP)

Most RADIUS-based OTP solutions can be integrated with DirectAccess. However, OTP solutions that use RADIUS challenge/response or employ CAPTCHA are not supported. In addition, RADIUS user accounts that are in new PIN or next token modes are not supported.

Smart Cards

Both physical and virtual smart cards are supported with DirectAccess.

Security Groups

Users that require exemption from strong user authentication must be part of an Active Directory security group configured for the purpose.

User Accounts

DirectAccess uses a predefined user account to monitor RADIUS server availability. A corresponding and matching user account must be created on the RADIUS server to eliminate failed authentication attempts.

Force Tunneling

Strong user authentication using RADIUS OTP cannot be configured with force tunneling. These options are mutually exclusive.

Manage Out

DirectAccess connectivity is bi-directional, enabling hosts on the corporate network to initiate outbound network communication to connected remote DirectAccess clients. In order to natively support manage-out functionality, IPv6 must be deployed on the corporate network.

ISATAP

If IPv6 has not been deployed on the corporate network, the Intrasite Automatic Tunnel Addressing Protocol (ISATAP) IPv6 transition technology can be leveraged to create an IPv6 overlay network used solely for this purpose. ISATAP is automatically configured on the server when DirectAccess is installed, and management clients can be configured to use the DirectAccess server as their ISATAP router.

Supportability

ISATAP is only supported for single-server DirectAccess deployments.

Summary

As you can see, there are a lot of moving parts involved in a DirectAccess implementation that make the initial planning vital to the success of the deployment. The Windows platform technologies that DirectAccess relies on are commonly deployed and well understood, making the deployment of DirectAccess less challenging for those with Windows systems-management experience.

CHAPTER 3

■ ■ ■

Install DirectAccess

Once the DirectAccess planning and design phase is complete, it's time to move on to preparing the first DirectAccess server. A physical server or virtual machine will be provisioned that meets the necessary minimum requirements for the deployment. The Windows Server 2016 operating system will be installed, joined to the domain, and updated as required. Additional preparation will include network interface configuration for multihomed servers, along with computer and SSL certificate installation. Finally, the DirectAccess role itself can be installed.

DirectAccess Server

After the physical or virtual server has been provisioned, the Windows Server 2016 operating system can be installed. Both server core and full graphical user interface (GUI) versions of Windows Server 2016 are supported. However, it is recommended that the server be configured with a GUI initially to make the installation and configuration of DirectAccess easier. Once the server has been tested, and prior to placing it into production, the GUI can be safely removed and the server managed remotely.

Operating System Installation

There are no special requirements for installing the Windows Server 2016 operating system. You can install the OS using the installation media provided by Microsoft, or it can be deployed using an automated provisioning process. Avoid installing the OS using an image that is heavily customized or has third-party firewall or antivirus software installed by default. These commonly interfere with the proper operation of DirectAccess. Instead, install the operating system from Microsoft media and then deploy DirectAccess. Once DirectAccess operation has been verified, any additional third-party software required can be installed.

Single-NIC Configuration

DirectAccess can be deployed with a single network adapter in both perimeter/DMZ and LAN deployments. There is no special configuration required for single-Network Interface Card (NIC) deployments. Simply provide an IPv4 address, subnet mask, and default gateway as required.

© Richard M. Hicks 2016
R. M. Hicks, *Implementing DirectAccess with Windows Server 2016*, DOI 10.1007/978-1-4842-2059-7_3

Dual-NIC Configuration

The most common network configuration for the DirectAccess server is multihomed, where the server is configured with two NICs. Dual NICs are required for edge-facing deployments. They are optional for perimeter/DMZ deployments. When the DirectAccess server is configured with two network adapters (multihomed), one network interface is defined as internal, the other as external. Which network the internal and external network interfaces reside on depends on the chosen topology.

- Edge-facing deployments

    - External interface connected to the public Internet using public IPv4 addressing

    - Internal interface connected to a perimeter or DMZ network or the LAN using private IPv4 addressing

- Perimeter/DMZ deployments

    - External interface connected to the perimeter or DMZ network using public or private IPv4 addressing

    - Internal interface connected to a perimeter or DMZ network or the LAN using private IPv4 addressing

Internal Interface

Open **Network Connections** by pressing **Window Key + X** and clicking **Network Connections**. Rename the network connections intuitively so they can be quickly identified in the future. Renaming them **Internal** and **External** should be sufficient. Network adapters can be renamed by right-clicking them and choosing **Rename** or by simply highlighting a network adapter and pressing **F2** (Figure 3-1).

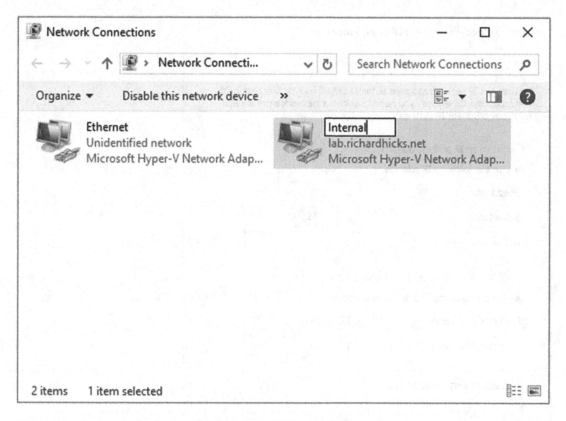

Figure 3-1. *Rename network connections*

To configure the Internal network interface, right-click the Internal network connection and choose **Properties**. Highlight **Internet Protocol Version 4 (TCP/IPv4)** and then click **Properties**. Provide an IPv4 address and a subnet mask. **DO NOT** specify a default gateway! Provide the IP addresses for DNS servers on the corporate LAN as necessary (Figure 3-2).

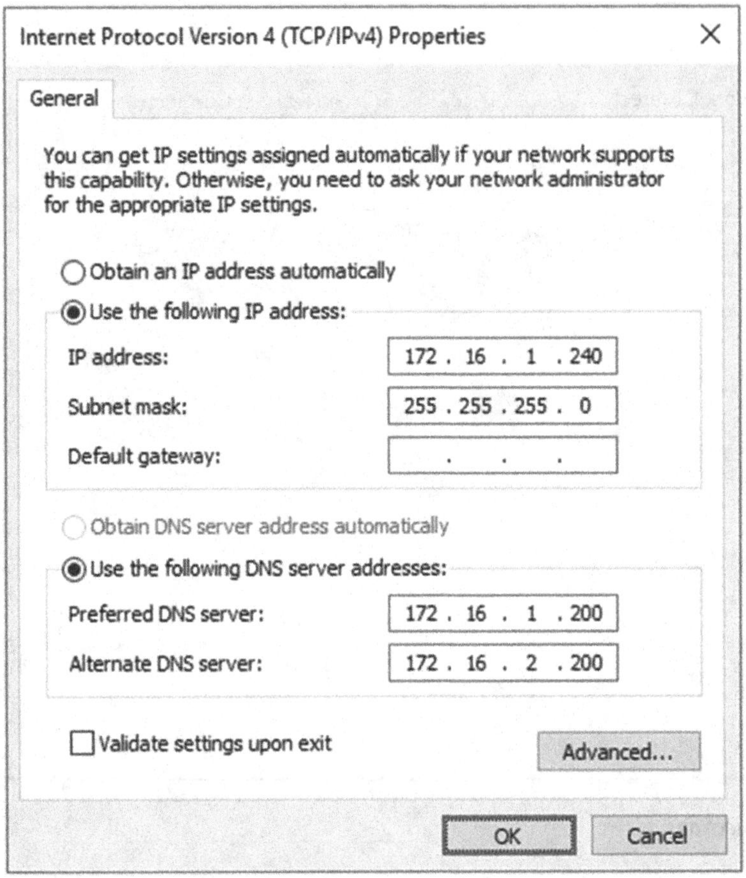

Figure 3-2. *Assign IPv4 address, subnet mask, and corporate DNS servers to the Internal network interface*

■ **Note** A multihomed Windows server must have a default gateway defined on **one interface only**. That interface must be the external, Internet-facing network interface. Any remote internal subnets will require static routes to be defined on the DirectAccess server to reach them.

External Interface

To configure the External interface, right-click the External adapter and choose **Properties**. Highlight **Internet Protocol Version 4 (TCP/IPv4)** and then click **Properties**. Provide an IPv4 address, subnet mask, and default gateway. **DO NOT** specify any DNS servers! (See Figure 3-3.)

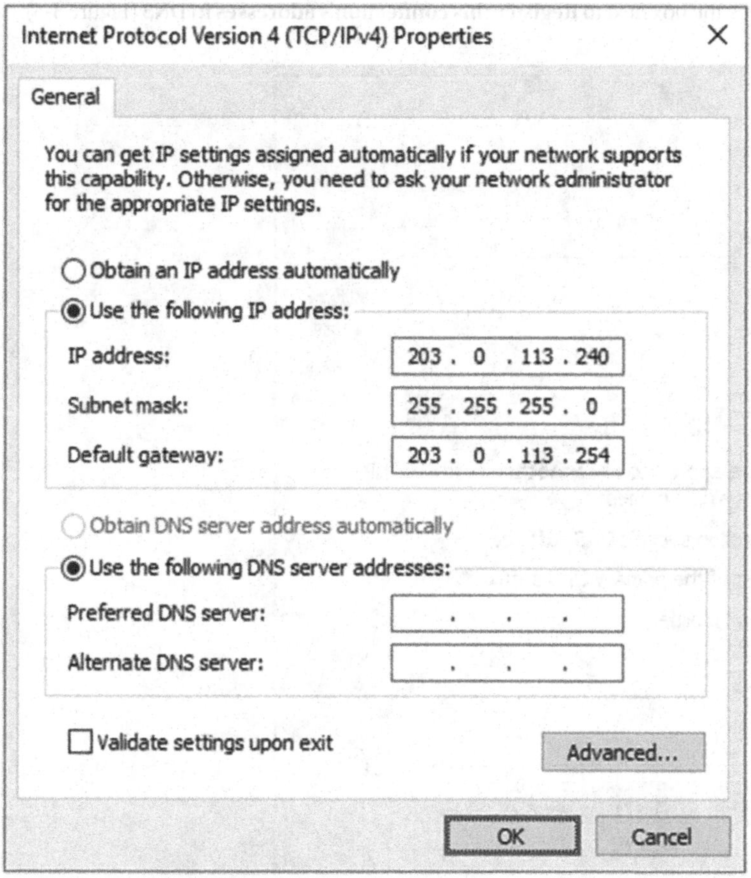

Figure 3-3. *Assign IPv4 address, subnet mask, and default gateway to External network interface*

Click **Advanced**. If Teredo support is required, click **Add** under the **IP addresses** section and specify the next consecutive public IPv4 address and subnet mask (Figure 3-4).

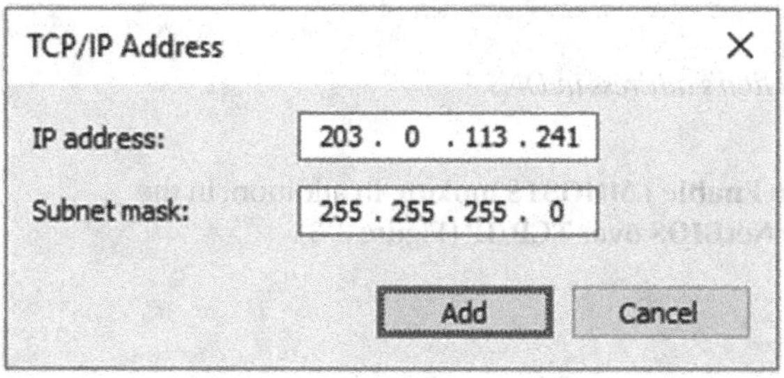

Figure 3-4. *Assign additional IPv4 addresses (if required)*

Select the **DNS** tab and uncheck the box next to **Register this connection's addresses in DNS** (Figure 3-5).

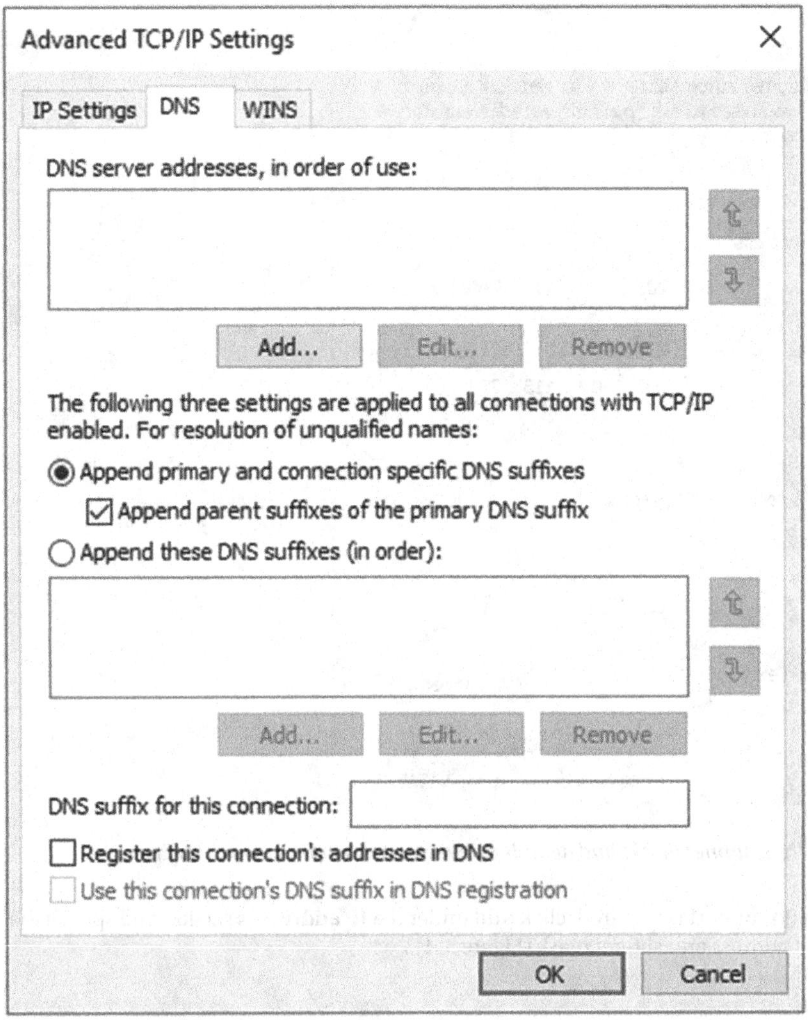

Figure 3-5. *Uncheck the option to register this connection's address in DNS*

Select the **WINS** tab and uncheck the box next to **Enable LMHOSTS lookup**. In addition, in the **NetBIOS setting** section select the option to **Disable NetBIOS over TCP/IP** (Figure 3-6).

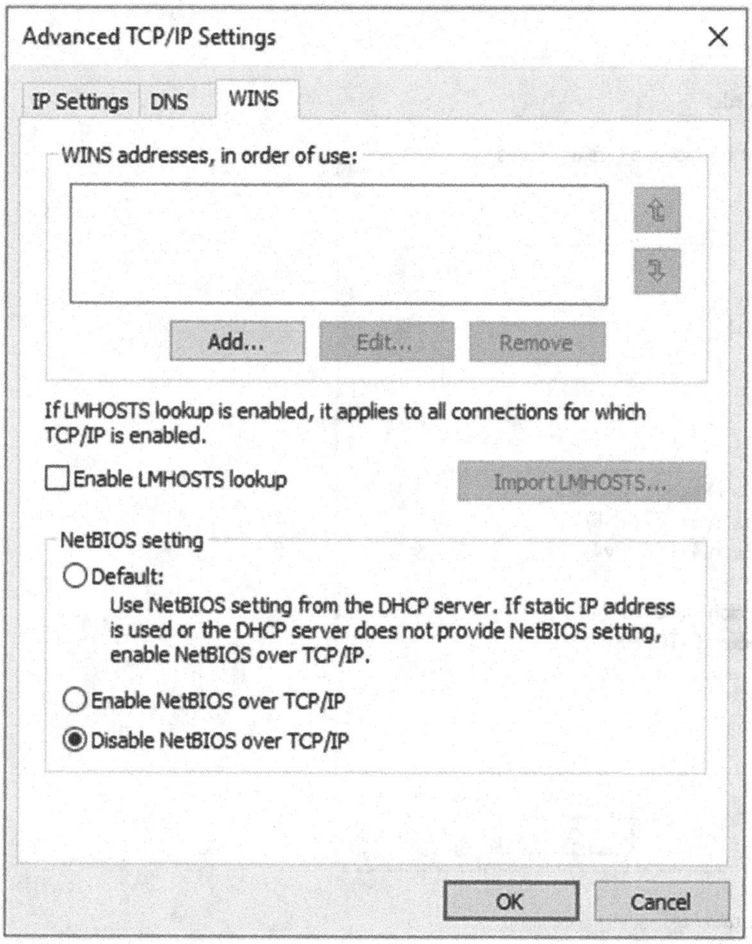

Figure 3-6. *Uncheck the option to enable LMHOSTS lookup and select the option to disable NetBIOS over TCP/IP*

■ **Note**   As the External network interface is public facing and connected to an untrusted network (public Internet or perimeter/DMZ network), it is recommended that all protocols and services other than IPv4 and IPv6 be disabled to reduce the attack surface of the DirectAccess server.

Back in the **Network Connections** window, click the **Organize** button, highlight **Layout**, and then select **Menu bar** (alternatively, you can simply press the Alt key to expose this menu). From the drop-down menu click **Advanced** and then **Advanced Settings**. Ensure that the Internal network interface is listed first. To adjust the connection order, highlight the Internal network adapter and then click the up arrow on the right side to move it to the top of the list (Figure 3-7).

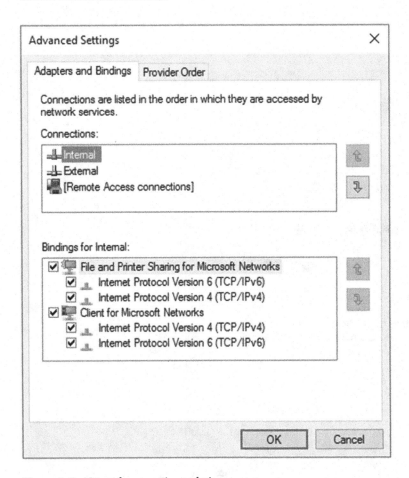

Figure 3-7. Network connection ordering

Static Routes

As the Internal network interface does not have a default gateway, it will be necessary to configure static routes to remote internal subnets that will need to be reachable from the DirectAccess server and by DirectAccess clients. For example, if the DirectAccess server is on the 172.16.1.0/24 subnet, but there are systems on the 172.16.2.0/24 subnet that must be accessible from the DirectAccess server, a static route will be defined by entering the following commands in an elevated PowerShell command window:

```
New-NetRoute -InterfaceAlias <Interface_Name> -DestinationPrefix <SubnetID/Mask>
-NextHop <Gateway_Address>
```

Using the preceding example, the command to create the static route would look like this:

```
New-NetRoute -InterfaceAlias Internal -DestinationPrefix 172.16.2.0/24 -NextHop 172.16.1.254
```

If there are multiple remote subnets on the Internal network, it is recommended that the route be summarized, if possible. For example, if there are additional subnets that are all in the 172.16.0.0/16 network, you can summarize them as follows:

```
New-NetRoute -InterfaceAlias Internal -DestinationPrefix 172.16.0.0/16 -NextHop 172.16.1.254
```

■ **Note** If you've read the first two chapters of this book you are no doubt keenly aware of the requirement for IPv6 to support DirectAccess. However, you'll notice that *no* IPv6 configuration is required when configuring network interfaces. That's by design. IPv6 configuration is performed automatically when DirectAccess is configured. If IPv6 is deployed on the Internal network, great! DirectAccess will make use of it, but there's no special IPv6 configuration required to support DirectAccess.

Join Domain and Apply Updates

The DirectAccess server must be joined to a domain. It is recommended that the server be renamed prior to doing this, but it can also be performed after being joined to the domain. Joining the server to the domain can be accomplished in the traditional way using the GUI, but I suggest using PowerShell so as to simplify and streamline the process. Using the **Add-Computer** PowerShell cmdlet, it is possible to rename the computer, join it to the domain, and place the server in a specific Organizational Unit (OU) with a single command:

```
Add-Computer -NewName <new_computer_name> -OUPath <OU_Path> -DomainName <domain_name>
```

For example:

```
Add-Computer -NewName EDGE1 -OUPath "OU=DirectAccess,DC=lab,DC=richardhicks,DC=net"
-DomainName lab.richardhicks.net -Restart
```

Once the DirectAccess server has been joined to the domain, proceed with installing Windows operating updates as necessary using Windows Update (Window Key + I ➤ Update & Security ➤ Check for Updates), Windows Server Update Services (WSUS), System Center Configuration Manager (SCCM), or any other third-party patch-management solution.

Third-Party Software

There is a high propensity for third-party software to interfere with the proper operation of DirectAccess. This occurs because commonly these non-Microsoft services are not IPv6 aware, or otherwise block protocols and services necessary for DirectAccess to work. As such, it is generally recommended that no third-party software be installed on the DirectAccess server.

In many cases, the installation of additional software on the DirectAccess server is unavoidable. Frequently, organizations have strict guidelines that dictate that management agents or antivirus or firewall software be installed before production use. Here, it is suggested that DirectAccess be installed, configured, and completely tested prior to installing third-party software. This will reduce the troubleshooting burden if the third-party software prevents DirectAccess from functioning correctly.

Certificates

For most deployment scenarios it will be necessary to install certificates on the DirectAccess server. DirectAccess requires two different types of certificates—a computer (machine) certificate and an SSL certificate.

Computer (Machine) Certificates

For DirectAccess deployments that require them, computer certificates are used for IPsec authentication and encryption. They must be issued to the DirectAccess server by an internal PKI. The certificate must include the Client Authentication Enhanced Key Usage (EKU).

Best practice is to not use the default Computer certificate template. Instead, it is recommended that a dedicated certificate template for DirectAccess IPsec be configured and deployed specifically for this purpose. To create a certificate template, open the Certificate Services management console on the Active Directory Certificate Services (AD CS) server. In the navigation tree, expand the server and then right-click **Certificate Templates** and choose **Manage**. Optionally, you can press **Windows Key + R** and enter **certtmpl.msc**.

Right-click the **Workstation Authentication** template and choose **Duplicate Template**. Select the **General** tab and provide a descriptive name for the new template. Specify an appropriate validity and renewal period based on your organization's security policy (Figure 3-8).

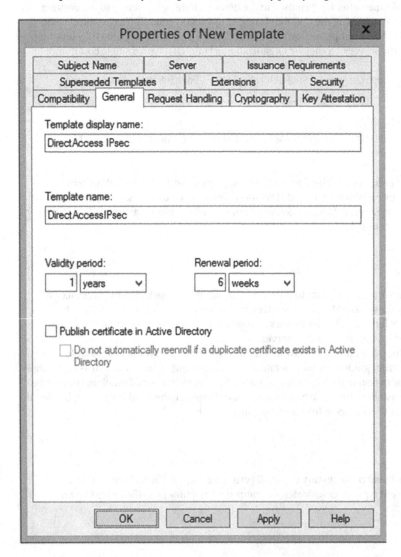

Figure 3-8. Configure the DirectAccess computer certificate template

Select the **Subject Name** tab and choose **DNS name** for the **Subject name format** (Figure 3-9).

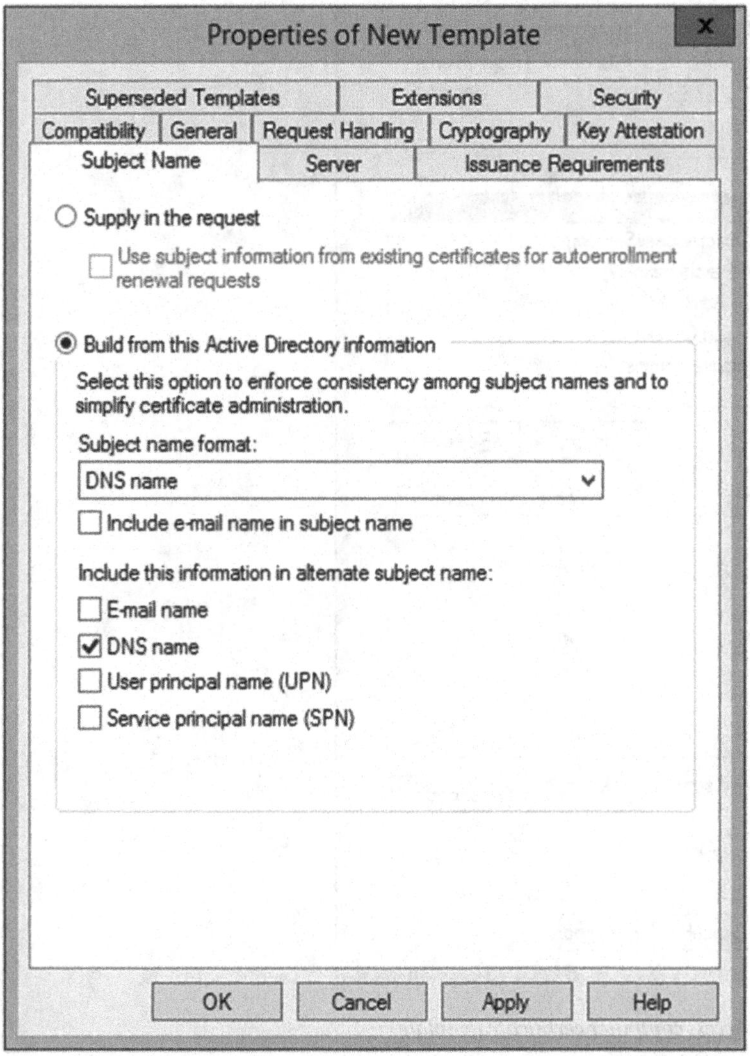

Figure 3-9. *Configure the DirectAccess computer certificate template*

Select the **Security** tab and click **Add**. Specify the names of the DirectAccess client security group and the name of each DirectAccess server. Optionally, a security group can be created for DirectAccess servers, and that group can be specified here. For the DirectAccess client group and the DirectAccess servers (or DirectAccess server group), check the **Allow** box for both **Enroll** and **Autoenroll**. Once complete, click **OK** (Figure 3-10).

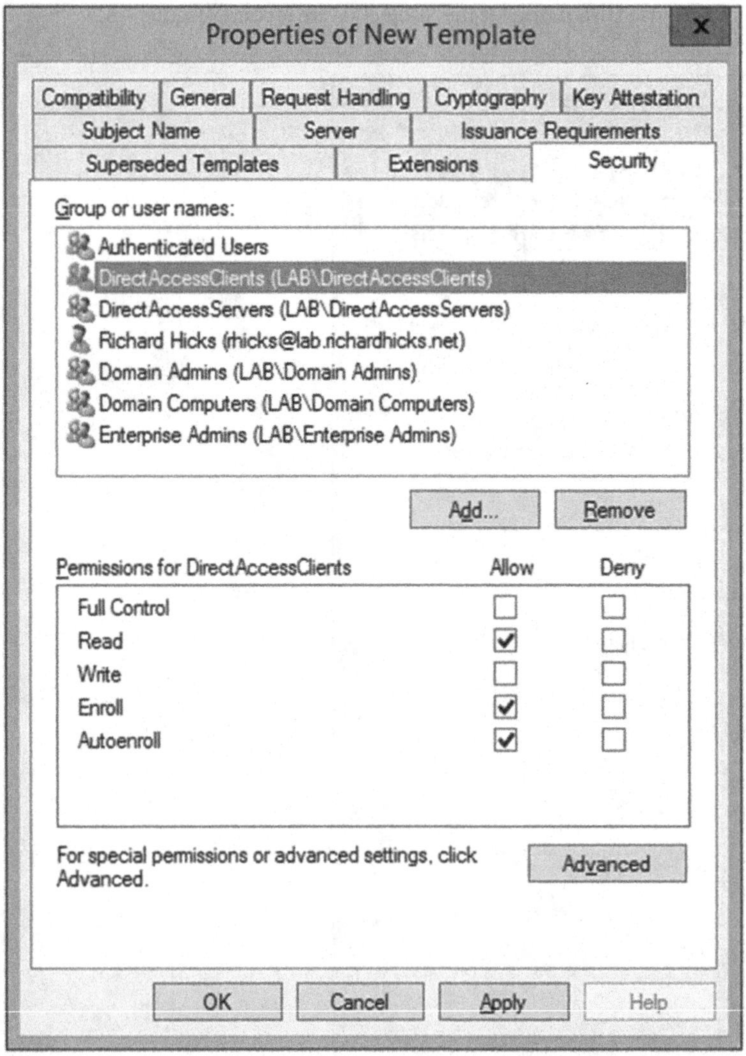

Figure 3-10. Configure the DirectAccess computer certificate template

---

■ **Note** If certificate autoenrollment will be used (recommended, see next section), it is advisable to also remove Domain Computers from the list of groups and user names on the Security tab.

In the Certification Authority management console, right-click **Certificate Templates** and choose **New** and **Certificate Template to Issue**. Highlight the DirectAccess IPsec certificate template and choose **OK** (Figure 3-11).

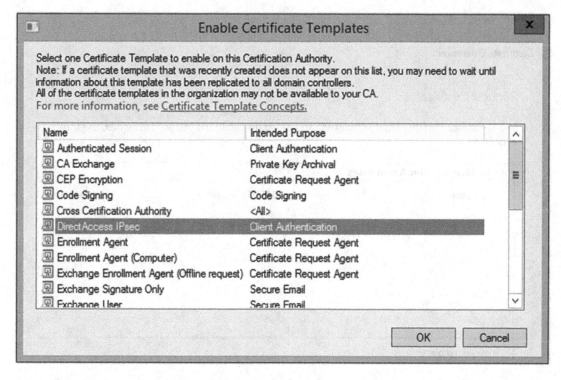

Figure 3-11. *Issue the DirectAccess computer certificate template*

Computer certificates can be requested and installed manually on the DirectAccess server using the Certificates management console snap-in. To request a computer certificate, press **Window Key + R** on the DirectAccess server to bring up the **Run** command box and enter **certlm.msc**

Expand **Certificates (Local Computer)**, right-click **Personal**, and choose **All Tasks** and **Request New Certificate**. Click **Next** twice, select the DirectAccess IPsec certificate template, and click **Enroll** (Figure 3-12).

Figure 3-12. *DirectAccess IPsec computer certificate request*

Automatic Enrollment

To streamline the provisioning of certificates for DirectAccess servers and clients, and to ensure that certificates are automatically renewed before they expire, it is recommended that certificate auto-enrollment be configured. This is accomplished by creating and deploying a Group Policy Object (GPO) in Active Directory.

To create and deploy a computer certificate auto-enrollment GPO, open the Group Policy Management console, expand the **Forest**, **Domains**, and the domain where the DirectAccess server and clients are joined. Right-click **Group Policy Objects** and click **New**. Provide a descriptive name for the new GPO and click **OK**.

Right-click the newly created GPO and choose **Edit**. Expand **Computer Configuration**, **Policies**, **Windows Settings**, and **Security Settings**, and highlight **Public Key Policies**. Double-click **Certificate Services Client - Auto-Enrollment** and select **Enabled** for the **Configuration Model**. Select the option to **Renew expired certificates, update pending certificates, and remove revoked certificates** and **Update certificates that use certificate templates** and click **OK** (Figure 3-13).

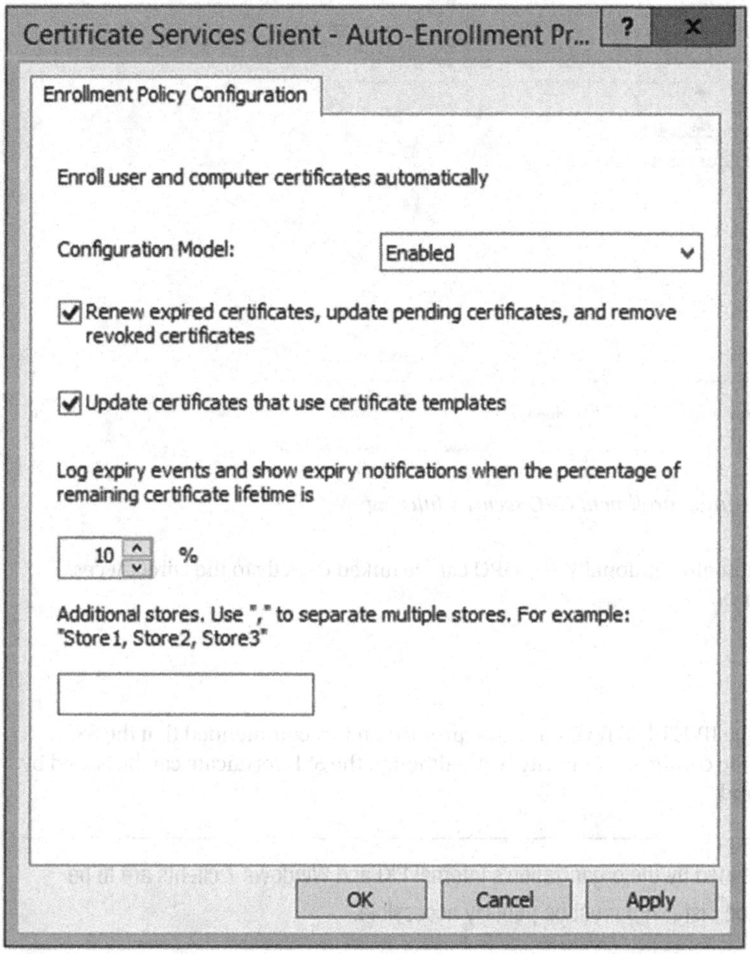

Figure 3-13. *Configure computer certificate auto-enrollment*

In the Group Policy Management Console, select the GPO and click **Add** under **Security Filtering**. Remove **Authenticated Users** and specify the DirectAccess client security group and all DirectAccess servers (or the DirectAccess servers security group; Figure 3-14).

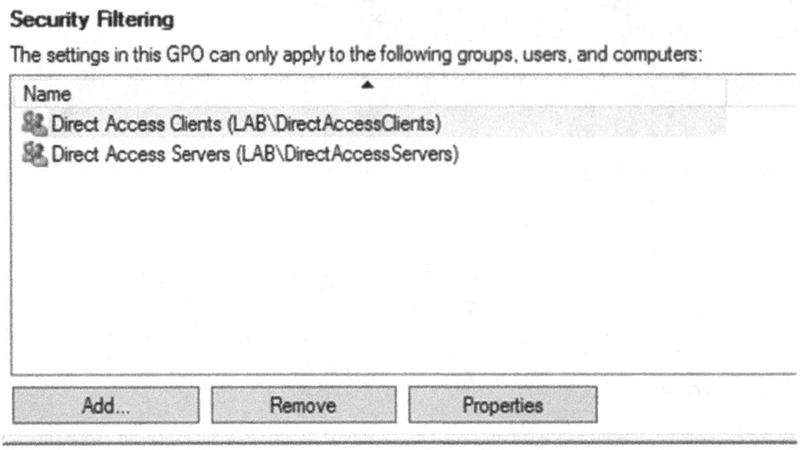

Security Filtering

The settings in this GPO can only apply to the following groups, users, and computers:

Name ▲
🖳 Direct Access Clients (LAB\DirectAccessClients)
🖳 Direct Access Servers (LAB\DirectAccessServers)

Add...	Remove	Properties

Figure 3-14. *Computer certificate auto-enrollment GPO security filtering*

Finally, link the GPO to the domain. Optionally, the GPO can be linked directly to the DirectAccess servers and clients OU, if necessary.

SSL Certificate

An SSL certificate is required for the IP-HTTPS IPv6 transition protocol. It is recommended that the SSL certificate be obtained from a public certificate authority (CA), although the SSL certificate can be issued by the organization's internal PKI.napd

---

■ **Note**   If an SSL certificate is issued by the organization's internal PKI and Windows 7 clients are to be supported, the Certificate Revocation List (CRL) must be publicly accessible.

The first step in requesting a public SSL certificate is to generate a Certificate Signing Request (CSR). This can be accomplished in a variety of ways, including using the Microsoft Management Console (MMC) Certificates snap-in, the certutil.exe command-line tool, and even the Internet Information Services (IIS) management tool. Another convenient method is to use the DigiCert Certificate Utility for Windows.[1] This handy free tool greatly simplifies the process of creating a CSR. Download and run the tool, highlight **SSL**, and then click **Create CSR**.

Choose **SSL** for the **Certificate Type** and enter the **Common Name**. The Common Name will be the public Fully Qualified Domain Name (FQDN) defined in the DirectAccess configuration (for example, da.richardhicks.net). If requesting a wildcard certificate, enter *.yourdomain.tld (for example *.richardhicks. net). Provide the remaining details as required and click **Generate** when finished (Figure 3-15).

---

[1]The DigiCert Certificate Utility for Windows can be downloaded for free from https://www.digicert.com/util/.

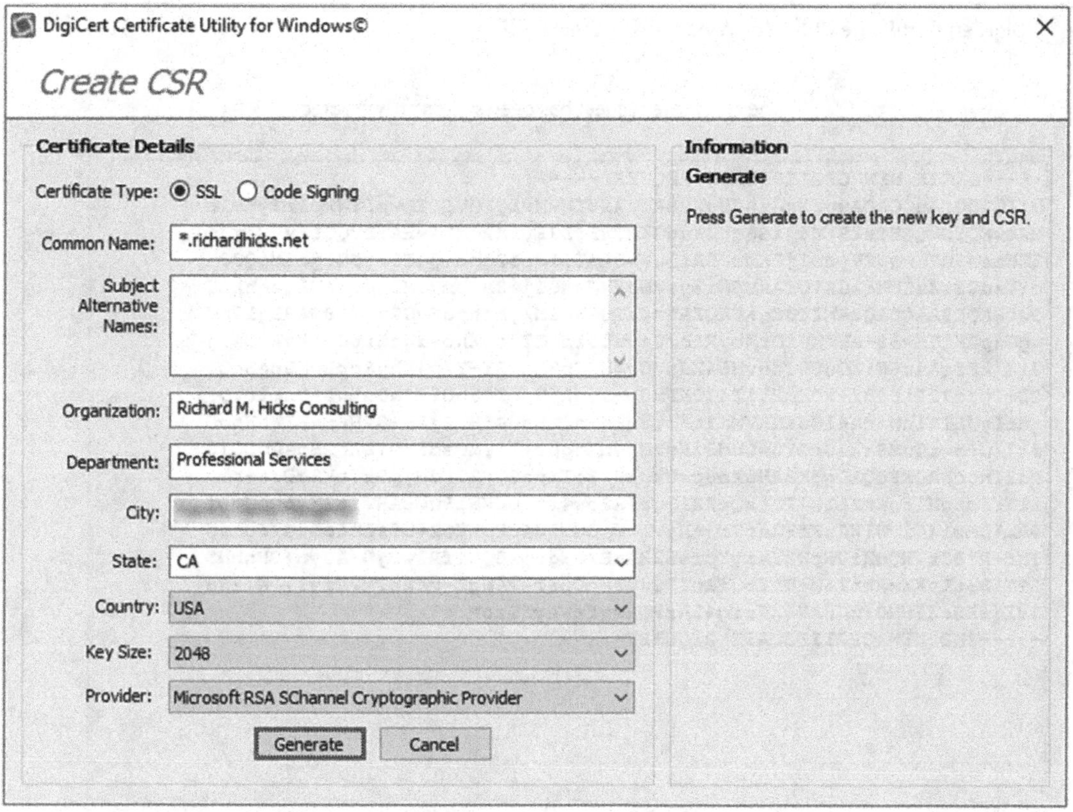

Figure 3-15. *Creating a Certificate Signing Request (CSR) using the Digicert Certificate Utility for Windows*

A new certificate request will be created. Copy the CSR or save it to a file, then submit it to a public CA (Figure 3-16).

Figure 3-16. *Certificate Signing Request (CSR)*

Once the CSR has been approved and processed by your CA, download the certificate and any additional intermediate certificates provided. Import any intermediate certificates using the Certificates MMC snap-in prior to importing the new certificate. Intermediate certificates should be imported into the Certificates (Local Computer) ➤ Intermediate Certification Authority ➤ Certificates store.

In the DigiCert utility click **Import** and specify the location of the certificate downloaded from the CA. Enter a new friendly name for the certificate and click **Finish** (Figure 3-17).

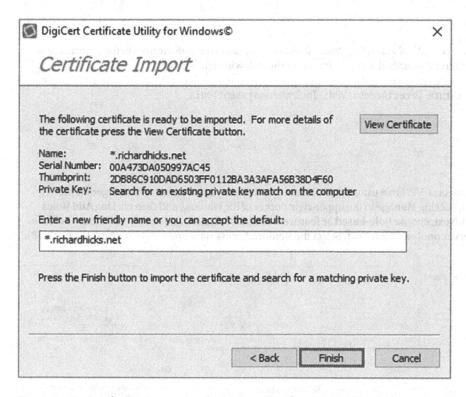

Figure 3-17. Certificate Import using the DigiCert Certificate Utility for Windows

Once the certificate has been successfully imported, select the certificate and choose **Export Certificate**. Select the option to export the private key. Additionally, select the option to **Include all certificates in the certification path if possible** and click **Next**. Provide a password and click **Next**. Finally, specify the location to save the file and click **Finish**.

To import the SSL certificate on the DirectAccess server, press **Window Key + R** to bring up the **Run** command box. Enter **mmc.exe**, click **File**, and then choose **Add/Remove Snap-In**. Highlight **Certificates** and click **Add**. Select **Computer Account** and click **Finish**. Choose **Local Computer (the computer this console is running on)** and click **Finish** and **OK**.

Expand **Certificates (Local Computer)**, right-click **Personal**, and choose **Import**. Click **Next**, specify the file name of the exported certificate, and click **Next** again. Provide the password for the certificate file, click **Next** twice, and then click **Finish**.

■ **Note** If any intermediate certificates appear in the Personal/Certificates store after importing the SSL certificate, move them to the Intermediate Certification Authority/Certificates store as necessary.

Installing the DirectAccess-VPN Role

Installing the DirectAccess-VPN role can be accomplished using either the GUI or PowerShell. PowerShell is the preferred method for installing the role, as it takes only a single PowerShell command to install the role and management tools.

PowerShell

Installing the DirectAccess-VPN role using PowerShell is simple and straightforward. On the DirectAccess server, open an elevated PowerShell window and enter the following command:

```
Install-WindowsFeature DirectAccess-VPN -IncludeManagementTools
```

That's it!

GUI

Installing the DirectAccess-VPN role using the GUI is accomplished by opening **Server Manager** on the DirectAccess server, clicking **Manage** in the upper-right corner of the window, and then clicking **Add Roles and Features**. Click **Next**, choose **Role-based or feature-based installation**, and click **Next**. Choose **Select a server from the server pool** and click **Next.** Select the **Remote Access** server role and click **Next** (Figure 3-18).

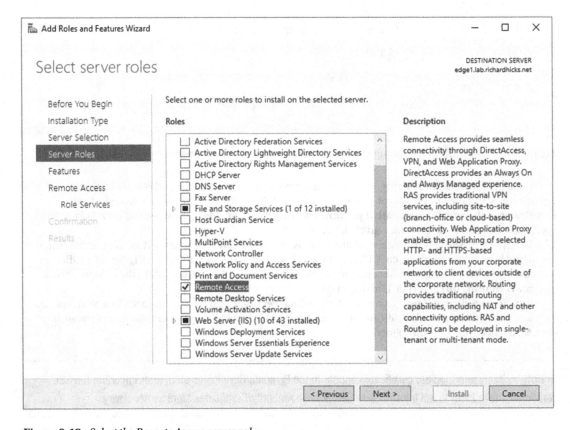

Figure 3-18. *Select the Remote Access server role*

Role features are automatically selected. Click **Next** twice and then select the **DirectAccess and VPN (RAS)** role service (Figures 3-19 and 3-20).

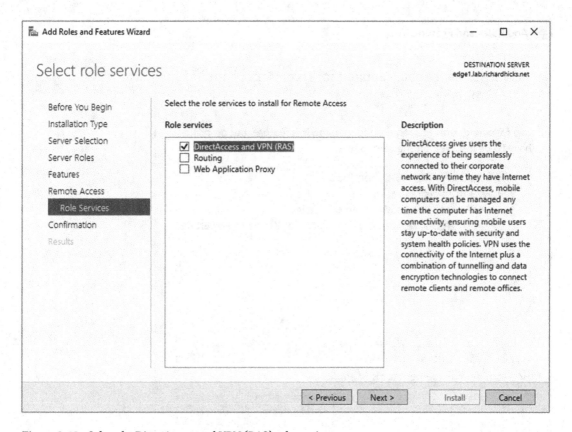

Figure 3-19. *Select the DirectAccess and VPN (RAS) role service*

Figure 3-20. *Add features that are required for DirectAccess and VPN (RAS)*

Confirm the installation selections and click **Install** (Figure 3-21).

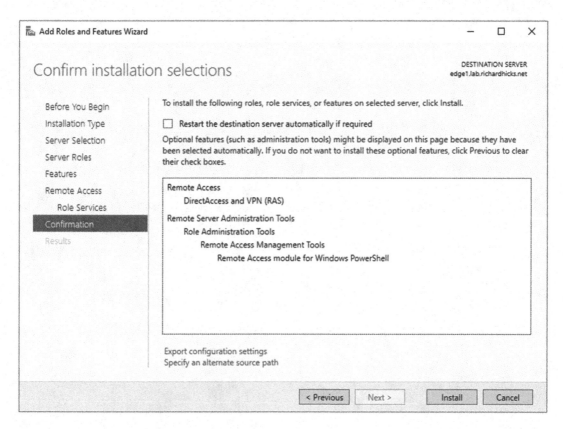

Figure 3-21. *Confirm your installation selections*

Configuring Additional Nodes

If multiple DirectAccess servers will be configured in a load-balanced cluster, each server must be prepared using the steps outlined in this chapter prior to joining the cluster. Each additional DirectAccess server will have to be provisioned and have network interface cards configured according to the chosen network topology. The servers must be joined to the domain, updated, and have all required certificates (computer and SSL) installed. Finally, the DirectAccess role can be configured.

Summary

Getting all of the pieces in place prior to installing the DirectAccess-VPN role is not a trivial task. Pay careful attention to network interface configuration, especially static route configuration for dual-NIC deployments. Use caution when deploying third-party software, as it often interferes with DirectAccess operation. Ensure that computer and SSL certificates are installed and configured properly too. Save yourself some time and use PowerShell to install the DirectAccess-VPN role, and don't forget that if you are planning to deploy multiple DirectAccess servers in a load-balanced cluster, all of the steps outlined in this chapter must be completed on each DirectAccess server prior to deployment.

CHAPTER 4

■■■

Configure DirectAccess with the Getting Started Wizard

There are two options for configuring DirectAccess using the Graphical User Interface (GUI). The first option is to use the Getting Started Wizard. The second is to use the Remote Access Setup Wizard. On the surface they would appear to perform the same function. However, the two options differ in subtle but important ways.

The Getting Started Wizard only requires the administrator to select a deployment option, choose a network topology, and provide a public hostname. It can be accomplished with as few as three mouse clicks. That's it! However, it configures DirectAccess in a highly simplified manner and with limited options that may not be suitable for many deployments.

Before We Begin

The Getting Started Wizard configures DirectAccess using default settings that are typically less than optimal. Its basic configuration lacks support for common requirements, such as support for Windows 7 clients, load balancing, strong user authentication, force tunneling, and geographic redundancy with multisite. As such, using the Remote Access Setup Wizard is often a better choice.

However, if the DirectAccess deployment is small and doesn't require Windows 7 client support or high availability, using the Getting Started Wizard to deploy DirectAccess is an acceptable option.

Getting Started Wizard

To launch the Getting Started Wizard, open the Remote Access Management Console on the DirectAccess server. The Remote Access Management Console can be found by clicking on the **Start** menu and navigating to **All Apps ➤ Windows Administrative Tools ➤ Remote Access Management Console**. Expand **Configuration**, highlight **DirectAccess and VPN**, and then click **Run the Getting Started Wizard** (Figure 4-1).

© Richard M. Hicks 2016

R. M. Hicks, *Implementing DirectAccess with Windows Server 2016*, DOI 10.1007/978-1-4842-2059-7_4

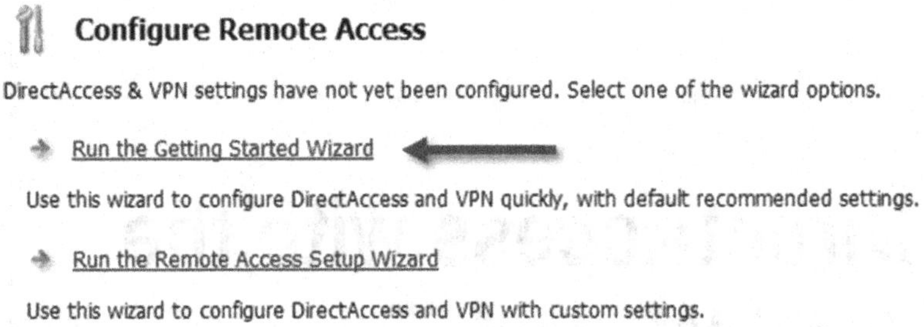

Configure Remote Access

DirectAccess & VPN settings have not yet been configured. Select one of the wizard options.

➔ Run the Getting Started Wizard ◀━━━━━

Use this wizard to configure DirectAccess and VPN quickly, with default recommended settings.

➔ Run the Remote Access Setup Wizard

Use this wizard to configure DirectAccess and VPN with custom settings.

Figure 4-1. Run the Getting Started Wizard

■ **Note**   The Getting Started Wizard and the Remote Access Setup Wizard will not appear if DirectAccess has already been configured.

Deployment Options

The Getting Started Wizard provides three options for configuring DirectAccess and VPN (Figure 4-2).

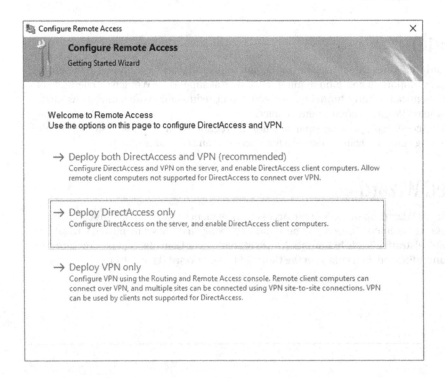

Figure 4-2. Configure Remote Access window

Deploy both DirectAccess and VPN (recommended)

Although the GUI suggests this option is "recommended," there are some very important reasons why VPN should not be installed on the DirectAccess server. The most critical reason is that it eliminates support for important scalability and performance features included in DirectAccess, namely null encryption for IP-HTTPS connections for Windows 8.x and Windows 10 clients. Having VPN and DirectAccess on the same server also makes the solution more complex, especially when configuring redundancy for DirectAccess (load balancing and multisite). As such, this configuration should be avoided if possible.[1]

Deploy DirectAccess only

This option should be selected.

Deploy VPN only

This is a book about DirectAccess, so this option is not applicable for our purposes.

Installing DirectAccess

To install DirectAccess without VPN, select the option to **Deploy DirectAccess only**. The Getting Started Wizard will perform a prerequisites check to ensure essential supporting components are installed.

■ **Note**   It is not uncommon to receive an error message at this point. Typical errors are IPv6 being disabled via Group Policy or the registry, WinRM not being configured, and IPv6 transition protocols being disabled. Resolve any issues before proceeding.

Network Topology

Select the desired network topology for the server (Figure 4-3). Options are **Edge**, **Behind an edge device (with two network adapters)**, and **Behind an edge device (with a single network adapter)**. Options that are not supported will be grayed out. For example, if the server has a private IPv4 address assigned to its External network interface, the **Edge** option will not be displayed. If the DirectAccess server has only one network interface, the **Edge** and **Behind an edge device (with two network adapters)** options will both be unavailable. In addition, enter the Fully Qualified Domain Name (FQDN) that will be used by DirectAccess clients to connect to the DirectAccess server. The FQDN must resolve to the public IPv4 address assigned to the DirectAccess server's External network interface, and it must match the subject name of the SSL certificate. For NAT deployments, it must resolve to the public IPv4 address assigned to the NAT device.

---

[1]The Web Application Proxy (WAP) role can also be configured on the same server as DirectAccess. Although technically supported, it too should be avoided if possible. The same reasons why VPN should not be installed on the DirectAccess server also apply to WAP. Best practice is to install DirectAccess on a server dedicated to the WAP role.

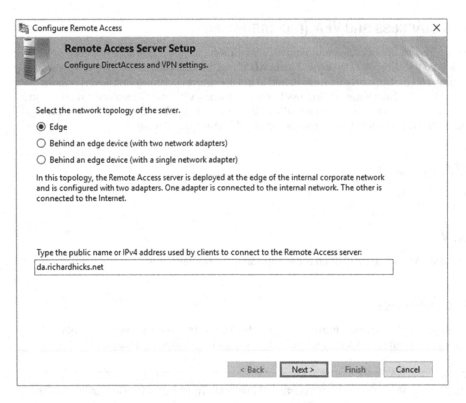

Figure 4-3. *Remote Access Server Setup window*

Apply Settings

Click **Finish** to apply the settings (Figure 4-4). Recall that the Getting Started Wizard uses predefined configuration settings that may not be applicable in all scenarios. In some cases, it may be necessary to make changes to the default settings created by the Getting Started Wizard. Click on the **Click here** link to review and edit settings, if necessary.

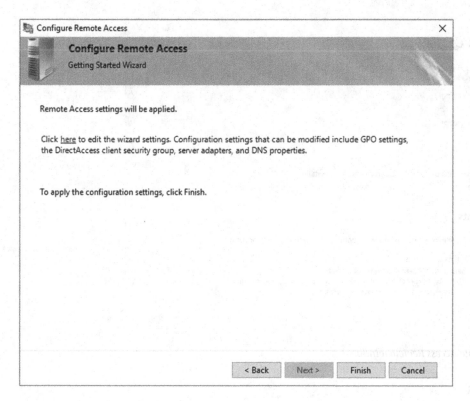

Figure 4-4. *Remote Access settings to be applied*

Review and Edit Settings

It is possible to edit some, though not all, of the settings configured using the Getting Started Wizard. Settings available to edit are GPO settings, remote client settings, remote access server settings, and infrastructure server settings (Figure 4-5).

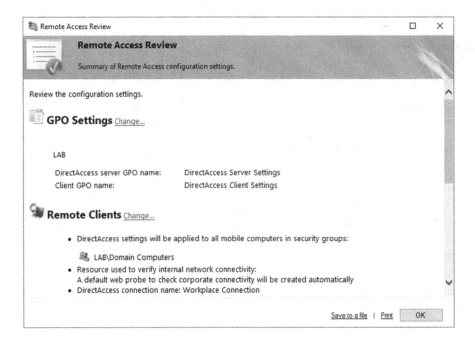

Figure 4-5. *Remote Access Review window*

GPO Settings

By default, the Getting Started Wizard will name the DirectAccess client and server settings' GPOs **DirectAccess Client Settings** and **DirectAccess Server Settings**, respectively (Figure 4-6). If different names are desired, click **Change** next to **GPO Settings** and provide new GPO names as required. If prestaged GPOs are to be used, click **Browse** and select them accordingly.

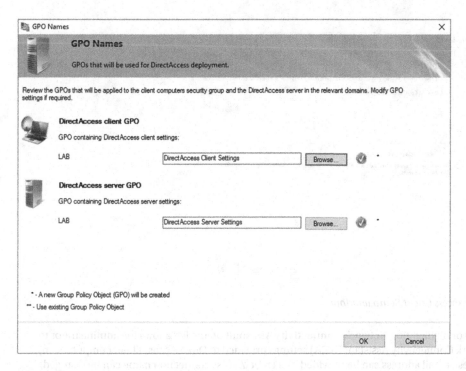

Figure 4-6. Edit GPO settings

Remote Clients

The Getting Started Wizard will configure the DirectAccess Client Settings GPO to apply to the **Domain Computers** security group. Additionally, it will also configure the GPO with a Windows Management Instrumentation (WMI) filter that further restricts the application of this GPO to only those computers with a mobile processor. For a variety of reasons, either or both of these settings may not be desirable. Click **Change** next to **Remote Clients** to specify a different security group or to disable the application of DirectAccess client settings only to mobile computers (Figure 4-7).

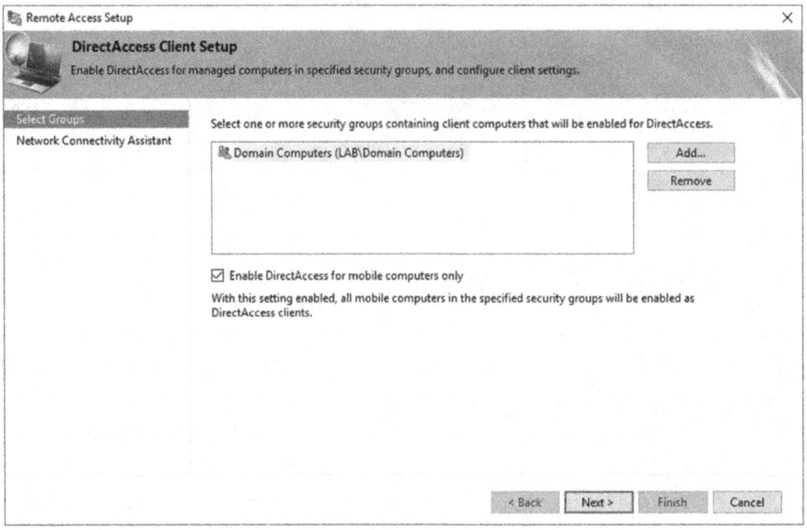

Figure 4-7. *DirectAccess Client Setup window*

Clicking **Next** or highlighting **Network Connectivity Assistant** on the left allows the administrator to change the Network Connectivity Assistant (NCA) settings provided to DirectAccess client computers. In addition, a help desk email address can be provided, the DirectAccess connection name can be changed, and DirectAccess clients can be allowed to use local name resolution, if necessary (Figure 4-8).

Figure 4-8. *DirectAccess Client Setup window*

■ **Note**   Providing a help desk email address is critically important for client-side troubleshooting. Without an email address specified here, it is not possible to collect diagnostic logs on the client.

Remote Access Server

If changes are to be made to the network topology, or perhaps if the public hostname requires editing, click **Change** next to **Remote Access Server** to access these settings. You can choose another network topology or make changes to the public hostname as required (Figure 4-9).

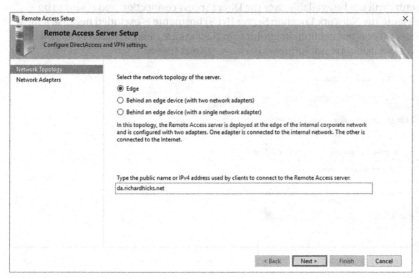

Figure 4-9. *Remote Access Server Setup window*

Clicking **Next** or highlighting **Network Adapters** on the left allows the administrator to make changes to the default network adapter selection (Figure 4-10). The Getting Started Wizard automatically chooses the option to use a self-signed certificate for IP-HTTPS connections. If a public SSL certificate is to be used, click **Browse** and choose the certificate accordingly.

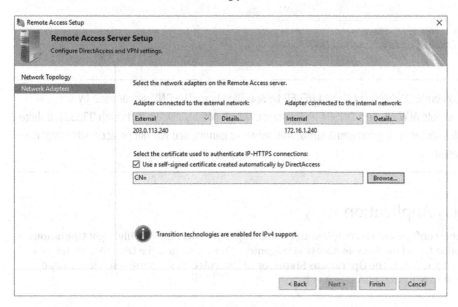

Figure 4-10. *Configure the network adapter and SSL certificate settings*

53

Infrastructure Servers

Clicking **Change** next to **Infrastructure Servers** allows the administrator to make changes to DNS suffixes and internal DNS servers for DirectAccess clients (Figure 4-11). A DNS name or suffix with a corresponding DNS server entry will be available over the DirectAccess connection. A DNS name or suffix without a corresponding DNS server entry will not be available over the DirectAccess connection and is said to be exempted or excluded. By default, the Network Location Server (NLS) hostname is excluded because it must not be reachable over the DirectAccess connection. In addition, exclusions are often required to ensure that public-facing resources such as websites are not tunneled back over DirectAccess.

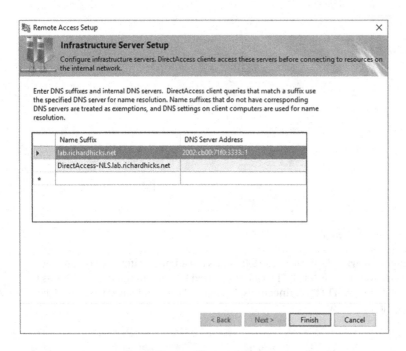

Figure 4-11. *Enter DNS suffixes and internal DNS servers*

■ **Note** Internal corporate DNS servers should NEVER be specified here. The DNS server used by DirectAccess clients should ALWAYS be a DNS64 IPv6 address, which notably always ends with 3333::1. If there is no entry for the DNS server for a given name suffix, this server or namespace will not be accessible over the DirectAccess connection.

Confirm Policy Application

Once the DirectAccess configuration is complete and the settings have been applied, highlight **Operations Status** in the navigation tree of the Remote Access Management Console to view the DirectAccess server's **Operations Status** (Figure 4-12). The **Operations Status** for all DirectAccess supporting services should indicate **Working** and have a green check next to it.

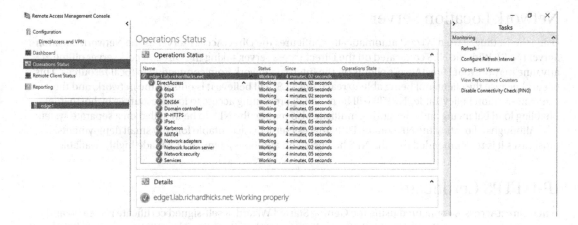

Figure 4-12. DirectAccess server Operations Status window

■ **Note**   Settings for the DirectAccess server are applied using Active Directory Group Policy. As such, it may take a period of time before those settings have been replicated in AD and are available to the DirectAccess server. Also, if the operations status of any supporting service is "unknown" and has a blue question mark next to it, continue to hit Refresh until its status has been updated.

Limitations and Drawbacks

Although the Getting Started Wizard allows the administrator to quickly and easily configure DirectAccess, there are some limitations and drawbacks to using this method.

DirectAccess Client Targeting

By default, the Getting Started Wizard applies DirectAccess client policies to all computers in the domain and filters the policy to apply only to mobile computers using a WMI filter. This assumes that all mobile computers in the organization should receive DirectAccess client settings. It also assumes that any non-mobile PCs, such as desktops or virtual machines, will not receive DirectAccess client settings. Often this is not the case. The application of DirectAccess client settings to all computers in the domain that have a mobile processor is often too broad, and further it prevents an administrator from knowing exactly which machines the DirectAccess client settings have been applied to.

Using a dedicated security group is ideal, because DirectAccess client settings can be targeted at specific machines with much more granularity. It allows for the application of DirectAccess client settings to non-mobile processor devices, such as desktop workstations and virtual machines. Security groups are also self-documenting, enabling administrators to quickly determine which systems have been provisioned for DirectAccess.

Network Location Server

Using the Getting Started Wizard automatically configures the DirectAccess server as the Network Location Server (NLS). With the NLS collocated on the DirectAccess server, taking the DirectAccess server offline at any time may prevent DirectAccess clients on the Internal network from connecting to local resources. This occurs because the client, not being able to reach the NLS, will believe it is outside the network, and the Name Resolution Policy Table (NRPT) will be enabled, preventing access to local resources by hostname. Enabling load balancing and configuring multisite also require the NLS to be installed on a separate system.

Although collocating the NLS on the DirectAccess server is acceptable for very small deployments, in most cases it is recommended that the NLS be hosted on another system and be made highly available.

IP-HTTPS Certificate

When DirectAccess is configured using the Getting Started Wizard, a self-signed certificate is created and provisioned for use with the IP-HTTPS IPv6 transition technology. Self-signed certificates provide little in terms of security, and they provide no inherent trust. Self-signed certificates are not managed, cannot be revoked, and cannot be rekeyed later, if required.

Client Support

Windows 7 clients are not supported when configuring DirectAccess with the Getting Started Wizard. This simplified deployment does not require a Public Key Infrastructure (PKI) to manage computer certificates for IPsec authentication and encryption. Instead, DirectAccess uses a component called the Kerberos Proxy on the DirectAccess server to authenticate to Active Directory as well as for IPsec encryption. Kerberos Proxy is only supported for clients with Windows 8 and later.

Deployment Flexibility

Most advanced deployment options—such as load balancing, multisite, strong user authentication, and force tunneling—will all require significant design changes in order to implement them after using the Getting Started Wizard. Often these changes will be disruptive. They may also require clients to be brought back to the corporate network, or connected out-of-band using traditional client-based VPN to receive the updated configuration.

Summary

For many, the Getting Started Wizard looks like the intuitive choice for configuring DirectAccess. The simplified deployment with reduced infrastructure requirements looks enticing, but from experience I can tell you it often causes more problems than it solves.

In some cases, using the Getting Started Wizard may be sufficient. For small deployments with limited requirements, the simplified deployment can be used without issue.

To address some of the challenges and shortcomings imposed by the Getting Started Wizard's restrictive default option selections, it is possible to edit many of the defaults prior to deployment. However, the process is cumbersome and unintuitive. If more than a few of these settings have to be changed, it is recommended that the Remote Access Setup Wizard be used instead. It provides much more granular control of configuration settings, offers better deployment flexibility for the future, and with the use of PKI is fundamentally more secure.

CHAPTER 5

■ ■ ■

Configure DirectAccess with the Remote Access Setup Wizard

In this chapter, DirectAccess will be configured using the Graphical User Interface (GUI), this time leveraging the Remote Access Setup Wizard instead of the Getting Started Wizard, as outlined in Chapter 4.

Using the Remote Access Setup Wizard provides several key advantages. It gives the administrator much more granular control over the initial configuration of DirectAccess. It also allows for flexible deployment configuration using optimal settings, and it provides crucial support for popular deployment options, such as Windows 7 client support.

Additionally, the Remote Access Setup Wizard lets the administrator deploy DirectAccess using common implementation best practices, such as using a security group for applying DirectAccess client settings, specifying a public SSL certificate for IP-HTTPS, and hosting the Network Location Server (NLS) on another server, just to name a few. It also exposes several advanced configuration settings, such as force tunneling, strong user authentication, management server definition, and end-to-end encryption.

Remote Access Setup Wizard

To launch the Remote Access Setup Wizard, open the Remote Access Management Console on the DirectAccess server. The Remote Access Management Console can be found by clicking on the **Start** menu and navigating to **All Apps ➤ Windows Administrative Tools ➤ Remote Access Management Console**. Expand **Configuration**, highlight **DirectAccess and VPN**, and then click **Run the Remote Access Setup Wizard** (Figure 5-1).

© Richard M. Hicks 2016
R. M. Hicks, *Implementing DirectAccess with Windows Server 2016*, DOI 10.1007/978-1-4842-2059-7_5

🔧 **Configure Remote Access**

DirectAccess & VPN settings have not yet been configured. Select one of the wizard options.

➔ Run the Getting Started Wizard

Use this wizard to configure DirectAccess and VPN quickly, with default recommended settings.

➔ Run the Remote Access Setup Wizard

Use this wizard to configure DirectAccess and VPN with custom settings.

Figure 5-1. *Run the Remote Access Setup Wizard*

■ **Note** The Getting Started Wizard and the Remote Access Setup Wizard will not appear if DirectAccess has already been configured.

Deployment Options

The Remote Access Setup Wizard provides three options for configuring DirectAccess and VPN (Figure 5-2).

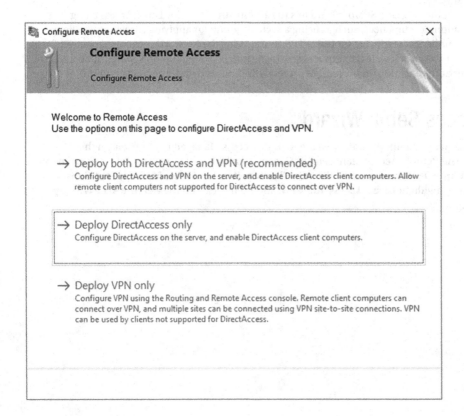

Figure 5-2. *Configure Remote Access*

Deploy both DirectAccess and VPN (recommended)

Although the GUI suggests this option is "recommended," there are some very important reasons why VPN should not be installed on the DirectAccess server. The most critical reason is that it eliminates support for important scalability and performance features included in DirectAccess, namely null encryption for IP-HTTPS connections. Having VPN and DirectAccess on the same server also makes the solution more complex, especially when configuring redundancy for DirectAccess (load balancing and multisite). As such, this configuration should be avoided if possible.[1]

Deploy DirectAccess only

This option should be selected.

Deploy VPN only

This is a book about DirectAccess, so this option is not applicable for our purposes.

Installing DirectAccess

To install DirectAccess without VPN, select the option to **Deploy DirectAccess only**. The Remote Access Setup Wizard will perform a prerequisites check to ensure essential supporting components are installed.

■ **Note**   It is not uncommon to receive an error message at this point. Typical errors are IPv6 being disabled via the registry, WinRM not being configured, and IPv6 transition technologies being disabled. Resolve any issues before proceeding.

Once the prerequisite check is complete, a four-step deployment wizard is displayed (Figure 5-3).

---

[1]The Web Application Proxy (WAP) role can also be configured on the same server as DirectAccess. Although technically supported, this too should be avoided if possible. The same reasons why VPN should not be installed on the DirectAccess server also apply to WAP. Best practice is to install DirectAccess on a server dedicated to the DirectAccess role.

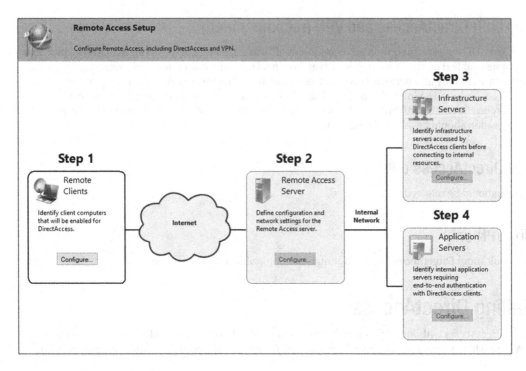

Figure 5-3. *Remote Access Setup Wizard's step-by-step deployment wizard*

Step 1: Remote Clients

Step 1 of the Remote Access Setup Wizard allows the administrator to select the DirectAccess deployment scenario, choose which security groups the DirectAccess client settings Group Policy Object (GPO) will be applied to, and define settings for the Network Connectivity Assistant for Windows 8.x and Windows 10 clients.

Deployment Scenario

Click **Configure** under **Remote Clients** on **Step 1** to select a deployment scenario (Figure 5-4). There are two options to choose from:

- **Deploy full DirectAccess for client access and remote management.** Select this option to grant DirectAccess computers and logged-on users full, unrestricted access to the Internal network when connected remotely.

- **Deploy DirectAccess for remote management only.** Select this option to grant DirectAccess computers limited access to the Internal network when connected remotely. Choosing this option restricts access only to infrastructure services, such as domain controllers and system-management servers. Users cannot access any other internal resources. However, administrators on the Internal network can still initiate connections outbound to connected DirectAccess clients.

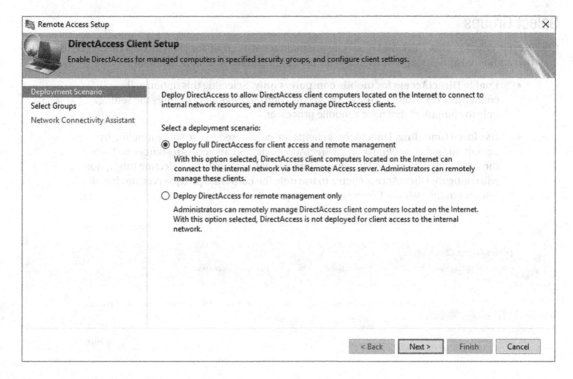

Figure 5-4. *Select a DirectAccess deployment scenario*

■ **Note**   When selecting the remote management only scenario, the Network Connectivity Assistant (NCA) will not be displayed in the Windows 8.x or Windows 10 GUI. In addition, the DirectAccess Connectivity Assistant (DCA) v2.0 should not be deployed to Windows 7 clients in this scenario.

Select Groups

Click **Next** to select groups. Click **Add** to specify a domain security group for DirectAccess clients (Figure 5-5). Two additional options are also available for the administrator to enable. They are:

- **Enable DirectAccess for mobile computers only.** Selecting this option will configure a WMI filter on the DirectAccess client settings GPO to apply the settings only to computers that have a mobile processor.

- **Use force tunneling.** DirectAccess clients are configured to use split tunneling by default. In split-tunneling mode, DirectAccess clients can access resources on both the corporate network and the public Internet at the same time. Selecting this option will configure DirectAccess clients to use only the corporate proxy server, forcing all Internet traffic over the DirectAccess connection.

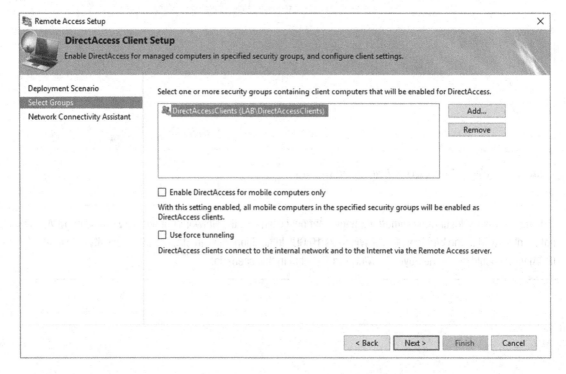

Figure 5-5. *Highlight Select Groups and optionally enable DirectAccess for mobile computers only and/or to use force tunneling*

■ **Note**   The use of force tunneling comes with some potential negative side effects. When force tunneling is enabled, all client Internet traffic is backhauled over the DirectAccess connection. The advantage is that web-browsing policies can be enforced by the on-premise proxy server. The disadvantage is that the additional overhead imposed by sending all web traffic over an encrypted connection (especially for HTTPS-protected websites, which are already encrypted) can result in a poor web-browsing experience for DirectAccess clients. Additionally, the use of strong user authentication is not supported when force tunneling is enabled.

Network Connectivity Assistant

Click **Next** to configure the Network Connectivity Assistant (NCA) (Figure 5-6).

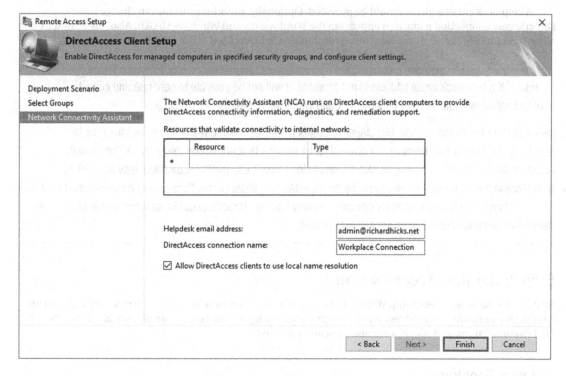

Figure 5-6.   *Configure the Network Connectivity Assistant*

■ **Note**   NCA settings apply only to Windows 8.x and Windows 10 clients. These settings are not used by Windows 7 clients. The DirectAccess Connectivity Assistant (DCA) v2.0 can optionally be deployed to provide similar functionality for Windows 7 clients, but must be configured separately. See "Chapter 9: Supporting Windows 7 Clients" for more information.

The **Resources that validate connectivity to the internal network** field is initially blank. Intuitively, information should be supplied here. However, it is not necessary (or recommended) to do so at this time. Resource validation is performed by Windows 8.x and Windows 10 clients by checking connectivity to this URL after the DirectAccess connection is made. During initial configuration, the DirectAccess deployment wizard will automatically populate this field with the URL `http://DirectAccess-WebProbeHost`, which is hosted on the DirectAccess server (a corresponding host record in DNS resolving to the internal IPv4 address of the DirectAccess server is also configured). This setting can later be changed after the initial configuration has been completed.

■ **Note**   If multiple resources are entered here, all must validate successfully for the remote client to indicate that a successful DirectAccess connection has been made.

A help desk email address should be provided. Optionally, the administrator can change the DirectAccess connection name as it appears in the Windows 8.x and Windows 10 GUI. Also, the option to allow DirectAccess clients to use local name resolution can be enabled. Click **Finish** to complete Step 1.

■ **Note**   If a help desk email address is not provided, it will not be possible to generate and collect troubleshooting information from Windows 8.x and Windows 10 clients.

Also, selecting the option to allow DirectAccess clients to use local name resolution allows the user to effectively disconnect the DirectAccess connection by clicking **Disconnect** on the Network Connectivity Assistant (NCA) GUI. However, only the Name Resolution Policy Table (NRPT) is disabled, leaving existing DirectAccess IPsec connections unaffected (new DirectAccess IPsec connections cannot be established until the computer is restarted). Administrators can still remotely manage DirectAccess clients when a user chooses to disconnect because IPsec tunnels are still established.

Step 2: Remote Access Server

Step 2 of the Remote Access Setup Wizard allows the administrator to select a network topology and provide a public name for the DirectAccess server, assign network adapters and choose an SSL certificate for IP-HTTPS connections, and specify user authentication methods.

Network Topology

Click **Configure** under **Remote Access Server** on **Step 2** to select a network topology (Figure 5-7). There are three options to choose from:

- **Edge**. Choose this topology when the DirectAccess server is configured with two network adapters and has a public IPv4 address assigned to the External interface.

- **Behind an edge device (with two network adapters)**. Choose this topology when the DirectAccess server is configured with two network adapters and has a private IPv4 address assigned to the External interface.

- **Behind an edge device (with a single network adapter)**. Choose this topology when the DirectAccess server is configured with a single network adapter.

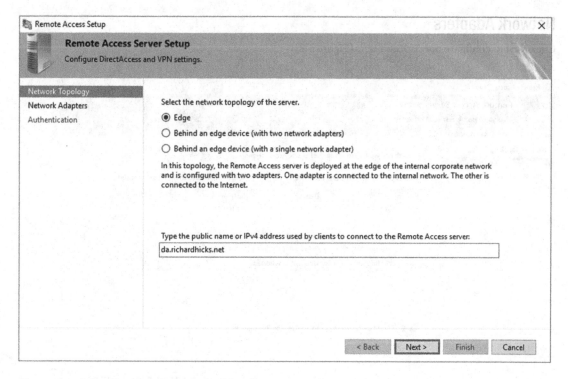

Figure 5-7. *Select the network topology of the server*

In addition, provide the public name or IPv4 address used by clients to connect to the remote access server.

___

■ **Note**   Although this field will accept an IPv4 address, it is strongly recommended that a fully qualified domain name (FQDN) be used instead. This FQDN must resolve to the public IPv4 address assigned to the DirectAccess server when configured with the Edge topology, or to the public IPv4 address assigned to the border router or edge firewall when the DirectAccess server is configured behind an edge device.

___

Network Adapters

Click **Next** to configure network adapters (Figure 5-8).

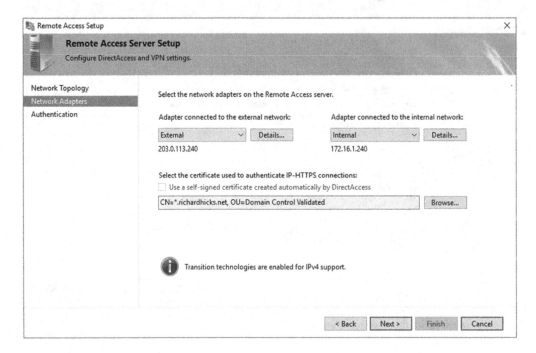

Figure 5-8. *Configure network adapters and select the IP-HTTPS SSL certificate*

The wizard automatically detects network adapters based on their configuration. Assuming they are configured correctly, no changes should be required. Also, if a public SSL certificate is available and matches the public name specified in the previous step, it will be automatically selected.

■ **Note**   If no suitable SSL certificate is found, the option of creating a self-signed certificate is selected. However, this should be avoided whenever possible.

Authentication

Click **Next** to configure authentication (Figure 5-9).

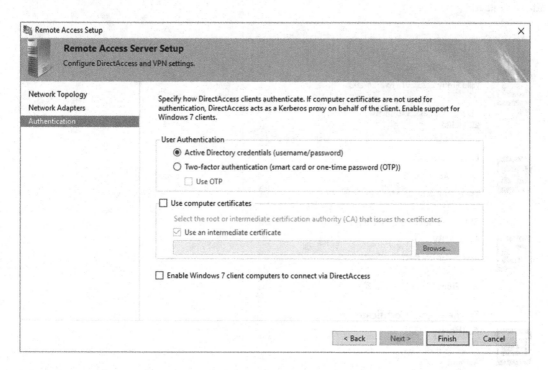

Figure 5-9. *Configure DirectAccess authentication*

Select the option to use **Active Directory credentials (username/password)**.

■ **Note** If two-factor authentication is required, it is still recommended to use Active Directory (AD) credentials for now. Configuring two-factor authentication is not trivial and is difficult to troubleshoot. It is best to ensure that DirectAccess is working with AD authentication alone first, then enable two-factor authentication afterward.

In addition to Active Directory credentials, it is recommended that computer certificates also be used for authentication. This will provide an additional level of security and assurance for DirectAccess clients and ensures maximum deployment flexibility in the future when enabling features that require certificate authentication.

To enable certificate authentication, select the option to **Use computer certificates**. If an intermediate Certification Authority (CA) is used to issue certificates to the DirectAccess server and clients, select the option to **Use an intermediate certificate** and click **Browse**. Select the certificate belonging to the CA that will be issuing certificates to the DirectAccess server and clients (Figure 5-10).

Figure 5-10. Select a CA certificate

■ **Note**   It is important to understand that this is not the certificate issued to the DirectAccess server. It is the certificate issued to the CA that will be used to issue computer certificates to DirectAccess servers and clients. If there is more than one certificate for a given CA, ensure that the exact certificate is chosen. To confirm, click the link below the certificate and view the properties. Click the Details tab and select **Thumbprint**. Confirm this thumbprint matches that of the CA server's certificate.

Finally, if Windows 7 clients are to be supported, select the option to **Enable Windows 7 client computers to connect via DirectAccess** and click **Finish**.

■ **Note**   Selecting the option to enable support for Windows 7 clients even for deployments that are exclusively Windows 8.x and Windows 10 is recommended for optimum security. This option forces machine certificate authentication for all DirectAccess clients.

Step 3: Infrastructure Servers

Step 3 of the Remote Access Setup Wizard allows the administrator to define a Network Location Server (NLS), configure DNS servers, define the DNS suffix search list, and specify management servers for use by DirectAccess clients.

Network Location Server

Click **Configure** under **Infrastructure Servers** on **Step 3** to configure a Network Location Server (Figure 5-11). There are two options to choose from:

- **The network location server is deployed on a remote web server (recommended)**. This is the preferred configuration option.

- **The network location server is deployed on the Remote Access server**. This option should be avoided whenever possible.

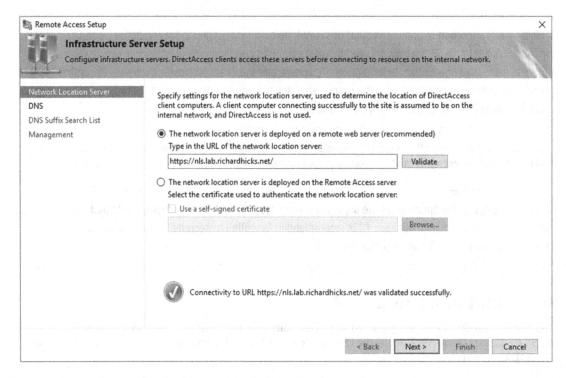

Figure 5-11. *Configure the Network Location Server (NLS)*

Select the option to deploy the network location server on a remote web server. Enter the URL (including HTTPS://) and click **Validate**. Ensure that connectivity to the URL validates successfully.

■ **Note**   For the network location server to be properly validated, the name of the NLS entered must match the subject name on the SSL certificate installed on the NLS web server.

DNS

Click **Next** to configure DNS settings for DirectAccess clients (Figure 5-12).

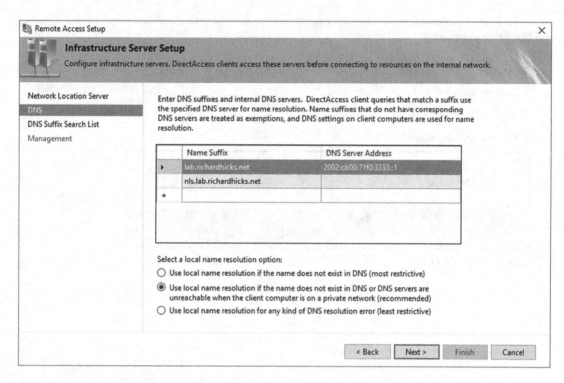

Figure 5-12. *Configure DNS and select local name-resolution options*

The settings here specify the configuration of the Name Resolution Policy Table (NRPT) on DirectAccess clients. The NRPT defines which DNS servers DirectAccess clients will use to resolve names in a particular namespace. The DirectAccess server's DNS suffix is automatically added and assigned a DNS server address. In addition, the name of the NLS is added but is not assigned a DNS server address. A name suffix without a corresponding DNS server address is effectively excluded, and DirectAccess clients will not be able to access this host (or resources in this namespace) over the DirectAccess connection.

___

■ **Note**   DNS configuration is simple and straightforward when the internal and external namespaces are distinct. However, when split DNS is employed and the internal and external namespaces are the same, additional configuration is required. Any resources that should be reachable externally and not over the DirectAccess connection will need to be excluded. NRPT exclusions are defined as table entries for which no DNS server is defined (blank), such as the Network Location Server (NLS). Examples would include public-facing websites, mail services, unified communications, and so forth. Also, the public name of the DirectAccess server must be excluded.

___

To add additional DNS suffixes, double-click an empty field, enter the DNS suffix name, and then click **Detect** (Figure 5-13). This will automatically populate the correct DNS server address. To exclude a specific server or an entire namespace from the NRPT, perform these steps without entering a DNS server address.

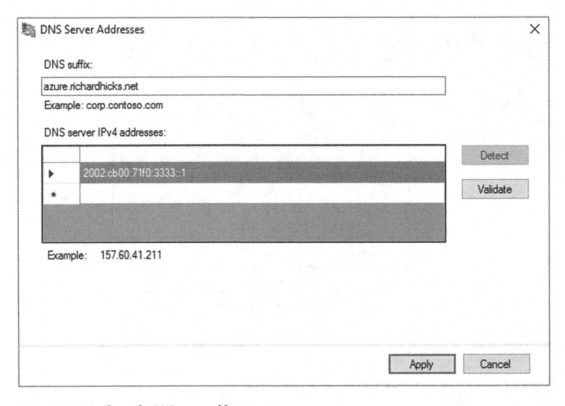

Figure 5-13. *Configure the DNS server addresses*

■ **Note** This method automatically populates the field with an IPv6 address ending in 3333::1. This IPv6 address is assigned to the Internal network interface of the DirectAccess server and is used by the DNS64 service. This is the preferred method for configuring DNS servers and ensures that DirectAccess clients always use the DNS64 service running on the DirectAccess server for name resolution.

Local name-resolution behavior using IPv6 Link Local Multicast Name Resolution (LLMNR) and NetBIOS over TCP/IP can also be configured. There are three local name-resolution options to choose from. They are:

- **Use local name resolution if the name does not exist in DNS (most restrictive).**
  This option is the most secure. When this option is selected, DirectAccess clients will only use local name resolution for host names that can't be resolved by internal DNS servers. However, if a host name can be resolved, or the internal DNS servers are not available, local name resolution will not be used.

- **Use local name resolution if the name does not exist in DNS or DNS servers are unreachable when the client computer is on a private network (recommended).**
  This is the recommended option and provides reasonable security, as it only allows the use of local name resolution on a private network when internal DNS servers are unavailable.

- **Use local name resolution for any kind of DNS resolution error (least restrictive).**
  This option provides the least security. If internal DNS servers are unavailable, or if any type of DNS error is encountered, local name resolution will be used.

DNS Suffix Search List

Click **Next** to configure the DNS suffix search list (Figure 5-14).

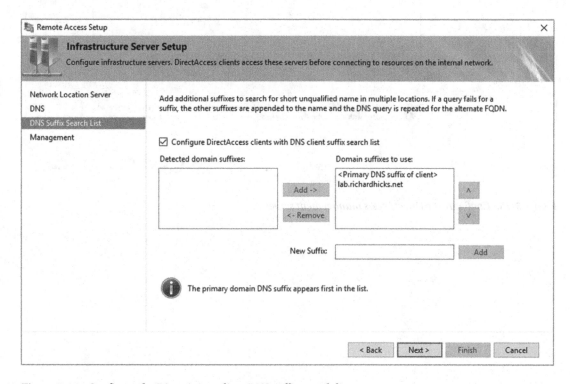

Figure 5-14. Configure the DirectAccess client DNS suffix search list

The option to **Configure DirectAccess clients with DNS client suffix search list** is enabled by default. This is recommended to ensure that DirectAccess clients can properly resolve single-label hostnames using internal DNS servers. To include additional DNS suffixes, enter a new suffix name and click **Add**.

Management

Click **Next** to configure management servers (Figure 5-15). Management servers are reachable by the DirectAccess client without requiring a user to be logged on. These may include patch-management servers, remediation servers, or any other server that must be accessible to the DirectAccess server prior to user logon.

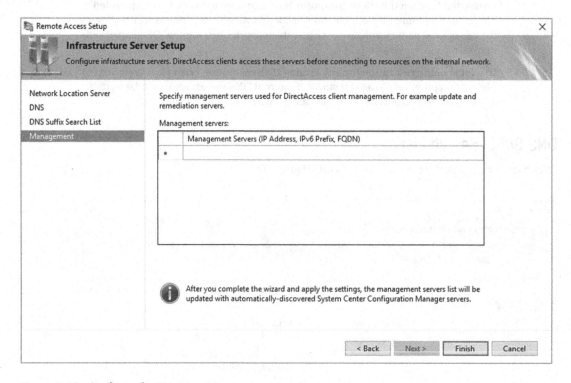

Figure 5-15. *Configure the DirectAccess management servers*

To add a management server, double-click a blank entry and provide the hostname or IPv4 address of the internal management server and click **OK** (Figure 5-16). Once complete, click **Finish**.

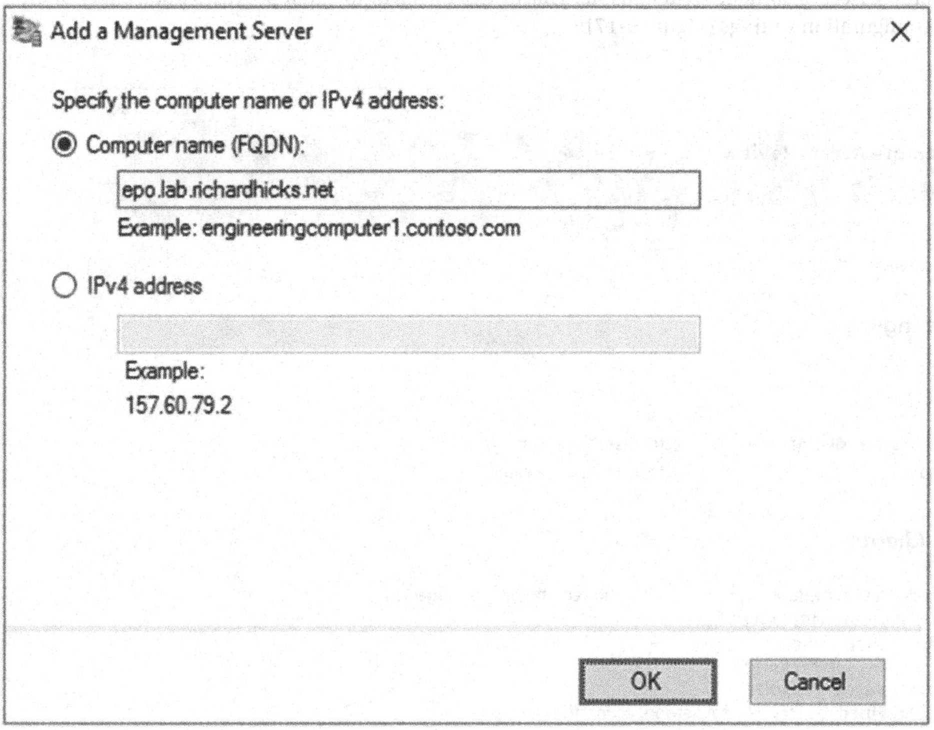

Figure 5-16. *Add a management server*

■ **Note**   It is not necessary to enter names or IP addresses for management servers that register SRV records in DNS. For example, management servers running Windows Server Update Services (WSUS) or System Center Configuration Manager (SCCM) will automatically be discovered and added to the management servers list during initial DirectAccess configuration. This may apply to some third-party management platforms as well.

Finish and Apply Changes

At the completion of Step 3, configuration changes can be applied by clicking **Finish** in the lower-right corner of the Remote Access Management console. This brings up a window that provides a summary of the remote access configuration settings (Figure 5-17).

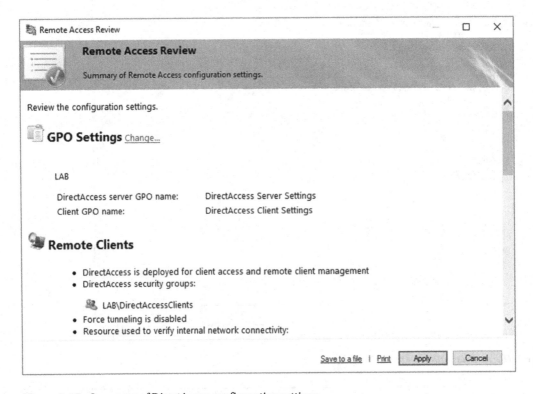

Figure 5-17. *Summary of DirectAccess configuration settings*

By default, the Remote Access Setup Wizard will name the DirectAccess client and server settings GPOs **DirectAccess Client Settings** and **DirectAccess Server Settings**, respectively. If different names are desired, click **Change** next to **GPO Settings** and provide new GPO names as required. If prestaged GPOs are to be used, click **Browse** and select them accordingly (Figure 5-18).

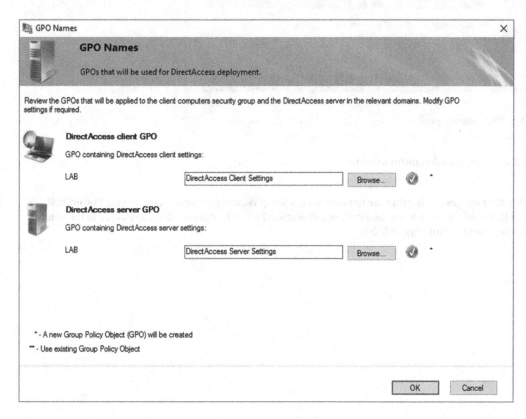

Figure 5-18. *Edit the GPO settings*

After reviewing the configuration settings, click **Apply**. Once the configuration has been applied successfully, click **More Details** to review warning messages, if any were raised (Figure 5-19).

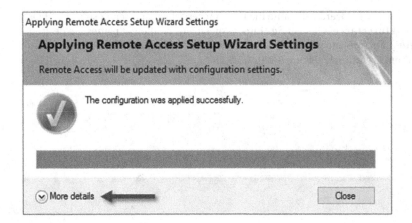

Figure 5-19. *Configuration status window*

All of the changes made using the Remote Access Setup Wizard are implemented using PowerShell commands. These commands can be saved as a PowerShell script by right-clicking anywhere in the window and choosing **Copy script** (Figure 5-20).

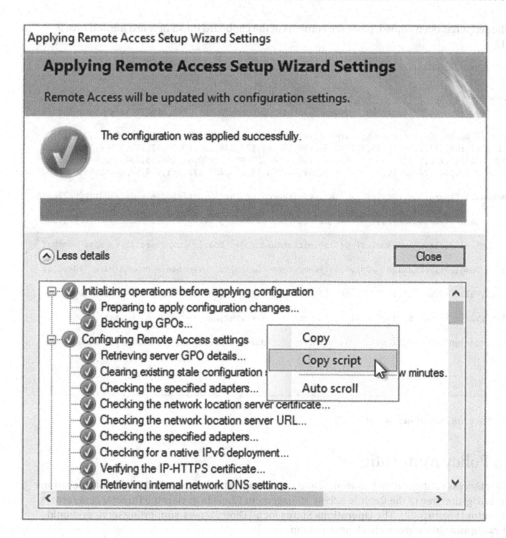

Figure 5-20. *Generate the PowerShell script*

Once the script has been copied, paste the contents of the clipboard into a new text file and save it (Figure 5-21).

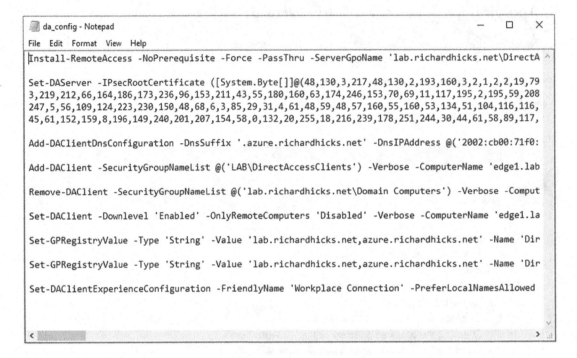

Figure 5-21. *Save the PowerShell script*

Confirm Policy Application

Once the DirectAccess configuration is complete and the settings have been applied, highlight **Operations Status** in the navigation tree of the Remote Access Management Console to view the DirectAccess server's **Operations Status** (Figure 5-22). The **Operations Status** for all DirectAccess-supporting services should indicate **Working** and have a green check next to them.

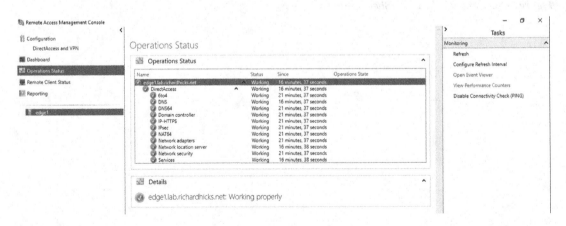

Figure 5-22. *DirectAccess server operation status*

Step 4: Application Servers (Optional)

Step 4 of the Remote Access Setup Wizard is optional. By default, DirectAccess client communication is authenticated and encrypted only between the DirectAccess client and the server. Communication between the DirectAccess server and hosts on the Internal network is not authenticated or encrypted.

If full end-to-end authentication—and, optionally, encryption—from the DirectAccess server to specific application servers is required, click **Edit** under **Application Servers** on **Step 4**. Select the option to **Extend authentication to selected application servers**, click **Add**, and specify an Active Directory security group that includes servers requiring end-to-end authentication (Figure 5-23).

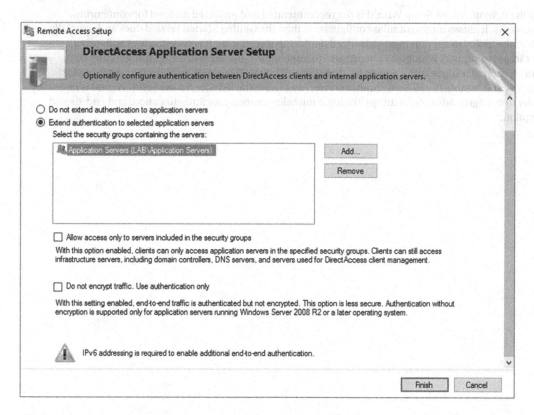

Figure 5-23. *Extend authentication to selected application servers*

Two additional configuration options are available to choose from. They are as follows:

- **Allow access only to servers included in the security groups.** Select this option to allow DirectAccess clients to access only the internal application servers included in the defined security groups. DirectAccess clients will still be able to access infrastructure and management servers.

- **Do not encrypt traffic. Use authentication only.** Select this option if only authentication is required and not encryption. Application servers must be running Windows Server 2008 R2 or later to support this option.

■ **Note** When configuring DirectAccess end-to-end authentication and encryption, application servers must be configured with an IPv6 address. If IPv6 has not been deployed on the Internal network, the ISATAP IPv6 transition protocol can be used for deployments where it is supported.

Summary

Using the Remote Access Setup Wizard is the recommended and preferred method for configuring DirectAccess. It allows more-granular configuration than the Getting Started Wizard does and, crucially, provides the ability to support more-advanced deployment scenarios. It is required for configuring DirectAccess to support Windows 7 clients, and to implement DirectAccess using configuration best practices, such as using security groups for deploying client settings, using a public SSL certificate for IP-HTTPS, and hosting the NLS on another server. Also, using the Remote Access Setup Wizard is necessary in order to configure advanced settings like force tunneling, strong user authentication, and end-to-end encryption.

CHAPTER 6

■ ■ ■

Configure DirectAccess Load Balancing

For many organizations, providing secure remote access is vital to the productivity of remote employees. Ensuring that the solution is highly available is critical, and eliminating single points of failure is crucial to making sure that planned or unplanned outages do not prevent mobile workers from accessing resources on the corporate network when they are outside the office.

In addition, many DirectAccess deployments require more than one server in order to adequately meet demands when supporting large numbers of connected DirectAccess clients.

To address both availability and scalability requirements, DirectAccess supports load balancing using either native Windows Network Load Balancing (NLB) or an external load balancer (ELB). With load balancing enabled and configured, single points of failure are eliminated and essential redundancy is provided. In addition, capacity can be added to support more DirectAccess clients, if required.

Load Balancing

In generic terms, load balancing is a concept where network traffic is distributed among multiple redundant systems for a variety of purposes. First is the obvious: improving availability. If multiple systems are available to process requests and one becomes unavailable for any reason (planned or unplanned), service is not interrupted, as other systems are available to handle the load. The second, and less obvious reason, is scalability. If one system does not have the capacity to handle all of the requests, additional capacity can be added by adding more servers.

DirectAccess Load Balancing

DirectAccess supports load balancing using either Windows Network Load Balancing (NLB) or a physical or virtual external load balancer (ELB).

Windows Network Load Balancing

Windows Network Load Balancing is a feature of the Windows Server 2016 operating system and is designed to distribute network traffic evenly to all hosts in the load-balanced cluster. It is a simple and cost-effective way to provide local redundancy for DirectAccess. A maximum of eight nodes are supported in a single DirectAccess server cluster with NLB.

© Richard M. Hicks 2016
R. M. Hicks, *Implementing DirectAccess with Windows Server 2016*, DOI 10.1007/978-1-4842-2059-7_6

NLB for DirectAccess supports two distinct operating modes: unicast (default) and multicast. Each has its own advantages and disadvantages.

Unicast Operating Mode

When NLB is enabled, the default operating mode is set to unicast. In this mode, the MAC address of each host in the cluster is overwritten with a common MAC address. Additionally, NLB prevents the network switch from learning this MAC address. By design, this induces switch flooding, which allows all hosts in the NLB cluster to "see" all traffic. The NLB driver then decides which host in the cluster will process the incoming request.

Multicast Operating Mode

NLB can also be configured in multicast operating mode. In this mode, each host in the cluster retains its original MAC address, and a multicast MAC address is assigned to the cluster's IPv4 address. In many environments, network routers will not deliver packets to a unicast IPv4 address associated with a *multicast* MAC address, so creating a static Address Resolution Protocol (ARP) entry on the router for the subnet where the DirectAccess servers reside is often required.

■ **Note**   NLB in multicast operating mode is required when the DirectAccess server is hosted in a VMware virtual environment. Details about how to configure NLB in multicast operating mode are covered later in this chapter.

NLB Drawbacks

NLB is simple and effective, but it comes with some potential drawbacks. DirectAccess is limited to eight nodes when using NLB, but four nodes should be considered the practical limit. In addition, NLB operates at Layer 2 of the Open Systems Interconnection (OSI) model.[1] Cluster members communicate with each other via heartbeat messages. These heartbeats are broadcast by all nodes in the cluster once per second, and all hosts on the network segment receive this traffic, including those that are not part of the cluster. This results in a lot of noise on the network, which can degrade network performance. NLB also consumes valuable CPU cycles on the DirectAccess server, which can negatively impact performance. All of these problems become exponentially worse as more hosts are added to the cluster.

■ **Note**   For more information about Windows Network Load Balancing, see **Overview of Network Load Balancing** on Microsoft TechNet (https://technet.microsoft.com/en-us/library/cc725691.aspx).

External Load Balancer

A better choice to provide load balancing for DirectAccess servers is to use a dedicated, purpose-built load-balancing appliance. External load balancers operate at Layers 3–7 of the OSI model and provide better performance than NLB does. In addition, external load balancers offer more intelligent traffic distribution and provide better visibility compared to NLB. A maximum of 32 nodes are supported in a single DirectAccess server cluster with an external load balancer.

---

[1]https://en.wikipedia.org/wiki/OSI_model.

The external load balancer can be physical or virtual. A physical appliance is recommended for optimum performance. Virtual appliances work well for smaller deployments.

Capacity Planning

When designing a load-balanced architecture, ensure that enough capacity exists, even in a failure state. For example, if two load-balanced servers are running at 70 percent capacity and one fails, the remaining server will not have enough reserve capacity to handle both its load and the failed server's load. The result will be a total outage, with the first server being overrun with requests.

Ideally, the load-balanced system should be designed such that a single server failure will not result in overloading the remaining servers. For example, if three servers are load-balanced, and each is running at 25 percent utilization, a failure of one server will result in increased utilization on the remaining servers, but they will still have enough reserve capacity to handle the additional load.

Preparing for Load Balancing

By definition, load balancing implies that there will be at least two servers. Before adding another DirectAccess server to create a cluster, the new server must be prepared as outlined in Chapter 3. It must have Windows Server 2016 installed and configured, it must be joined to the domain, and it must have the necessary certificates installed. It must also have the DirectAccess role installed.

■ **Important**   DO NOT *configure* DirectAccess on the second server! Install the DirectAccess-VPN role only. The server will be added to the cluster and configured from the first server.

Add NLB Feature

Adding the NLB feature can be accomplished using either the GUI or PowerShell. PowerShell is the preferred method for installing the feature, as it takes only a single PowerShell command to install the role and management tools.

■ **Note**   It is not necessary to install the NLB feature when using an external load balancer.

PowerShell

To install the NLB feature, open an elevated PowerShell window on the DirectAccess server and enter the following command:

```
Install-WindowsFeature NLB -IncludeManagementTools
```

■ **Note**   Repeat this step on each DirectAccess server that will be joined to the cluster.

GUI

To install the NLB feature using the GUI, open the **Server Manager** on the DirectAccess server, click **Manage** in the upper-right corner of the window, and then click **Add Roles and Features**. Click **Next**, choose **Role-based or feature-based installation**, and click **Next**. Choose **Select a server from the server pool** and click **Next** twice, then select the **Network Load Balancing** feature (Figure 6-1).

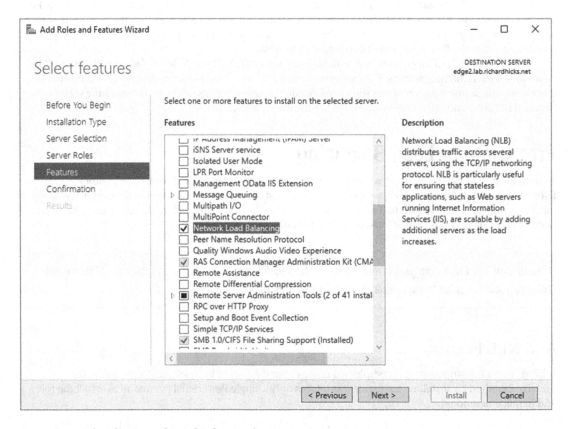

Figure 6-1. *Select the Network Load Balancing feature*

Click **Add Features** when prompted to add features that are required for Network Load Balancing (Figure 6-2) and click **Next**.

Figure 6-2. Add features required for Network Load Balancing

Confirm installation selections and click **Install** (Figure 6-3).

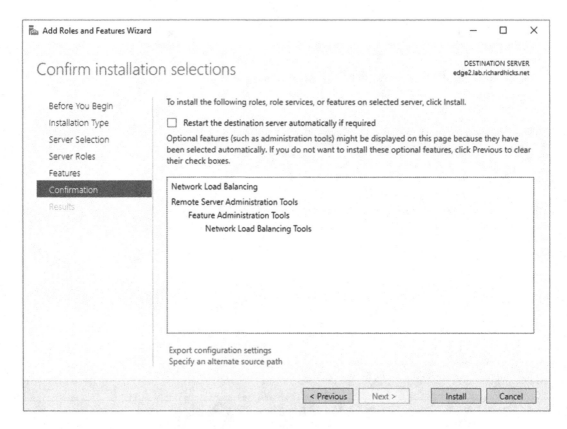

Figure 6-3. *Confirm your installation selections*

Hyper-V and NLB

Special consideration is required when enabling NLB on DirectAccess servers hosted in a Hyper-V virtual environment. By default, Hyper-V virtual switches will not send or receive traffic for hosts where the MAC address has been changed in the operating system, which happens when NLB is configured in unicast operating mode. To resolve this issue, MAC address spoofing must be enabled on each DirectAccess server virtual network interface. To do this, open the Hyper-V manager and right-click **Settings** on the DirectAccess virtual server. Expand **Network Adapter** and highlight **Advanced Features**. Check the box next to **Enable MAC address spoofing** (Figure 6-4). Repeat this process for each network adapter on the DirectAccess server and on each DirectAccess server that will be part of the cluster.

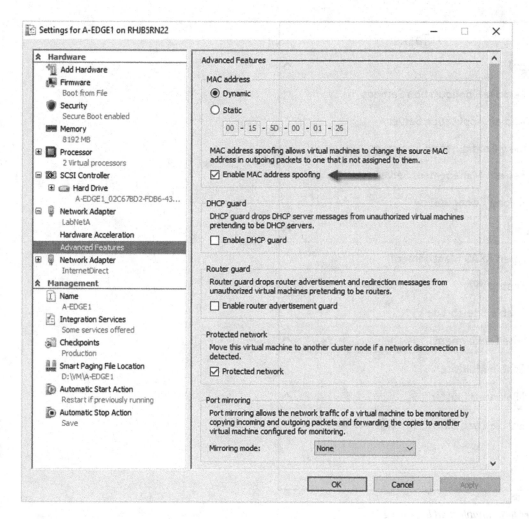

Figure 6-4. *Enable MAC address spoofing*

Enable Network Load Balancing (NLB)

To enable load balancing using Windows Network Load Balancing, open the Remote Access Management console on the first DirectAccess server, highlight **DirectAccess and VPN** in the navigation tree, and click **Enable Load Balancing** under **Load Balanced Cluster** in the **Tasks** pane (Figure 6-5).

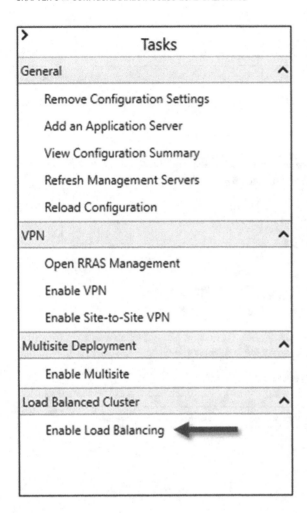

Figure 6-5. *Enable load balancing*

■ **Note**   To enable load balancing on a multisite DirectAccess entry point, highlight the entry point in the navigation tree and click **Enable Load Balancing** under **Load Balanced Cluster** in the **Tasks** pane.

Click **Next** and choose **Use Windows Network Load Balancing (NLBn** (Figure 6-6).

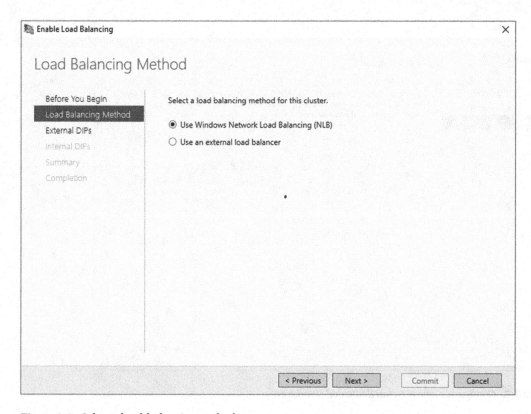

Figure 6-6. Select a load-balancing method

The existing dedicated IP address (DIP) assigned to each network interface on the *first* DirectAccess server will become the virtual IP address (VIP) for the cluster.[2] A new dedicated IP address for the DirectAccess server must then be assigned (Figures 6-7 and 6-8). Provide new IP addresses to be assigned to this DirectAccess server and click **Next**.

[2]https://www.youtube.com/watch?v=3tdqgY9Y-uo

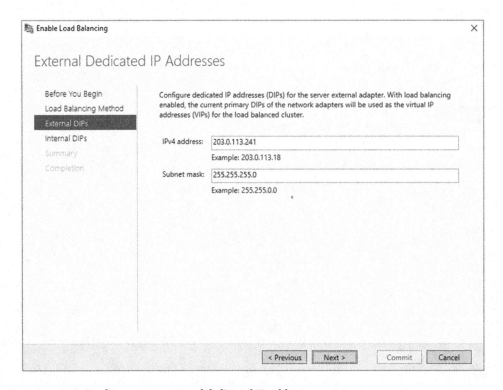

Figure 6-7. Configure a new external dedicated IP address

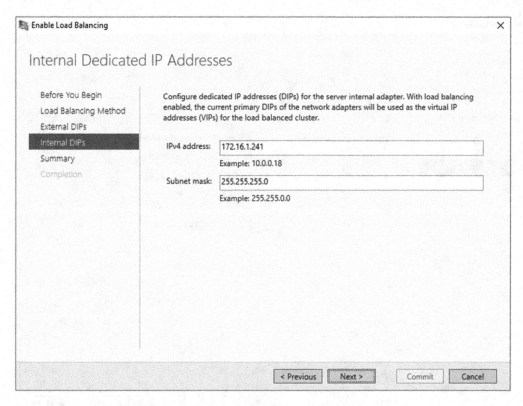

Figure 6-8. *Configure a new internal dedicated IP address*

Confirm the load-balancing settings and click **Commit** (Figure 6-9).

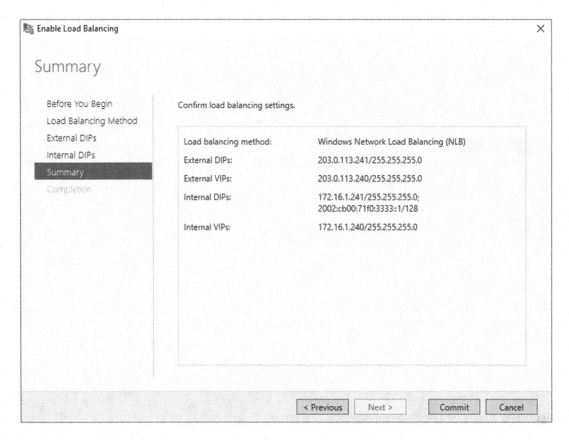

Figure 6-9. Confirm load-balancing settings

■ **Note**   Initial configuration of NLB for DirectAccess must ALWAYS be performed using the Remote Access Management console. NLB settings are managed exclusively by DirectAccess. Initial configuration of NLB should NEVER be performed using the native Network Load Balancing manager. Once NLB has been configured, viewing the NLB status and changing the cluster operation mode using the NLB manager is acceptable.

VMware and NLB

Special consideration is required when enabling NLB on DirectAccess servers hosted in a VMware virtual environment. NLB operates in unicast mode by default, and all nodes in the cluster share the same MAC address. In physical environments, the operating system masks the MAC address for outgoing traffic, preventing the switch from learning it. This induces switch flooding, which is by design and is crucial to the operation of NLB. However, the VMware hypervisor knows the virtual server's MAC address and proactively shares that information with the virtual switch when the virtual machine starts. Fundamentally, this breaks NLB and results in all cluster traffic being delivered to a single node in the cluster.

To resolve this issue, it will be necessary to change the default NLB operation mode from unicast to multicast. To do this, it will be necessary to install the Network Load Balancing Manager on a separate Windows system. The NLB manager can be installed on Windows client operating systems by installing the Remote Server Administration Tools (RSAT),[3] or on any Windows Server 2012 R2 or Windows Server 2016 host by opening an elevated PowerShell command window and entering the following command:

```
Install-WindowsFeature RSAT-NLB
```

Once complete, open the Network Load Balancing manager, choose **Cluster** from the drop-down menu, and then choose **Connect to existing**. Enter the hostname of the DirectAccess server and click **Connect** (Figure 6-10). Select the **Internal DA cluster** and click **Finish**. For dual-NIC deployments, repeat these steps for the **Internet DA cluster**.

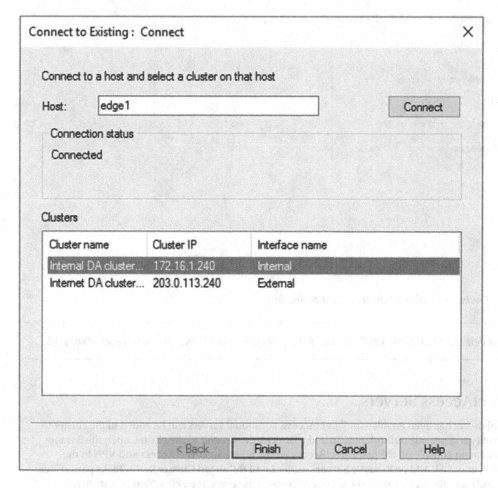

Figure 6-10. *Connect to thr DirectAccess NLB clusters*

---

[3]The Remote Server Administration Tools for Windows 10 can be downloaded here: https://www.microsoft.com/en-us/download/details.aspx?id=45520

Expand **Network Load Balancing Clusters**, then right-click **Internal DA cluster** and choose **Cluster Properties**. Select the **Cluster Parameters** tab and choose **Multicast** for the cluster operation mode (Figure 6-11). For dual-NIC deployments, repeat these steps for the **Internet DA cluster**.

Figure 6-11. *Enable the Multicast cluster operation mode*

■ **Note**   For detailed information about running NLB on VMware, visit `https://kb.vmware.com/kb/1556`.

Add DirectAccess Servers

Once load balancing has been enabled for DirectAccess, additional servers can be added to the cluster to increase capacity and provide redundancy. To add a DirectAccess server to the cluster, open the Remote Access Management console on the first DirectAccess server, highlight **DirectAccess and VPN** in the navigation tree, and click **Add or Remove Servers** under **Load Balanced Cluster** in the **Tasks** pane. Click **Add Server** and enter the hostname of the second DirectAccess server, then click **Next** (Figure 6-12).

■ **Note**   To add a server to a multisite DirectAccess entry point, highlight the entry point in the navigation tree and click **Add or Remove Servers** under **Load Balanced Cluster** in the **Tasks** pane.

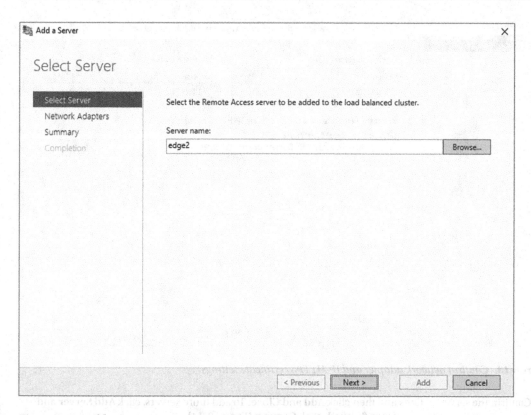

Figure 6-12. *Add a remote access server to a load-balanced cluster*

■ **Reminder**   Ensure that servers being added to the DirectAccess cluster are properly configured and meet all installation prerequisites prior to adding the. Most important, the DirectAccess-VPN and NLB roles must be installed but not configured. In addition, ensure that all required certificates (IPsec and IP-HTTPS) are in place before proceeding.

Review the network adapter and IP-HTTPS certificate settings and click **Next** (Figure 6-13).

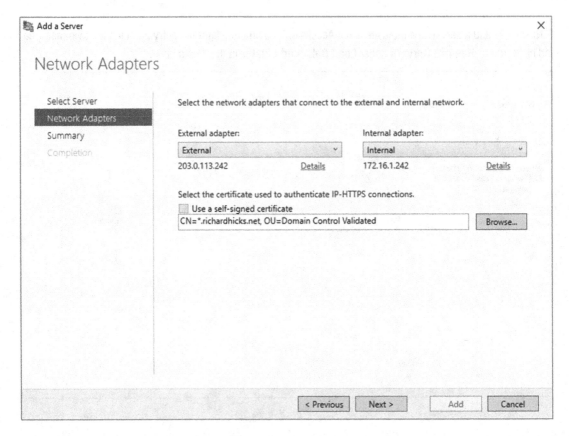

Figure 6-13. Confirm network adapter and IP-HTTPS certificate settings

Confirm the server settings and then click **Add** and **Close**. To add more servers, click **Add Server** and repeat the process as necessary. Once finished, click **Commit** (Figure 6-14).

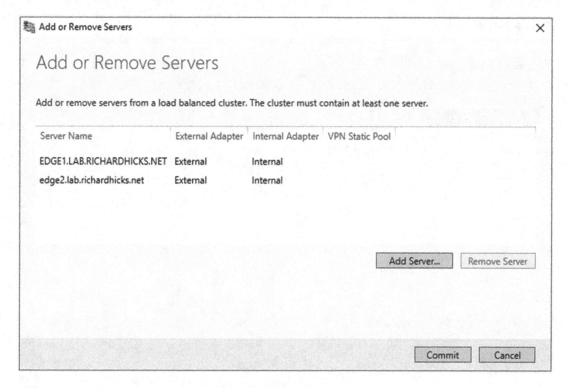

Figure 6-14. *Add or remove servers from a load-balanced cluster*

Enable External Load Balancer (ELB)

Enabling load balancing for DirectAccess using an external load balancer (ELB) is similar to configuring NLB. However, the NLB role does not need to be installed when enabling ELB. To configure ELB, follow the steps outlined previously for enabling NLB, this time choosing the option to **Use an external load balancer** (Figure 6-15).

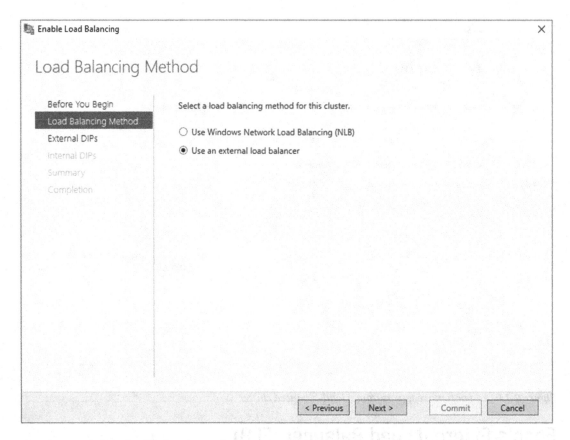

Figure 6-15. *Select a load-balancing method*

VIP Assignment

As described earlier in this chapter, the DIPs on the first DirectAccess server become the VIPs for the cluster. However, unlike NLB, the ELB VIP is not actually assigned anywhere. Rather, it is reserved for use on the ELB device, if necessary.

Assigning the VIP to the ELB is optional. For example, a common DirectAccess network topology has the External network interfaces residing in a perimeter or DMZ network. The ELB has a public IPv4 address assigned as a VIP, with the perimeter/DMZ DIPs of the DirectAccess servers configured as pool members.

There is no need to load balance the *Internal* network interfaces when the DirectAccess servers are configured with two network interfaces, unless the web-probe host URL is being hosted on the DirectAccess servers. In this scenario, assign a different resource for the web-probe host (*DirectAccess and VPN configuration, Step 1n Network Connectivity Assistant*). Alternatively, the VIP can be assigned to the ELB, and TCP port 80 can be load balanced to the Internal network interface of each DirectAccess server.[4]

---

[4]https://directaccess.richardhicks.com/2014/08/12/directaccess-clients-in-connecting-state-when-using-external-load-balancer/

Load Balancer Configuration

Prescriptive guidance for configuring the external load balancer itself differs greatly between vendors and is outside the scope of this book. However, in general terms, configuring an external load balancer for DirectAccess is fundamentally the same as load balancing a secure web server. The external load balancer should be configured to load balance HTTPS traffic on TCP port 443. It should also be configured to perform SSL bridging; SSL termination (offloading) is not supported.[5] The external DIPs of each DirectAccess server are configured as pool members. Consult the load balancer vendor for detailed information.

■ **Note**   Load balancing for Teredo traffic isn't recommended, because it is complex and prohibitively difficult to implement correctly. If load balancing for Teredo is required, configuration guidance can be found here: https://www.f5.com/pdf/deployment-guides/f5-uag-dg.pdf.

Summary

Enabling DirectAccess load balancing allows administrators to improve availability for the remote access solution by eliminating single points of failure in their architecture. It also provides important scalability to accommodate large deployments where many DirectAccess clients will be supported.

NLB can be deployed quickly and is a cost-effective way to improve reliability. However, NLB has some potentially serious drawbacks, especially for large deployments. In practice, NLB should be considered for small to mid-sized deployments only. An external load balancer should be deployed for the best overall experience.

---

[5]Some load balancers can be configured to provide SSL offload for DirectAccess IP-HTTPS traffic. Although not supported, it can be an effective way to improve performance and scalability on DirectAccess servers in some scenarios. More details can be found here: http://directaccess.richardhicks.com/2013/07/10/ssl-offload-for-ip-https-directaccess-traffic-from-windows-7-clients-using-f5-big-ip/.

CHAPTER 7

Configure DirectAccess Geographic Redundancy

Where load balancing provides local redundancy and high availability, multisite DirectAccess provides geographic redundancy and failover for DirectAccess clients across multiple locations. If an outage occurs that affects all DirectAccess servers in one location—for example, a datacenter's connection to the Internet fails—DirectAccess clients will still be able to connect to an entry point in another location.

Multisite DirectAccess also accommodates geographically dispersed clients. If an organization has DirectAccess clients connecting from many different regions, the DirectAccess experience is improved when those clients can connect to an entry point closer to their physical location.

Client Support

Multisite DirectAccess can be leveraged by all supported DirectAccess clients. However, not all multisite features are available to all of them.

Windows 8.x and Windows 10

Windows 8.x and Windows 10 clients are aware of all entry points in the organization. When a Windows 8.x/10 client initiates a DirectAccess connection, it will check the status of all entry points and connect to the closest one. "Closest" is defined as the entry point that responds the quickest to a probe sent automatically by the client.

Optionally, an administrator can allow Windows 8.x and Windows 10 clients to manually select an entry point to connect to, if required.

Windows 7

Windows 7 clients can be provisioned in a multisite deployment, but their functionality is limited. Windows 7 clients must be assigned to a specific entry point and are unaware of other entry points in the organization. They will always connect to their assigned entry point and will not fail over.

■ **Note** There's a common misconception that Windows 7 clients can transparently fail over to another entry point if a Global Server Load Balancer (GSLB) is used. A Windows 7 client can't establish a DirectAccess connection just because the entry point's public hostname can be resolved to another entry point. Using GSLB to point the client to another entry point only swings the IPv6 transition tunnel to the new entry point. However, the DirectAccess client still expects to connect to its assigned DirectAccess servers using specific IPv6 addresses. Although the Windows 7 client will successfully establish a transition tunnel, the tunnel endpoint IPv6 addresses inside the transition tunnel will be incorrect, and IPsec will fail. This will prevent access to internal resources.

Preparing for Multisite

A number of prerequisites must be in place prior to implementing multisite DirectAccess. Considerations for DirectAccess servers, Active Directory Security groups, and SSL certificates must be made.

DirectAccess Servers

Much like preparing a DirectAccess server for load balancing, DirectAccess servers that will be added to a multisite configuration must meet all installation prerequisites. Windows Server 2016 must be installed and joined to the domain, all necessary certificates must be installed, and the DirectAccess-VPN role must be installed. Again, it is not necessary to *configure* DirectAccess directly on these servers. All DirectAccess configuration will be performed from a previously deployed DirectAccess server.

Security Groups

If Windows 8.x and Windows 10 clients are to be supported exclusively, no additional security groups are required. However, if Windows 7 clients are to be supported as well, one additional security group per entry point is required. For example, a multisite DirectAccess deployment with two entry points will require three security groups in total. One security group will be dedicated to Windows 8.x and Windows 10 clients, with one security group for each entry point dedicated to Windows 7 clients.[1]

■ **Note** It is crucial that DirectAccess clients belong to **only one** security group. Windows 8.x and Windows 10 clients must not reside in Windows 7 groups, and Windows 7 clients must not be included in the Windows 8.x/10 group. If a Windows 7 client is to be moved from one entry point to another, remove the client from its current security group first before placing it in another. When performing in-place upgrades from Windows 7 to Windows 8.x or Windows 10, it is recommended that the client be removed from the DirectAccess security group before being upgraded. Once the upgrade is complete, the client can be placed in the Windows 8.x/10 DirectAccess client security group.

---

[1]This assumes that all DirectAccess clients are members of a single domain. Additional security groups may be required if DirectAccess clients reside in more than one domain.

DNS

Each additional entry point will require its own unique public hostname. This hostname must resolve in public DNS to the IPv4 address assigned to the DirectAccess server's External network interface, or to the IPv4 address assigned to the edge security device protecting the DirectAccess server.

IP-HTTPS Certificate

The IP-HTTPS certificate installed on the DirectAccess server(s) must match the public hostname for the entry point. Optionally, a wildcard certificate can be deployed.

Enable Multisite

The process of enabling multisite DirectAccess involves first converting the existing DirectAccess server(s) to an entry point, then creating additional entry points and adding servers as necessary.

■ **Important**   Enabling multisite DirectAccess will disconnect clients that are connected remotely! They will not be able to reconnect until they perform a group policy update. This will require clients to be reconnected to the LAN or connect out-of-band via client-based VPN.

Create the First Entry Point

To enable multisite DirectAccess, open the Remote Access Management console, highlight **DirectAccess and VPN** in the navigation tree, and click **Enable Multisite** under **Multisite Deployment** in the **Tasks** pane (Figure 7-1).

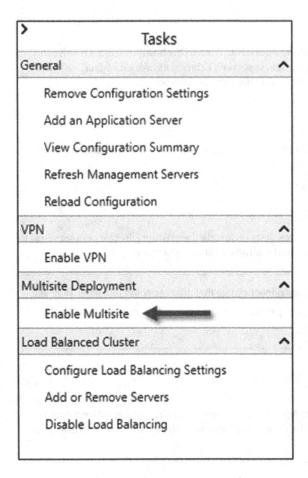

Figure 7-1. *Enabled multisite*

Click **Next** and provide a descriptive name for the multisite DirectAccess deployment. The existing DirectAccess server(s) will become the first entry point, so also provide a name for the new entry point (Figure 7-2).

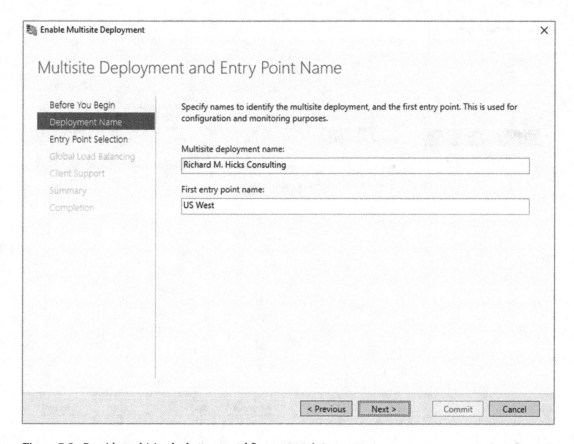

Figure 7-2. Provide multisite deployment and first entry point names

---

■ **Note**　The multisite deployment name and entry point name are purely administrative. They are not hostnames or Fully-Qualified Domain Names (FQDNs) and do not resolve in DNS.

Windows 8.x and Windows 10 clients will automatically select the best entry point to connect to. Optionally, the administrator can allow DirectAccess clients to manually select an entry point, if desired. Choose whether to allow DirectAccess clients to automatically and manually select, or to restrict them to using automatic entry-point selection only, and click **Next** (Figure 7-3).

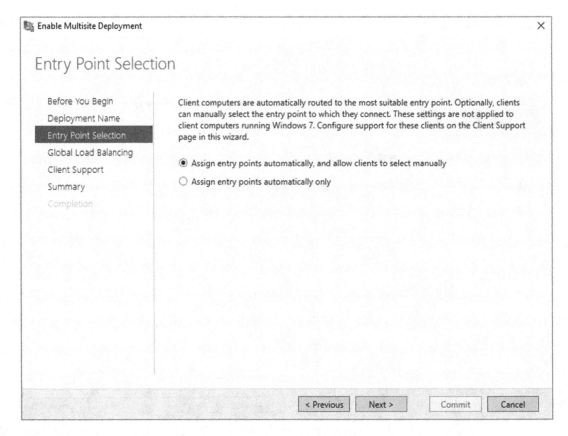

Figure 7-3. *Choose an entry-point selection option for Windows 8.x/10 clients*

Select **No, do not use global load balancing** to allow Windows 8.x and Windows 10 clients to automatically select an entry point on their own (Figure 7-4).

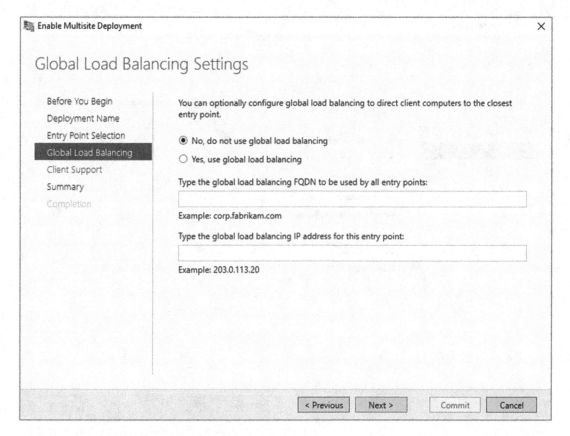

Figure 7-4. *Global load-balancing settings*

Optionally, Select **Yes, use global load balancing** to integrate a Global Server Load Balancer (GSLB) solution to enhance entry-point selection for DirectAccess clients (Figure 7-5).

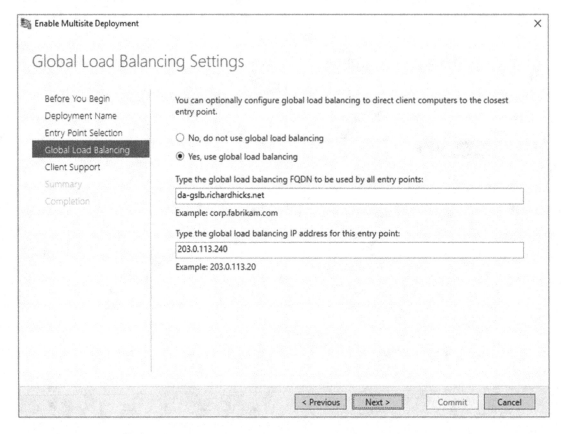

Figure 7-5. *Optionally, configure global load balancing*

If Windows 8.x and Windows 10 clients are to be supported exclusively, select the option to **Limit access to client computers running Windows 8 or a later operating system**. If Windows 7 clients will connect to this entry point, select the option to **Allow client computers running Windows 7 to access this entry point**. Click **Add**, choose the appropriate security group, and then click **Next** (Figure 7-6).

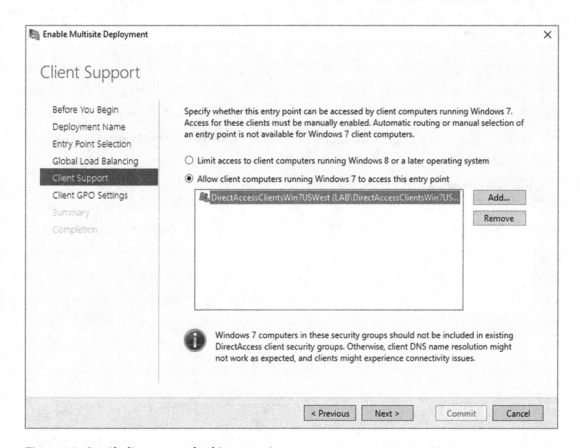

Figure 7-6. Specify client support for this entry point

A new Active Directory Group Policy Object (GPO) will be created to apply settings to Windows 7 clients for this entry point. Review and optionally adjust the name of the GPO, then click **Next** (Figure 7-7).

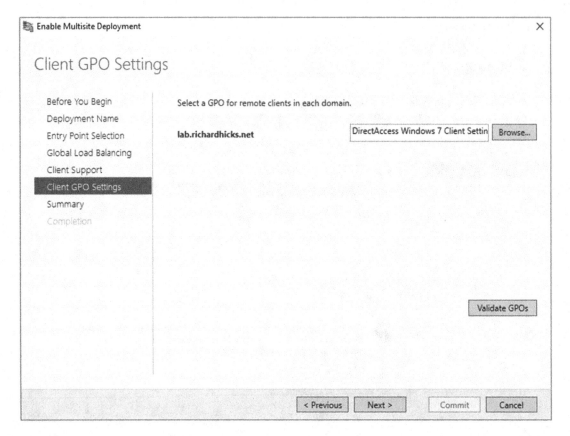

Figure 7-7. *Select a GPO for Windows 7 clients*

Confirm the multisite deployment settings and click **Commit** (Figure 7-8).

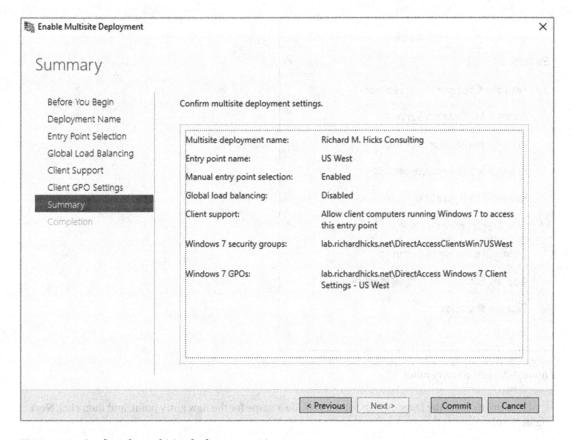

Figure 7-8. *Confirm the multisite deployment settings*

Add Additional Entry Points

Once the first entry point is configured, a second entry point can be established by highlighting **DirectAccess and VPN** in the navigation tree, highlighting the root node of the enterprise, and then clicking **Add an Entry Point** under **Multisite Deployment** in the **Tasks** pane (Figure 7-9).

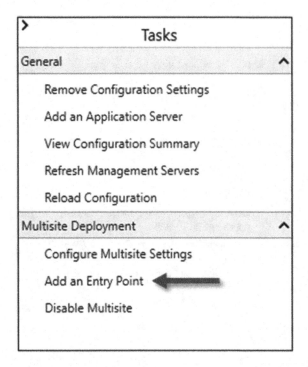

Figure 7-9. *Add an entry point*

Enter the name of the DirectAccess server, provide a name for the new entry point, and then click **Next** (Figure 7-10).

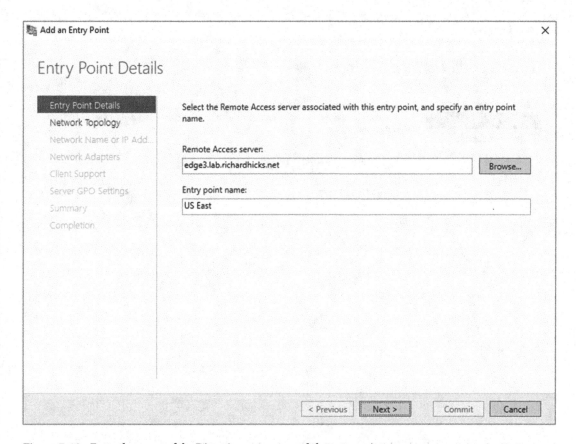

Figure 7-10. *Enter the name of the DirectAccess server and the entry point*

If global load balancing is enabled, enter the public IPv4 address for this entry point (Figure 7-11).

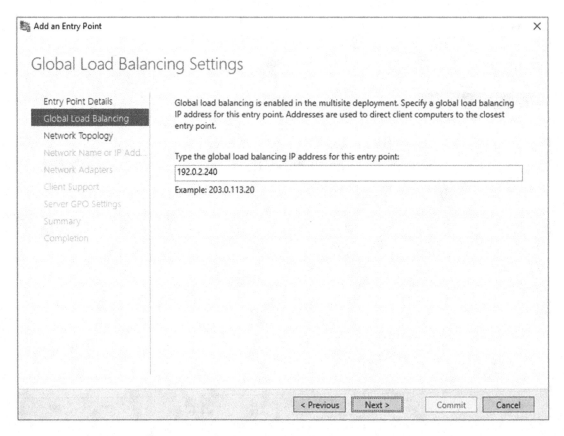

Figure 7-11. *Enter the global load-balancing IP address for this entry point*

Select the appropriate network topology for the new entry point. If the DirectAccess server does not have two network adapters or a public IPv4 address assigned to the external adapter, some choices may be unavailable. Choose a network topology and click **Next** (Figure 7-12).

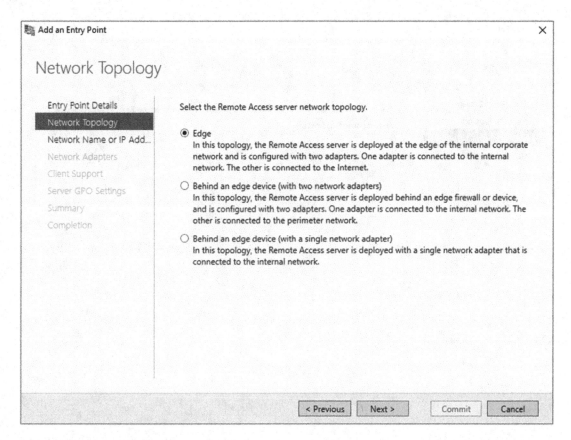

Figure 7-12. *Select a network topology*

Enter the public hostname for the new entry point and click **Next** (Figure 7-13).

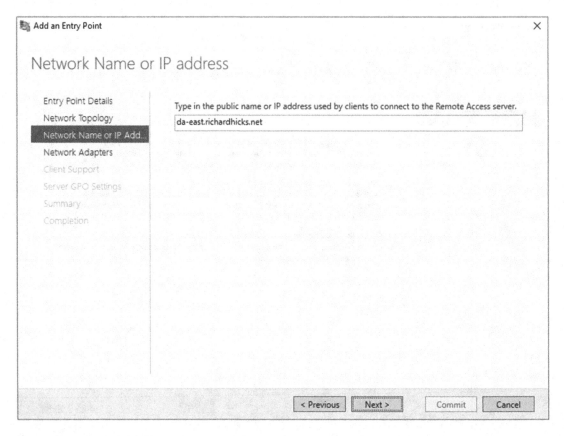

Figure 7-13. *Enter the public hostname for the entry point*

■ **Note** Although the GUI suggests that an IP address can be provided here, it is strongly recommended that an FQDN be used instead.

Review the network adapter and IP-HTTPS certificate settings and click **Next** (Figure 7-14).

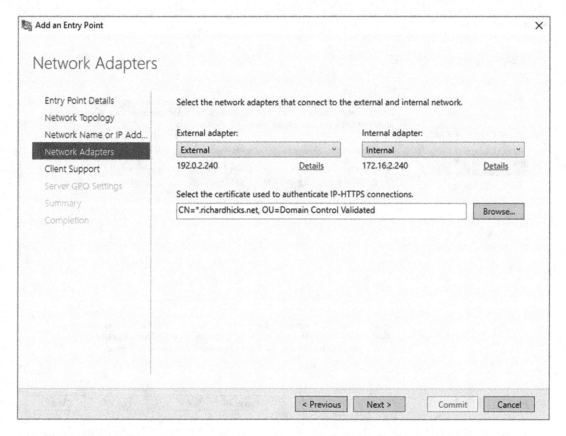

Figure 7-14. Configure network adapter and IP-HTTPS certificate settings

If this entry point will support only Windows 8.x and Windows 10 clients, select the option to **Limit access to client computers running Windows 8 or a later operating system**. If Windows 7 clients will connect to this entry point, select the option to **Allow client computers running Windows 7 to access this entry point**. Click **Add**, choose the appropriate security group, and then click **Next** (Figure 7-15).

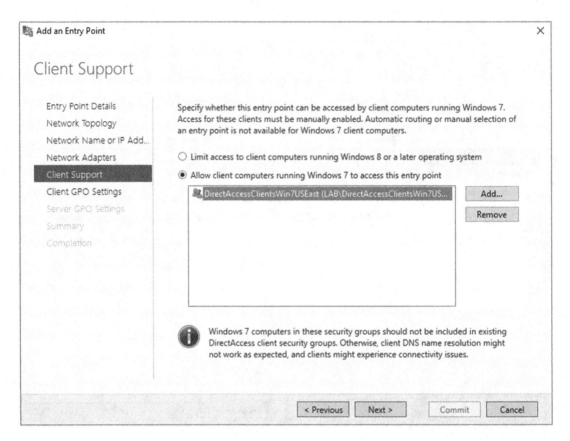

Figure 7-15. Specify client support for this entry point

A new GPO will be created with which to apply settings to Windows 7 clients for this entry point. Review and optionally adjust the name of the GPO and click **Next** (Figure 7-16).

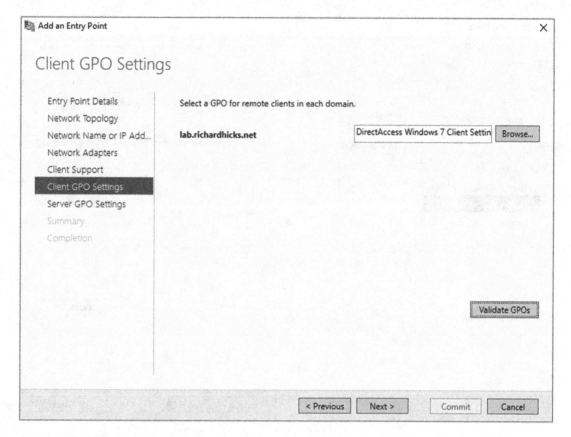

Figure 7-16. Select a GPO for Windows 7 clients

Another new GPO will be created, this time to apply settings to all DirectAccess servers belonging to this entry point. Review and optionally adjust the name of the GPO, then click **Next** (Figure 7-17).

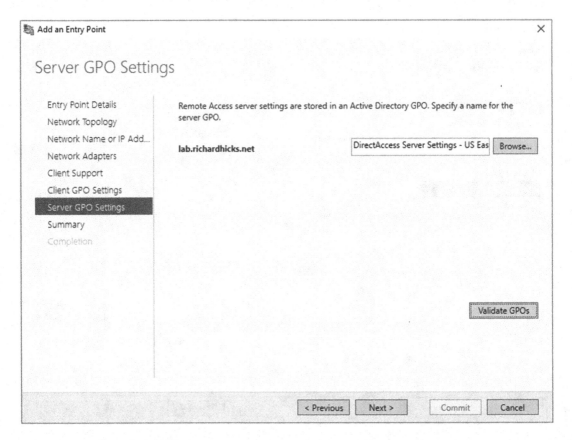

Figure 7-17. *Select a GPO for the DirectAccess servers*

Confirm the deployment settings for this entry point and then click **Commit** (Figure 7-18).

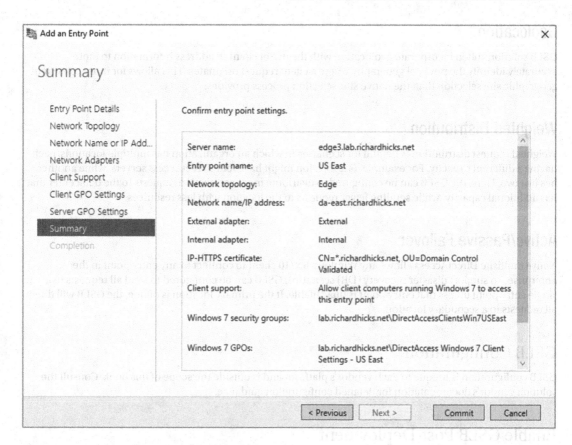

Figure 7-18. Confirm the multisite deployment settings

Enable Load Balancing for an Entry Point

To enable load balancing for a newly provisioned entry point, or to add servers to an existing load-balanced entry point, follow the procedures outlined in Chapter 6.

Multisite and GSLB

Multisite DirectAccess can be enhanced using a Global Server Load Balancing (GSLB) solution. GSLB can be deployed using dedicated appliances or with Cloud-based services, such as Microsoft Azure Traffic Manager.[2]

GSLB Deployment Scenarios

Using a GSLB enables important new deployment scenarios, such as geolocation, weighted distribution, and active/passive failover.

---

[2]https://directaccess.richardhicks.com/2016/04/04/directaccess-multisite-geographic-redundancy-with-microsoft-azure-traffic-manager/

Geolocation

GSLB solutions often incorporate geolocation with the use of client IP address information to more accurately identify the physical geography where a client request originates. This allows for more consistent geographic site selection than the native site-selection process provides.

Weighted Distribution

Weighted request distribution is helpful for scenarios in which an organization has multiple locations, each having a different capacity. For example, one location might have four DirectAccess servers, while another has just two. Here, the GSLB can be configured to distribute more connection requests to the datacenter that has additional capacity, while sending fewer requests to the location with less resources.

Active/Passive Failover

Native multisite DirectAccess allows any Windows 8.x/10 client to connect to any entry point in the enterprise. To support disaster recovery (DR) scenarios, GSLB can be configured to send all requests to a single entry point unless that entry point is unavailable. If the primary location is offline, the GSLB will direct all requests to a secondary location.

GSLB Configuration

GSLB configuration is unique to each vendor's platform and is outside the scope of this book. Consult the solution vendor's documentation for detailed configuration guidance.

Enable GSLB Post-Deployment

To enable GSLB after multisite DirectAccess has been configured, highlight **DirectAccess and VPN** in the navigation tree, highlight the root node of the enterprise, and then click **Configure Multisite Settings** under **Multisite Deployment** in the **Tasks** pane (Figure 7-19).

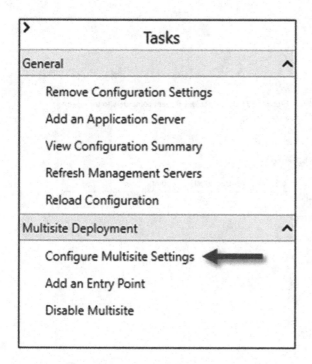

Figure 7-19. *Configure multisite settings*

Click **Global Load Balancing** and select the option **Yes, use global load balancing**, then click **Next** (Figure 7-20) .

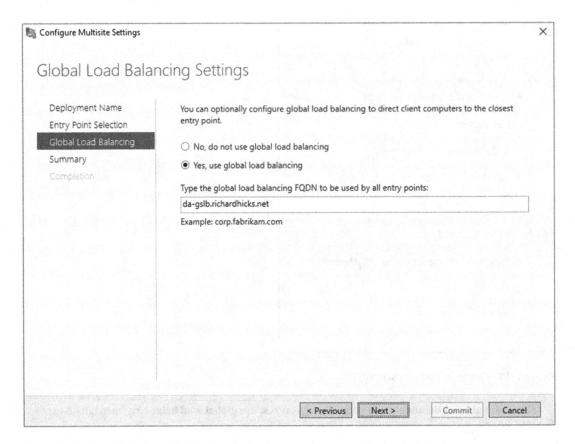

Figure 7-20. *Configure global load balancing*

Confirm the multisite deployment settings and click **Commit** (Figure 7-21).

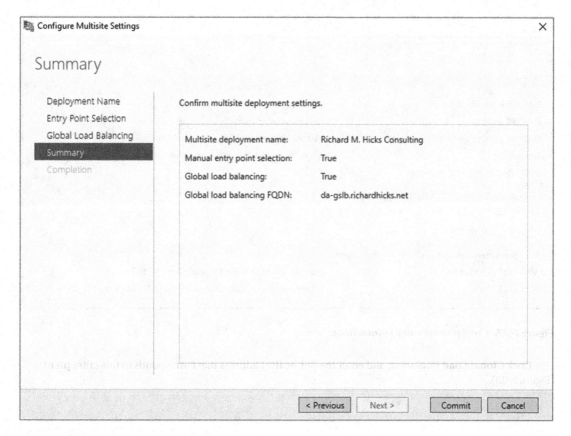

Figure 7-21. *Confirm your multisite deployment settings*

After the settings have been applied, the global load-balancing IP address must be set for each entry point in the organization. Highlight **DirectAccess and VPN** in the navigation tree, highlight an entry point, and then click **Configure Entry Point Settings** (Figure 7-22).

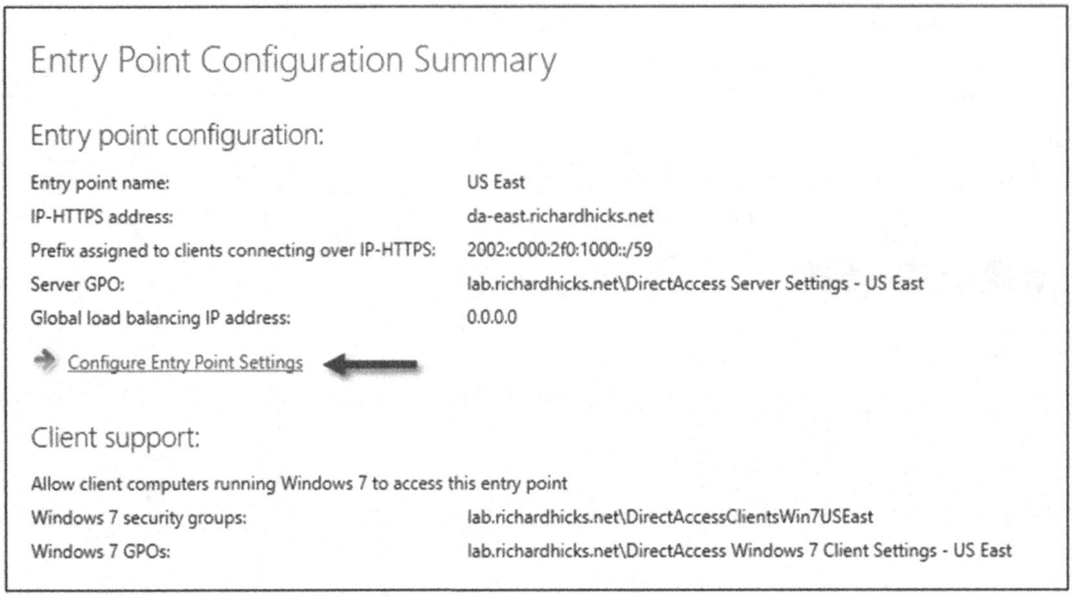

Entry Point Configuration Summary

Entry point configuration:

Entry point name:	US East
IP-HTTPS address:	da-east.richardhicks.net
Prefix assigned to clients connecting over IP-HTTPS:	2002:c000:2f0:1000::/59
Server GPO:	lab.richardhicks.net\DirectAccess Server Settings - US East
Global load balancing IP address:	0.0.0.0

➡ Configure Entry Point Settings ⬅━━━━━

Client support:

Allow client computers running Windows 7 to access this entry point

Windows 7 security groups:	lab.richardhicks.net\DirectAccessClientsWin7USEast
Windows 7 GPOs:	lab.richardhicks.net\DirectAccess Windows 7 Client Settings - US East

Figure 7-22. Configure the entry point settings

Click **Global Load Balancing** and enter the public IPv4 address that corresponds to this entry point (Figure 7-23).

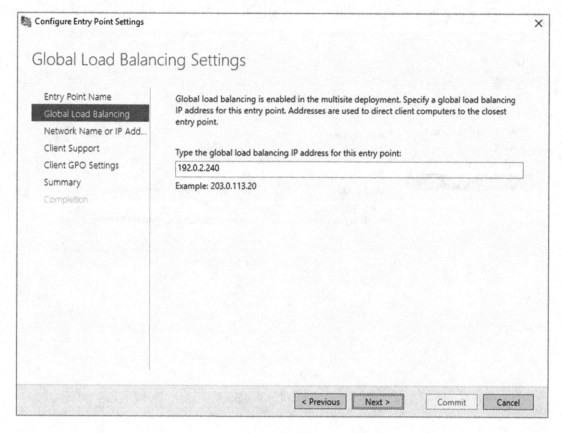

Figure 7-23. *Enter the global load-balancing IP address for this entry point*

Click **Next** four times, then click **Commit** (Figure 7-24). Repeat these steps for each entry point in the enterprise.

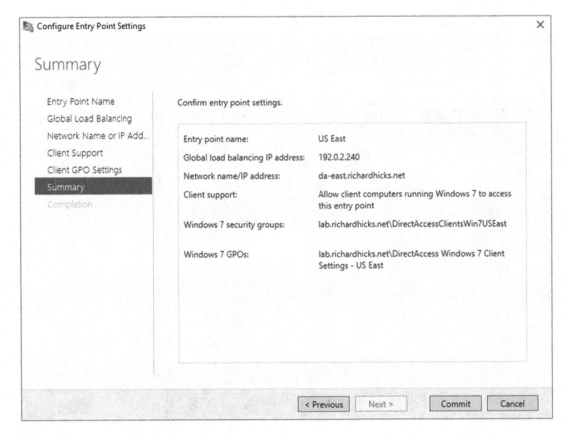

Figure 7-24. Confirm your entry point settings

The global load-balancing IP address for each entry point can also be configured using PowerShell and the Set-DAEntryPoint cmdlet. Run this command on any DirectAccess server in the enterprise. The syntax is as follows:

```
Set-DAEntryPoint -Name [entry_point_name] -GslbIP [ip_address]
```

For example:

```
Set-DAEntryPoint -Name "US West" -GslbIP 203.0.113.240
Set-DAEntryPoint -Name "US East" -GslbIP 192.0.2.240
```

GSLB Operation

When a Windows 8.x or Windows 10 client establishes a DirectAccess connection, it will attempt to resolve the GSLB FQDN to an IP address. The GSLB will respond, based on its configuration, with an IP address corresponding to a preferred entry point. The client does not connect directly to this IP address, however. Instead, it looks up the IP address in its entry point table and chooses the IPHTTPS profile that matches the IP address returned by the GSLB. The client then connects to the URL defined in that profile.

You can view the DirectAccess entry point table on a Windows 8.x or Windows 10 client by using the following PowerShell command (Figure 7-25):

```
Get-DAEntryPointTableItem
```

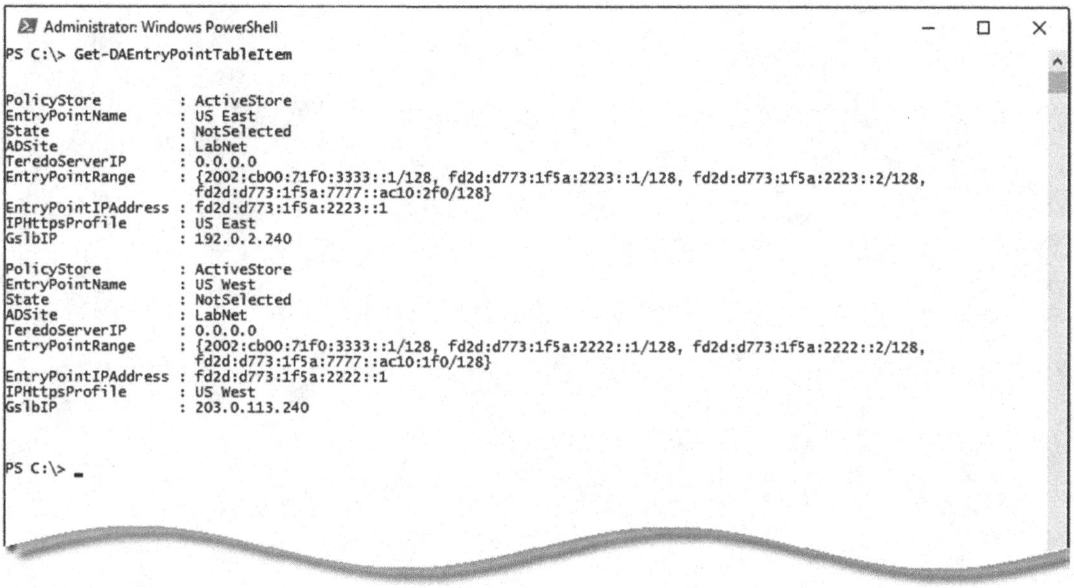

Figure 7-25. *Display the DirectAccess entry point table*

Summary

Multisite DirectAccess can be deployed to eliminate the datacenter itself as a potential single point of failure. In addition, multisite configuration can be used to ensure that geographically disperse clients connect to an entry point close to their physical location.

Full support for multisite DirectAccess is available with Windows 8.x and Windows 10 clients. Windows 7 clients can still be deployed, but they must be assigned to a single site and will not fail over.

Load balancing and multisite DirectAccess are not mutually exclusive. In fact, they work together to provide the most highly available solution, ensuring that a server failure in a single location, or even the failure of an entire datacenter, does not prevent remote users from connecting remotely.

GSLB can be used to enhance the multisite experience and enable new deployment scenarios not natively supported in Windows Server 2016, such as weighted distribution, proximity-based access, and active/passive failover.

CHAPTER 8

Enable Two-Factor Authentication

By default, users log in to DirectAccess client machines using only their username and password. To improve the overall security of the solution and to provide a higher level of assurance for remote users, two-factor authentication can be enabled.

DirectAccess supports multifactor user authentication using either smart cards (physical or virtual) or RADIUS-based one-time password (OTP) solutions. Each has its own unique advantages and disadvantages.

Smart Cards

Smart cards are an effective way of providing a high level of assurance for the logged-on user. To gain access to corporate resources over the DirectAccess connection, the user must have their physical smart card and know the personal identification number (PIN) associated with the card. This makes credential theft much more difficult. In addition, requiring a physical card to log in ensures that a user cannot log on to more than one device at a time.

Physical Smart Cards

Smart cards are most commonly physical, requiring the user to have them in their possession to log on to their device. Along with having the card, they must also know their PIN to gain access to the card itself. Physical smart cards provide enhanced protection for encryption keys, secure processing for cryptographic operations, and anti-hammering capabilities to prevent brute-force attacks on the card.

Virtual Smart Cards

Virtual smart cards replicate the security and functionality of physical smart cards without requiring additional hardware to support them. Instead of using proprietary hardware, virtual smart cards leverage the Trusted Platform Module (TPM)[1] that is already included with most modern computers. The TPM provides enhanced protection for encryption keys, secure processing for cryptographic operations, and anti-hammering capabilities to prevent brute-force attacks, just as physical smart cards do. Virtual smart cards stored on the TPM essentially make the client computer the second factor of authentication for the user.

---

[1]https://en.wikipedia.org/wiki/Trusted_Platform_Module

R. M. Hicks, *Implementing DirectAccess with Windows Server 2016*, DOI 10.1007/978-1-4842-2059-7_8

One-Time Passwords

OTP is another effective way to provide a higher level of assurance for DirectAccess users. To gain access to corporate resources over the DirectAccess connection, the user must provide their PIN plus their OTP. OTPs are generated in a variety of ways. Commonly, the OTP can be obtained from a physical token or be generated using an application running on a PC or a smartphone.

Supported OTP Solutions

Any OTP solution that uses RADIUS will work with DirectAccess. However, DirectAccess does not support the use of OTP solutions that implement challenge/response. The user must be able to provide their PIN and OTP when signing on to DirectAccess.

■ **Note** Microsoft Azure Multifactor Authentication (MFA) is an example of a popular OTP solution that does not work with DirectAccess. Azure MFA challenges the user by calling their phone number after receiving an authentication request from the server. The user must respond by answering the call and pressing a number on their keypad, and optionally providing a PIN, to be successfully authenticated. Azure MFA is not supported for use with DirectAccess because the user cannot provide their PIN and OTP when prompted by the Windows 8.x/10 DirectAccess Network Connectivity Assistant (NCA) or the Windows 7 DirectAccess Connectivity Assistant (DCA).

Prerequisites

The following topics describe the requirements for enabling and configuring DirectAccess to support multifactor authentication.

Client Authentication

DirectAccess must be configured to use computer certificates for client authentication when enabling multifactor authentication using smart cards or OTP. The use of Kerberos Proxy is not supported.

■ **Note** Kerberos Proxy is used for authentication when DirectAccess is configured using the Getting Started Wizard or when certificate authentication is enabled and the option to enable Windows 7 client computers to connect via DirectAccess is not selected (Remote Access setup wizard, DirectAccess and VPN, Step 2, Authentication).

Certification Authority

For smart cards, the certification authority requirements depend largely on the smart card implementation. For OTP, a Microsoft Enterprise Certification Authority (CA) is required. The CA can be running on Windows Server 2003 or later. A CA running on Windows Server 2008 R2 or later is recommended. The same CA used to issue IPsec certificates to DirectAccess clients can be used to issue OTP certificates. In addition, the CA must be included in the management computers list so that it is accessible over the infrastructure (first) IPsec tunnel.

■ **Note**   To add the CA to the DirectAccess management servers list, open the Remote Access management console and click **Edit** on **Step 3**. Click **Management** and then enter the hostname of the CA. Alternatively, the CA can be added to the management servers using the **Add-DAMgmtServer**[2] PowerShell cmdlet.

If OTP authentication is enabled in a multiforest environment, the CA used to issue OTP certificates should be located in the resource forest only. Certificate enrollment should then be configured across forest trusts.

OTP and Force Tunneling

OTP authentication cannot be enabled if DirectAccess is configured to use force tunneling. OTP authentication takes place outside of the DirectAccess IPsec tunnel. However, force tunneling disallows this, which causes the OTP authentication request to fail.

Windows 7 Clients

The DirectAccess Connectivity Assistant (DCA) v2.0 must be installed on Windows 7 clients to support OTP authentication. Detailed guidance for configuring the DCA on Windows 7 is covered in Chapter 9, "Supporting Windows 7 Clients."

DirectAccess Configuration

Strong user authentication should be enabled only after DirectAccess has been installed and configured, remote DirectAccess connectivity has been established, and validation testing has been performed to ensure that the solution is working correctly. This will streamline the troubleshooting process in the event that DirectAccess doesn't work correctly after enabling multifactor authentication.

Enable Smart Card Authentication

The following steps will describe the process of configuring DirectAccess to enforce multifactor authentication using physical or virtual smart cards.

Configure DirectAccess

To configure DirectAccess to require multifactor authentication using smart cards, open the Remote Access Management console and highlight **DirectAccess and VPN** under **Configuration** in the navigation tree. Click **Edit** on **Step 2**, click **Authentication**, and then select **Two-factor authentication (smart card or one-time password (OTP))** under **User Authentication** (Figure 8-1).

---

[2]https://technet.microsoft.com/en-us/library/hh918394.aspx

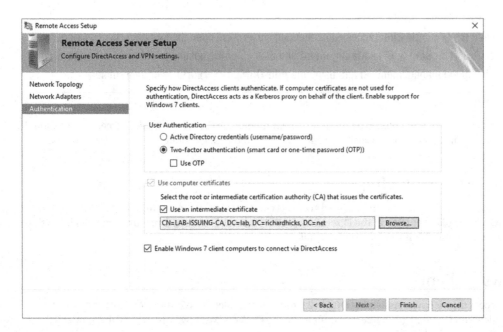

Figure 8-1. *Enable two-factor authentication*

Optionally, multifactor authentication can be enabled by opening an elevated PowerShell command window and executing the following command:

```
Set-DAServer -UserAuthentication TwoFactor
```

Smart Card End User Experience

With DirectAccess configured to require smart card authentication, the user will log on to their device using the Ctrl+Alt+Delete sequence as usual. After logging in, the user will not have access to any corporate resources without first supplying their smart card credentials.

■ **Note**   If the user is unable to provide their multifactor authentication credentials, access will be restricted to infrastructure servers only.

To complete the authentication process on the DirectAccess client, press **Window Key + I**, click **Network & Internet**, and then highlight **DirectAccess**. The connectivity status indicator will show that action is needed (Figure 8-2).

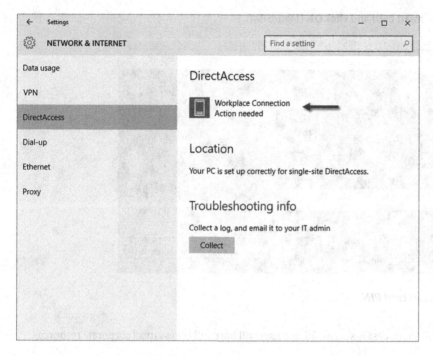

Figure 8-2. *Workplace connection action needed*

Click **Workplace Connection** and then click **Continue** (Figure 8-3).

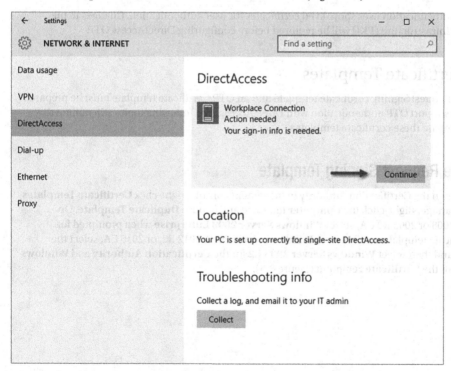

Figure 8-3. *Workplace connection sign-in info needed*

Enter the PIN for the smart card and click **OK** (Figure 8-4).

Figure 8-4. *Enter your smart card PIN*

Once the authentication process is successful, the user will have full access to all corporate resources.

Enable OTP Authentication

DirectAccess OTP authentication uses short-lived certificates for user authentication. Changes to the internal Public Key Infrastructure (PKI) will be required before configuring DirectAccess OTP.

Configure Certificate Templates

An OTP Certificate Request Signing certificate template and an OTP Certificate template must be prepared on the CA server to support OTP authentication with DirectAccess. The following topics will outline the steps required to prepare these certificate templates.

OTP Certificate Request Signing Template

On the CA server, open the Certification Authority management console, right-click **Certificate Templates**, and then choose **Manage**. Right-click the **Computer** template and choose **Duplicate Template**. On a Windows Server 2008 or 2008 R2 CA, select **Windows Server 2008 Enterprise** when prompted for the duplicate certificate template version. On a Windows Server 2012, 2012 R2, or 2016 CA, select the **Compatibility** tab and then select **Windows Server 2008 R2** for the **Certification Authority** and **Windows 7/Server 2008 R2** for the **Certificate recipient** (Figure 8-5).

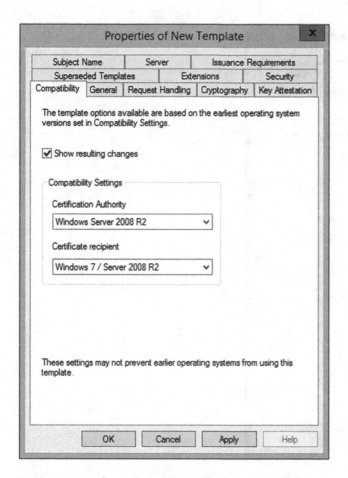

Figure 8-5. *Configure the certificate template compatability*

Select the **General** tab and provide a descriptive name for the **Template Display Name**. Specify a **Validity period** of two days and a **Renewal period** of one day (Figure 8-6).

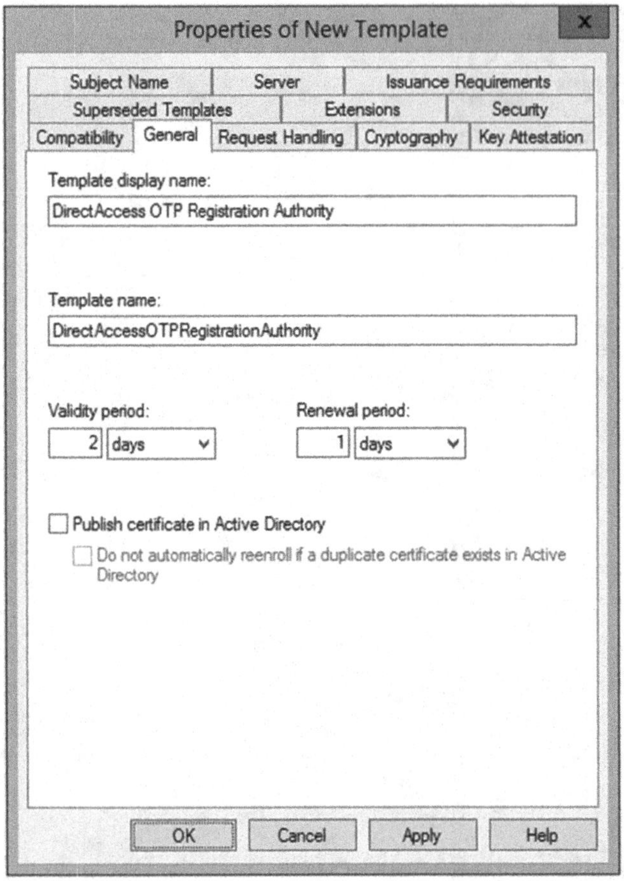

Figure 8-6. *Enter the template display name*

Select the **Security** tab and click **Add**. Click **Object Types** and then select **Computers** and click **OK**. Enter the names of each DirectAccess server. Click **OK** when finished. For each DirectAccess server, grant **Read**, **Enroll**, and **Autoenroll** permissions. Select **Authenticated Users** and remove any permissions other than **Read**. Select **Domain Computers** and remove the **Enroll** permission. Select **Domain Admins** and grant **Full Control** permission. Do the same for **Enterprise Admins** (Figure 8-7).

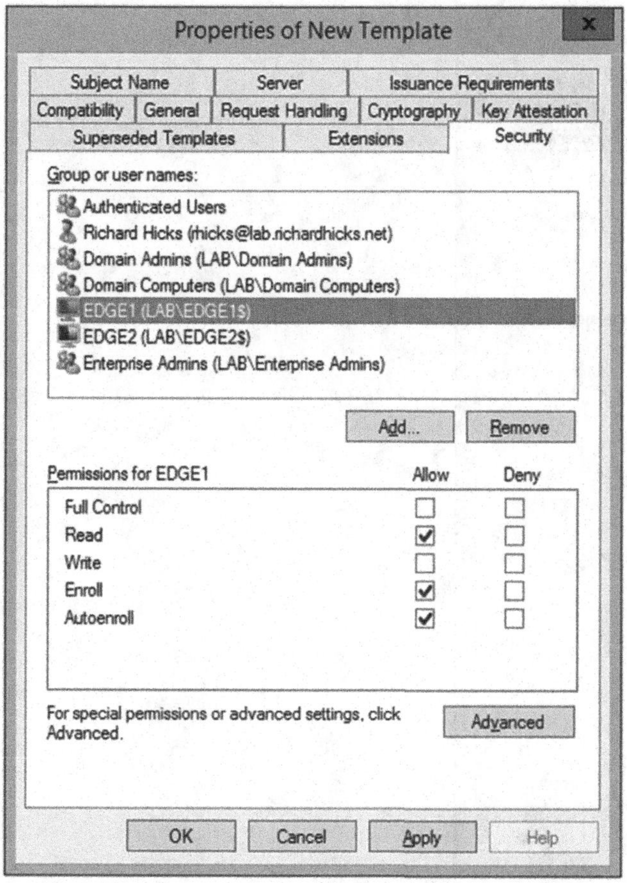

Figure 8-7. Configure the security permissions

Select the **Subject Name** tab and choose the option to **Build from this Active Directory information**. Select **DNS name** in the **Subject name format** drop-down list and confirm that DNS name is checked under **Include this information in alternate subject name** (Figure 8-8) .

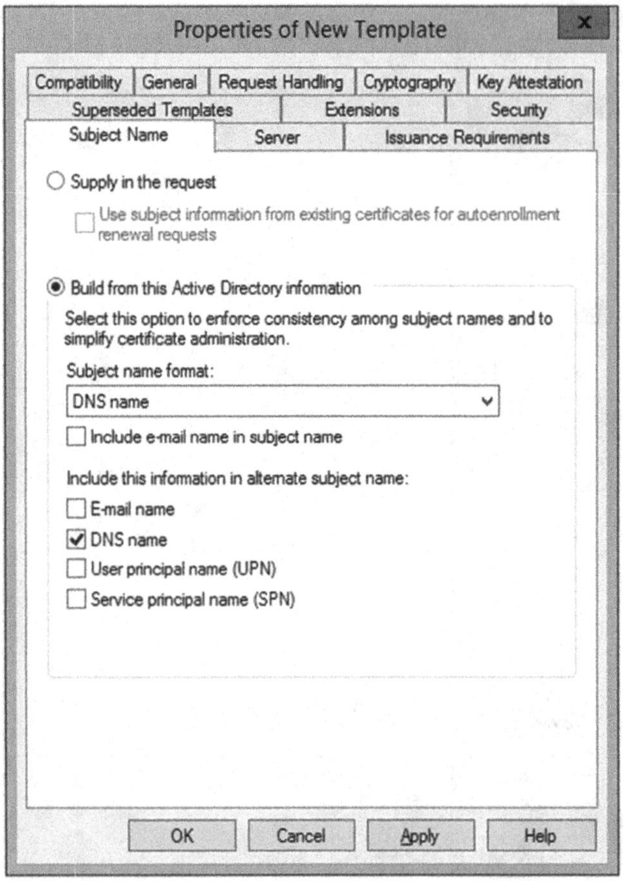

Figure 8-8. Enable the DNS name subject name format

Select the **Extensions** tab, highlight **Application Policies**, and click **Edit**. Remove all existing application policies and then click **Add** and then **New**. Provide a descriptive name for the new application policy and enter **1.3.6.1.4.1.311.81.1.1** for the **Object Identifier**. Click **OK** for all remaining dialog boxes (Figure 8-9).

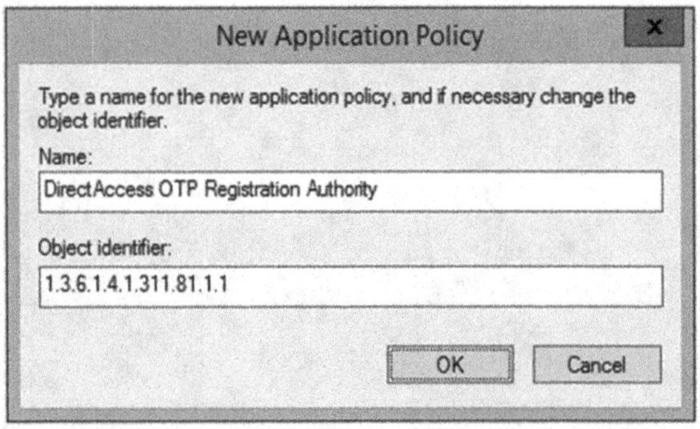

Figure 8-9. Create a new application policy

OTP Certificate Template

Right-click the **Smartcard Logon** certificate template and choose **Duplicate Template**. On a Windows Server 2008 or 2008 R2 CA, select **Windows Server 2008 Enterprise** when prompted for the duplicate certificate template version. On a Windows Server 2012, 2012 R2, or 2016 CA, select the **Compatibility** tab and then select **Windows Server 2008 R2** for the **Certification Authority** and **Windows 7/Server 2008 R2** for the **Certificate recipient** (Figure 8-10) .

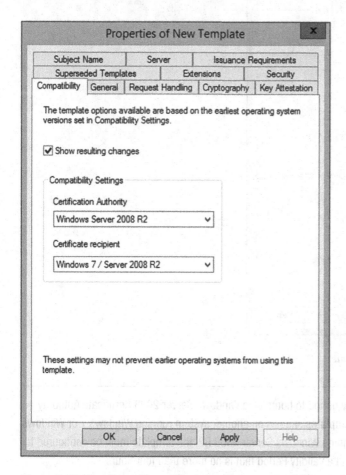

Figure 8-10. *Configure the certificate template compatability*

Select the **General** tab and provide a descriptive name for the **Template Display Name**. Specify a validity period of one hour and a renewal period of zero hours (Figure 8-11) .

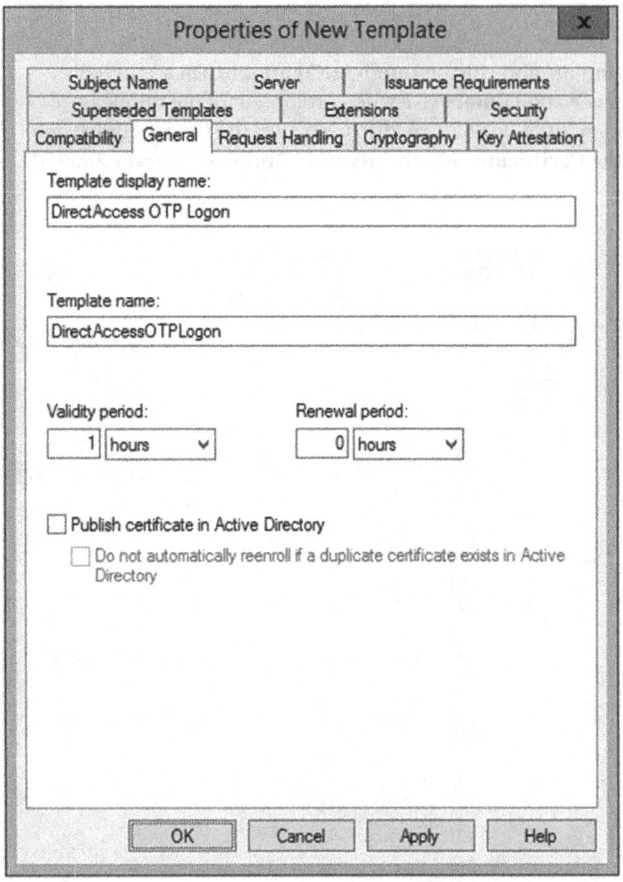

Figure 8-11. *Enter the template display name*

■ **Note**   It is not possible to set the validity period to hours on a Windows Server 2003 Certificate Authority (CA). As a workaround, use the Certificate Templates snap-in on another system running Windows 7 or Windows Server 2008 R2 or later. Also, if the CA is running Windows Server 2008 R2, the template must be configured to use a Renewal Period of one or two hours and a Validity Period that is no more than four hours.

Select the **Security** tab, then highlight **Authenticated Users** and grant **Read** and **Enroll** permissions. Select **Domain Admins** and grant **Full Control** permission. Do the same for **Enterprise Admins** (Figure 8-12).

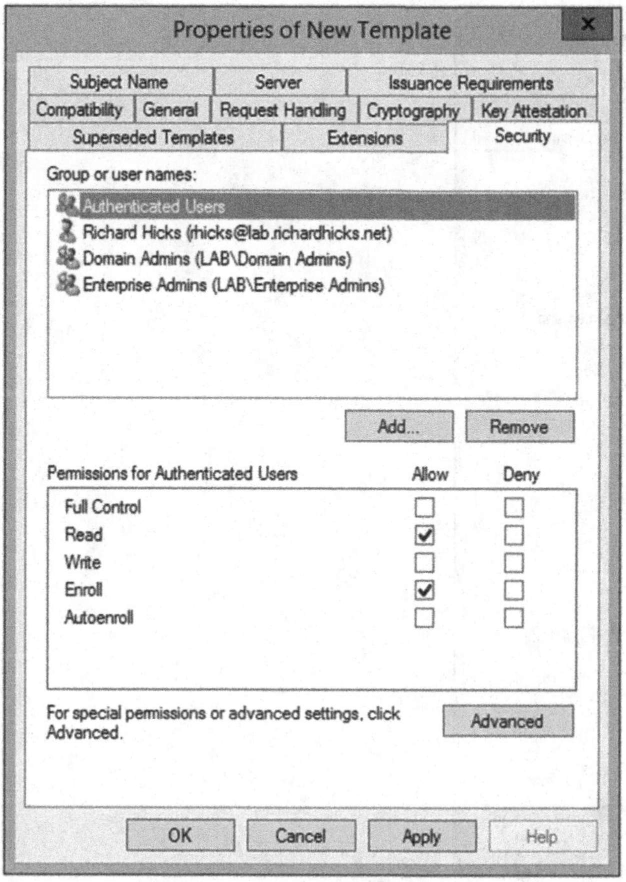

Figure 8-12. *Configure the security permissions*

Select the **Subject Name** tab and choose the option to **Build from this Active Directory information**. Select **Fully distinguished name** in the **Subject name format** drop-down list and confirm that **User principal name (UPN)** is checked under **Include this information in alternate subject name** (Figure 8-13).

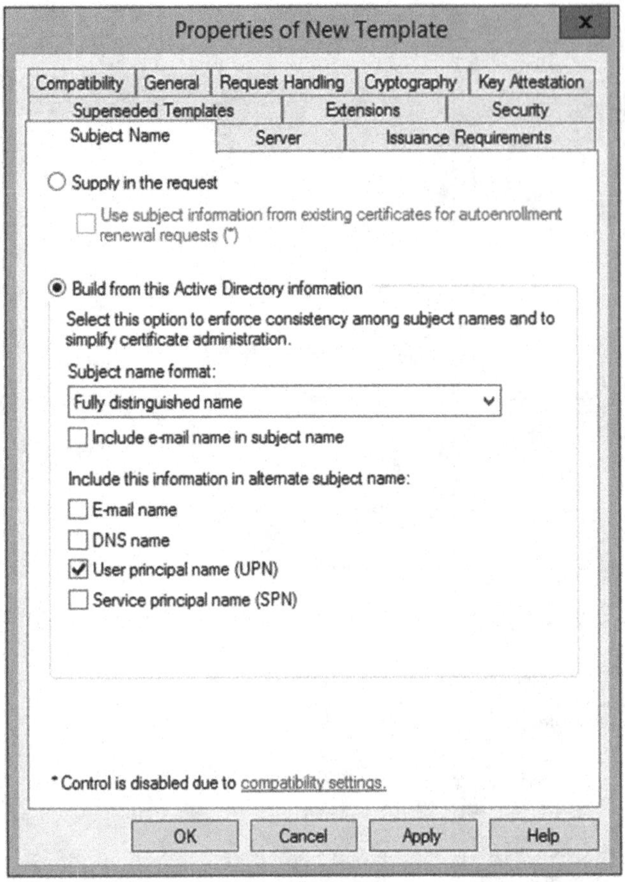

Figure 8-13. *Enable the Fully distinguished name subject name format*

Select the **Server** tab and choose the option **Do not store certificates and requests in the CA database**. Unselect the checkbox next to **Do not include revocation information issued in certificates** (Figure 8-14).

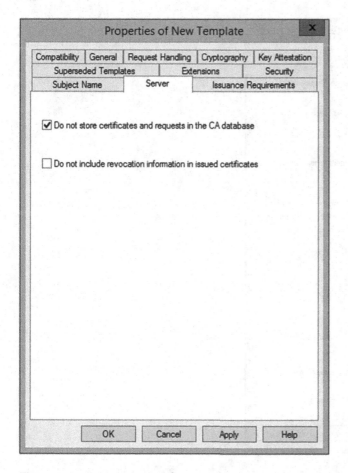

Figure 8-14. *Do not store certificates and requests in the CA database*

Select the **Issuance Requirements** tab and set .the value for **This number of authorized signatures** to 1. Confirm that **Application Policy** is selected from the **Policy type required in signature** drop-down list and choose the OTP certificate request signing template created previously (Figure 8-15).

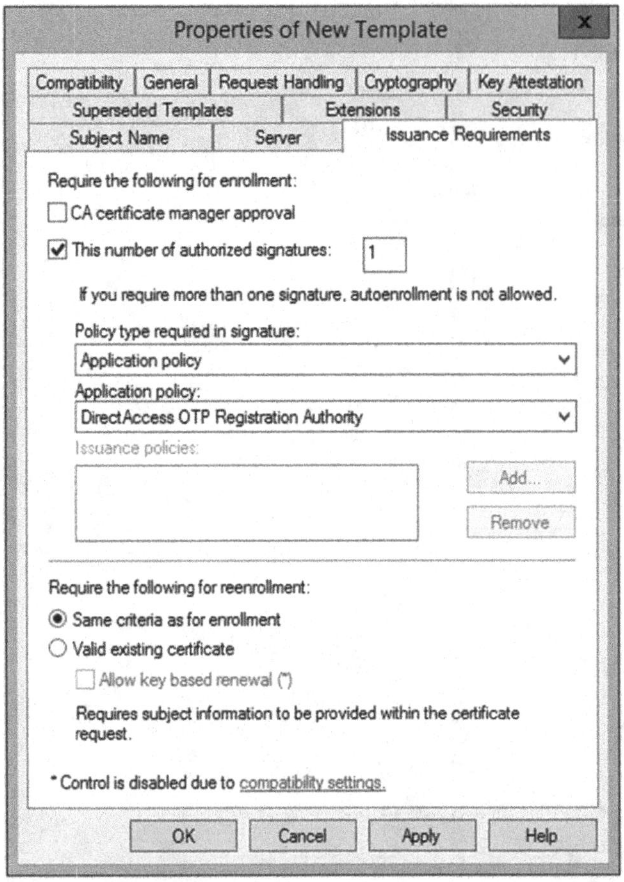

Figure 8-15. *Configure the issuance requirements*

Select the **Extensions** tab, highlight **Application Policies**, and click **Edit**. Highlight **Client Authentication** and click **Remove**. Ensure that the only application policy listed is **Smart Card Logon**. Click **OK** for all remaining dialog boxes (Figure 8-16) .

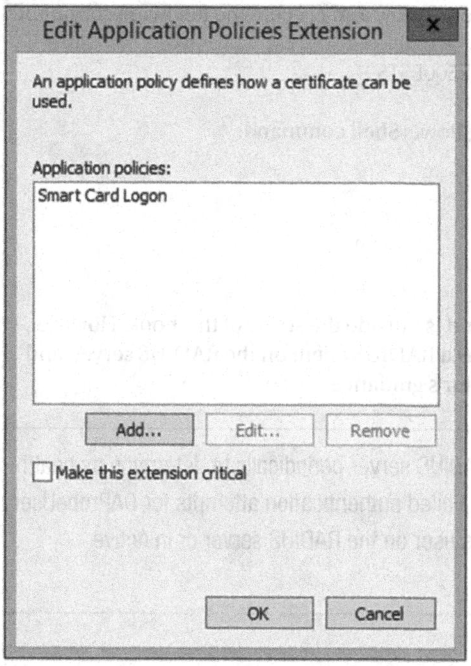

Figure 8-16. *Configure the application policies*

Configure Certification Authority (CA)

In the Certificate Authority management console, right-click **Certificate Templates**, choose **New**, and then select **Certificate Template to Issue**. Highlight both of the certificate templates created previously and click **OK** (Figure 8-17).

Figure 8-17. *Enable the new certificate templates*

On the CA server, open an elevated PowerShell command window and execute the following command:

```
certutil.exe -setreg dbflags +DBFLAGS_ENABLEVOLATILEREQUESTS
```

Once complete, restart the CA by executing the following PowerShell command:

```
Restart-Service CertSvc
```

Configure RADIUS OTP

Configuring the RADIUS OTP server differs for each vendor and is outside the scope of this book. However, at a high level, the DirectAccess server should be configured as a RADIUS client on the RADIUS server, and users and tokens should be provisioned according to the vendor's guidance.

■ **Note**   The DirectAccess server will probe the configured RADIUS server periodically to determine its health status and report it in the remote access management console. Failed authentication attempts for DAProbeUser on the RADIUS server are normal. It is not required to create this user on the RADIUS server or in Active Directory. These failed login attempts can be safely ignored.

Configure DirectAccess

To configure DirectAccess to require multifactor authentication using OTP, open the Remote Access Management console and highlight **DirectAccess and VPN** under **Configuration** in the navigation tree. Click **Edit** on **Step 2**, click **Authentication**, and then select **Two-factor authentication (smart card or one-time password (OTP))** under **User Authentication**. In addition, select the option to **Use OTP** and click **Next** (Figure 8-18).

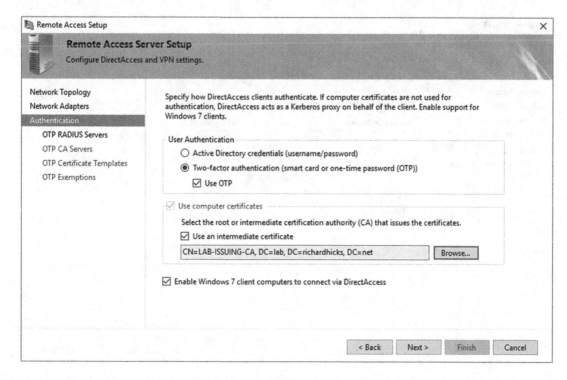

Figure 8-18. *Enable two-factor authentication and OTP*

Add the RADIUS servers that will be used for OTP authentication. Provide the hostname, FQDN, or IP address of the server, the shared secret, specify the service port, and click **OK** and then **Next** (Figure 8-19).

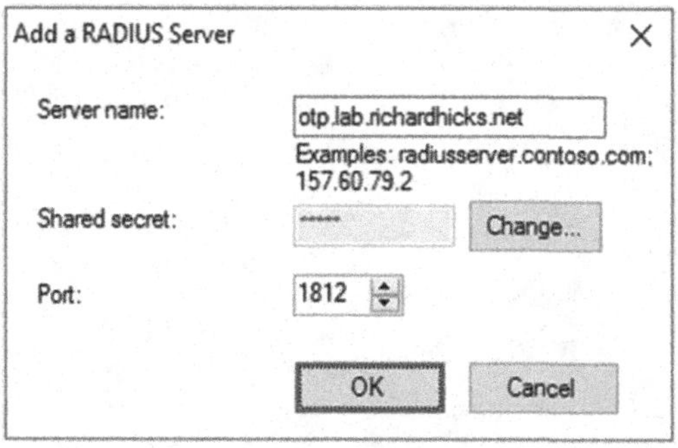

Figure 8-19. *Add a RADIUS server*

Select the CA server that will be used to issue certificates to DirectAccess clients for OTP authentication, then click **Add** and **Next** (Figure 8-20).

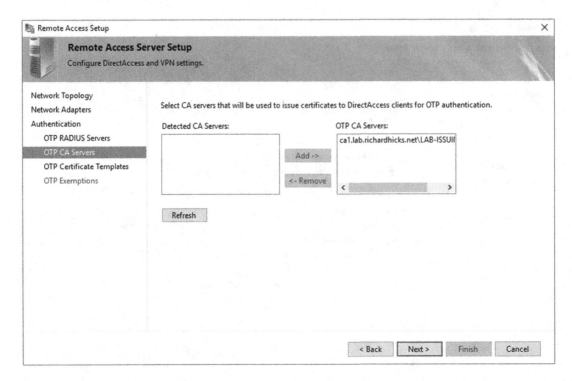

Figure 8-20. *Select the CA servers*

Select the certificate templates to be used for the enrollment of certificates that are issued for OTP authentication. Also, select a certificate template to be used for enrolling the certificate used by the DirectAccess server to sign OTP certificate enrollment requests; click **Next** (Figure 8-21).

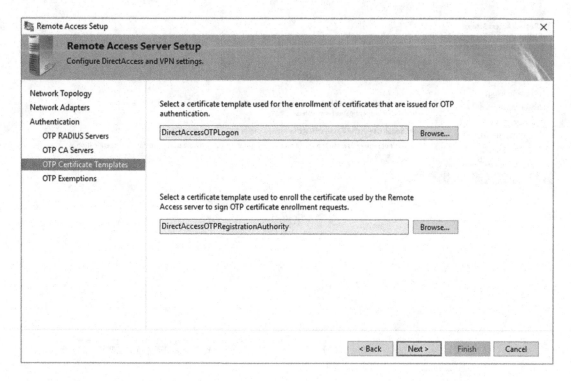

Figure 8-21. *Select certificate templates for OTP*

All users are required to authenticate using OTP by default. If some users need to be exempt from using OTP, select the option **Do not require users in the specified security group to authenticate using two-factor authentication,** specify the appropriate security group, then click **Finish** (Figure 8-22).

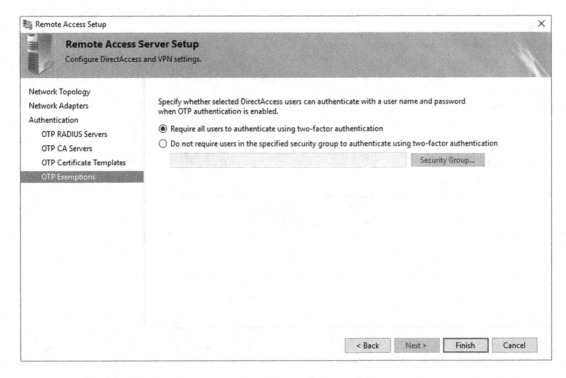

Figure 8-22. *Specify users who can authenticate without OTP (optional)*

Click **Edit** on **Step 3**, select **Management**, add the CA server used for OTP authentication to the list of management servers, then click **OK** and **Finish** twice. Now click **Apply** and **Close** (Figure 8-23).

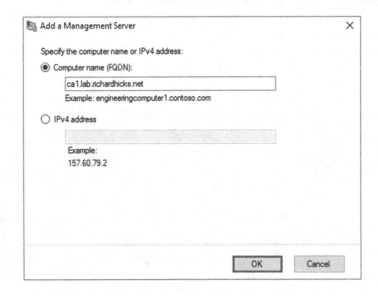

Figure 8-23. *Add a CA server to the management servers list*

OTP End User Experience

With DirectAccess configured to require OTP authentication, the user will log on to their device using the Ctrl+Alt+Delete sequence as usual. After logging in, the user will not have access to any corporate resources without first supplying their PIN and OTP.

■ **Note**   If the user is unable to provide their multifactor authentication credentials, access will be restricted to infrastructure servers only.

To complete the authentication process on the DirectAccess client, press **Window Key + I**, click **Network & Internet**, and then highlight **DirectAccess**. The connectivity status indicator will show that action is needed (Figure 8-24).

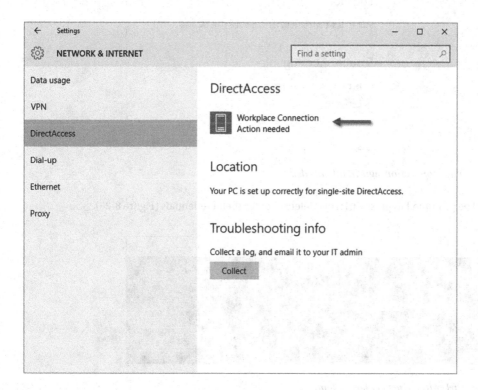

Figure 8-24. *Workpalce connection action needed*

Click **Workplace Connection** and then click **Continue** (Figure 8-25).

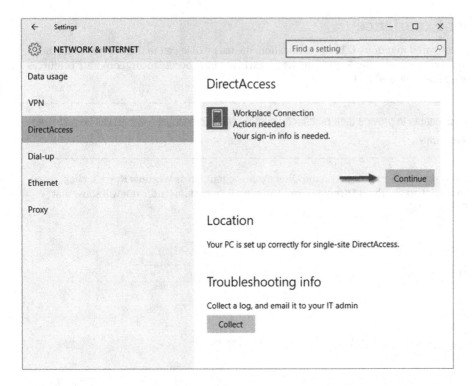

Figure 8-25. *Workplace connection sign-in info needed*

The user will be prompted to press Ctrl+Alt+Delete to enter their credentials (Figure 8-26).

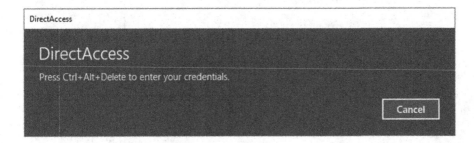

Figure 8-26. *Press Ctrl+Alt+Delte to enter credentials*

After pressing Ctrl+Alt+Delete, the user is prompted to enter their OTP credentials (PIN+OTP) (Figure 8-27).

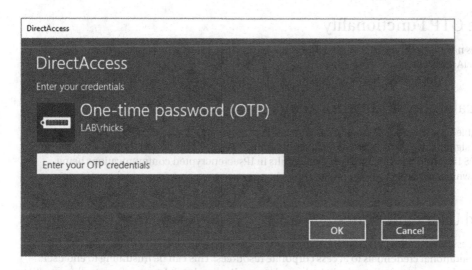

Figure 8-27. Enter OTP credentials (PIN + OTP)

Once the authentication process is successful, the user will have full access to all corporate resources.

Deployment Considerations

There are a number of important considerations to be made when enabling strong user authentication using smart cards or OTP. The following topics will describe some of the potential negative side effects of multifactor authentication with DirectAccess.

Increased Complexity

Strong user authentication with smart cards or OTP solutions add to the complexity of a DirectAccess deployment, making it more difficult to support and troubleshoot.

Added Expense

Multifactor authentication solutions can add to the expense of implementing DirectAccess. Typically, there are hardware, licensing, and support costs associated with most smart card and OTP solutions. Smart cards and OTP tokens can be expensive, although this can be mitigated with the use of virtual smart cards or soft tokens.

Limited Flexibility

OTP and force tunneling cannot be enabled at the same time. These deployment options are mutually exclusive, forcing the administrator to choose between one option and the other.

Incomplete OTP Functionality

DirectAccess does not support new PIN or next token modes. Further, there is no support for an OTP PIN change on a DirectAccess client.

Reduced Scalability and Performance

When OTP is enabled, the number of concurrent DirectAccess connections supported by each DirectAccess server is reduced significantly. This happens because enabling OTP disables support for null encryption with the IP-HTTPS IPv6 transition technology. This results in IPsec-encrypted communications being encrypted again, which increases the load on the DirectAccess server.

Diminished User Experience

When a DirectAccess client connects remotely, there is no visible cue or any intuitive indication that the user needs to provide additional credentials to access corporate resources. This can be frustrating to end users and has the potential to generate calls to the help desk when applications and data aren't accessible over the DirectAccess connection.

Summary

Enabling strong user authentication using smart cards or one-time passwords is an effective way to improve the overall security posture of the DirectAccess implementation, but it comes at a price.

Multifactor authentication fundamentally breaks the seamless and transparent nature of DirectAccess. The added complexity also makes the solution more difficult to support. Smart cards and OTP solutions increase costs and degrade the user experience. Additionally, OTP limits scalability and reduces performance on the DirectAccess server.

CHAPTER 9

Support Windows 7 Clients

Windows 10 clients are recommended in order to get the best DirectAccess experience, both from the administrator's perspective as well as the end user's. Performance is better in Windows 10, and administration and troubleshooting are easier as well. Windows 7 clients are still supported with DirectAccess in Windows Server 2016, but with some important limitations and unique requirements.

Deployment Considerations

The following topics will highlight some important deployment considerations for supporting Windows 7 clients.

Multisite Support

Windows 7 clients do not perform automatic site selection when they are provisioned in a DirectAccess multisite deployment. Windows 7 clients must be assigned to a single entry point in the enterprise. They are not aware of any other entry points and cannot transparently fail over to another if their assigned entry point is unavailable.

■ **Note** There's a common misconception that Windows 7 clients can transparently fail over to another entry point if a Global Server Load Balancer (GSLB) is used. A Windows 7 client can't establish a DirectAccess connection just because the entry point's public hostname can be resolved to another entry point. Using GSLB to point the client to another entry point only swings the IPv6 transition tunnel to the new entry point. However, the DirectAccess client still expects to connect to its assigned DirectAccess servers using specific IPv6 addresses. Although the Windows 7 client will successfully establish a transition tunnel, the tunnel endpoint IPv6 addresses inside the transition tunnel will be incorrect, and IPsec will fail. This will prevent access to internal resources.

Degraded Performance

Windows 7 clients incur a performance penalty when the DirectAccess server is deployed behind a networking device performing Network Address Translation (NAT). IP-HTTPS is the only supported IPv6 transition technology in this deployment scenario. 6to4 and Teredo are not supported.

© Richard M. Hicks 2016

R. M. Hicks, *Implementing DirectAccess with Windows Server 2016*, DOI 10.1007/978-1-4842-2059-7_9

Crucially, Windows 7 clients support only encrypted SSL/TLS cipher suites when using IP-HTTPS. DirectAccess communication is already encrypted, so this double encryption increases CPU utilization by the client.

Reduced Scalability

Supporting Windows 7 clients also reduces the number of concurrent connections a DirectAccess server can support at one time. Since the server must perform double encryption for many clients at once, the added protocol overhead greatly increases CPU utilization by the DirectAccess server, limiting the number of active DirectAccess connections the server can efficiently handle.

■ **Note**   Some load balancers can be configured to provide SSL offload for DirectAccess IP-HTTPS traffic. Although not supported, it can be an effective way to improve performance and scalability on the DirectAccess servers in some scenarios. More details can be found here: `http://directaccess.richardhicks.com/2013/07/10/ssl-offload-for-ip-https-directaccess-traffic-from-windows-7-clients-using-f5-big-ip/`.

DirectAccess Connectivity Assistant (DCA) v2.0

The Network Connectivity Assistant (NCA), included in the Windows 8.x and Windows 10 client operating systems, validates remote corporate network connectivity via the DirectAccess connection and provides a visual indication of the current status of the connection. It also provides a facility to generate and view diagnostic logs and to email them to an administrator.

Windows 7 does not include the NCA, but it can be configured with the optional DirectAccess Connectivity Assistant (DCA) v2.0,[1] which provides functionality similar to that of the NCA.

■ **Note**   DCA 2.0 *must* be installed on Windows 7 clients when the deployment requires one-time password (OTP) authentication.

Configuring DCA 2.0

DCA configuration settings are managed exclusively with the Active Directory group policy. It will be necessary to deploy custom group policy templates prior to configuring the DCA. Once complete, a new Group Policy Object (GPO) will be created that contains the DCA settings. In addition, a Windows Management Instrumentation (WMI) filter will be created to ensure that only Windows 7 clients receive the DCA settings.

---

[1]`https://support.microsoft.com/en-us/kb/2666914`.

Deploy Group Policy Templates

The group policy template files required for DCA 2.0 configuration are included in the downloaded .zip file. Extract the contents of the .zip file and copy the .ADMX and .ADML files contained therein to a domain controller. The **DirectAccess_Connectivity_Assistant_2_0_GP.admx** file should be copied to the **%WINDIR%\PolicyDefinitions** folder, and the **DirectAccess_Connectivity_Assistant_2_0_GP.adml** file should be copied to the **%WINDIR%\PolicyDefinitions\en-US** folder.

Create Group Policy Object

Open the Group Policy Management Console (GPMC), right-click **Group Policy Objects**, and click **New**. Provide a descriptive name for the new GPO and click **OK** (Figure 9-1).

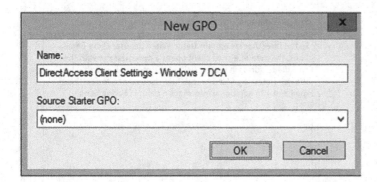

Figure 9-1. *Create a new GPO*

■ **Note**   Some DCA settings are unique for each entry point in a multisite deployment. Separate GPOs for DCA settings for each entry site in the enterprise will be required.

Right-click the new GPO and choose **Edit**. Expand **Computer Configuration**, **Policies**, and then **Administrative Templates**. Highlight **DirectAccess Connectivity Assistant** and then double-click **Support Email**. Select **Enabled** and enter a support email address. Click **Next Setting** when finished (Figure 9-2).

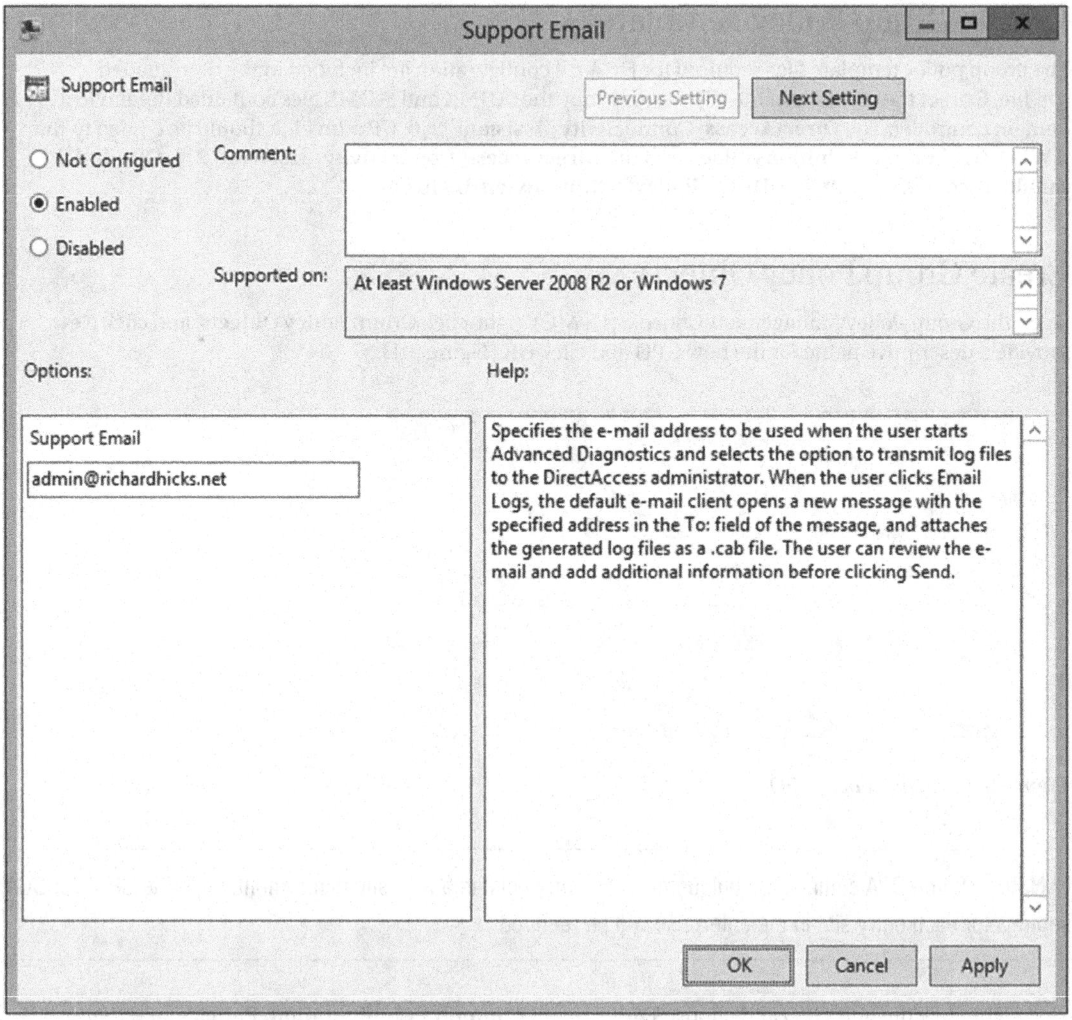

Figure 9-2. *Enter a support email address*

■ **Note** The Support Email configuration is optional but recommended. It is not possible to generate diagnostic logs on the client using the DCA without defining a support email address.

Select **Enabled** and then click **Show** next to **DTEs**. Double-click a blank field and enter the Dynamic Tunnel Endpoint (DTE) IPv6 addresses using the format **PING:<DTE>**. Click **Next Setting** when finished (Figure 9-3).

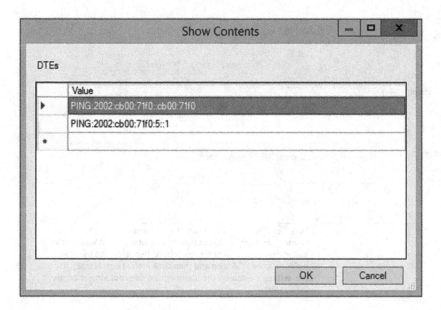

Figure 9-3. *Configure the DTEs*

■ **Note**   To obtain the IPv6 DTE addresses, open an elevated PowerShell command window on the DirectAccess server and execute the following command:

Get-Item –Path HKLM:\\SYSTEM\CurrentControlSet\Services\RaMgmtSvc\Config\Parameters

---

The **LocalNamesOn** setting is an optional setting that effectively allows the end user to disconnect the DirectAccess connection. It does this by disabling the Name Resolution Policy Table (NRPT), allowing all name-resolution requests to be sent to the DNS server that is configured on the DirectAccess client's local network adapter. Choose an option and click **Next Setting** (Figure 9-4).

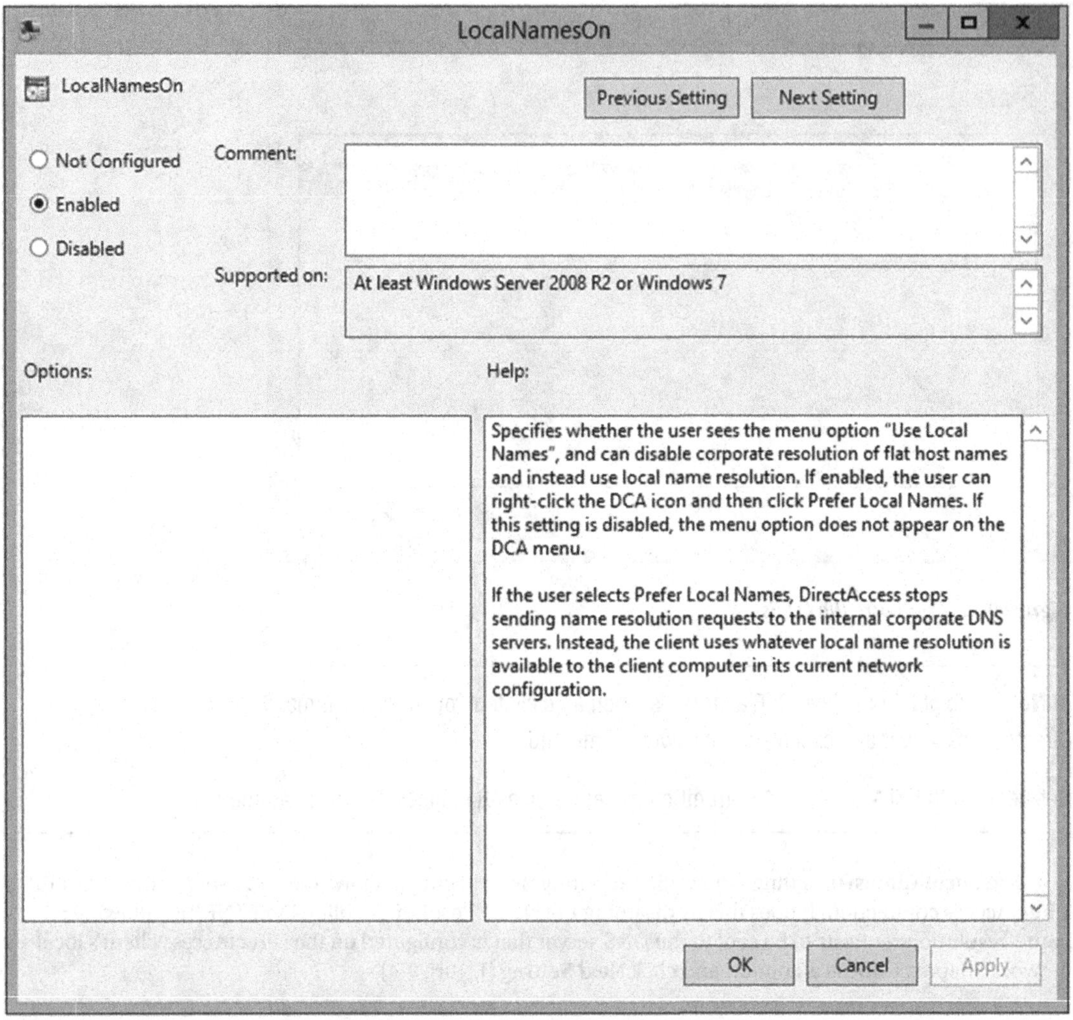

Figure 9-4. Enable local name resolution (optional)

Select **Enabled** and click **Show** next to **Corporate Resources**. Double-click a blank field and enter the URL of an internal web resource using the format **HTTP:<URI>** (Figure 9-5).

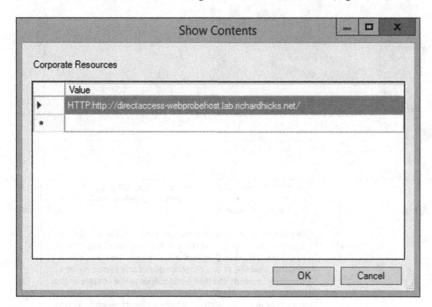

Figure 9-5. Enter the URL of an internal web resource

■ **Note**   DirectAccess creates an entry in DNS for DirectAccess-WebProbeHost, which resolves to the internal IPv4 address of the DirectAccess server by default. For load-balanced configurations, it resolves to the Virtual IP Address (VIP) of the load-balanced cluster. This URL can be used, but any internal web server, with the exception of the NLS, can also be specified here. It is recommended that only one resource be entered. It is not required or recommended that multiple resources be provided. In addition, the use of HTTP resources is encouraged over Internet Control Message Protocol (ICMP) as ICMP is not always a reliable indicator of network connectivity status and may cause issues with one-time password (OTP) authentication.

The **Admin Script** setting is an optional setting that allows the administrator to define a script to be executed on the client during the diagnostic log-generation process. The output of the script will be included in the .cab file that is created when **Advanced Diagnostics** is initiated by the user. The script file can be any file that can be run at a command prompt and that sends output to the console as text. The script must not take longer than 45 seconds to run. In addition, the script file must be local to the computer and stored in a location that cannot be modified by a standard user account, as the DCA runs the script with elevated permissions. Click **Next Setting** when finished (Figure 9-6).

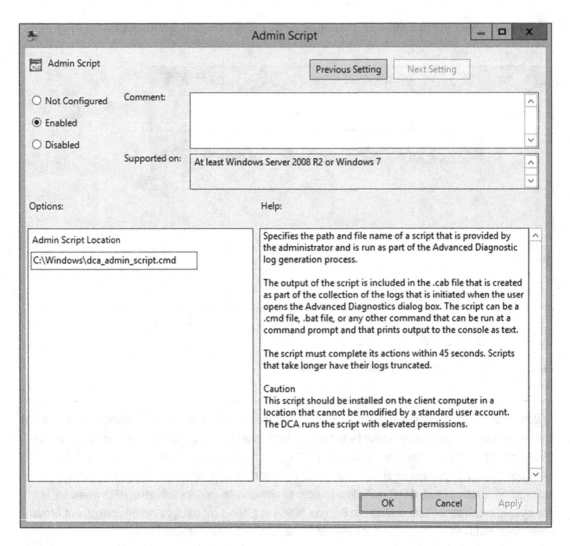

Figure 9-6. *Enable an admin script (optional)*

Create WMI Filter

■ **Note** This step is optional for multisite deployments. In a multisite scenario, Windows 7 clients are members of a dedicated security group. The GPO can be targeted at the Windows 7 client group for the entry point without requiring a WMI filter.

In the Group Policy Management Console (GPMC) right-click **WMI Filters** and choose **New**. Provide a descriptive name and click **Add**. Enter the following WMI query and click **OK**, and then click **Save** (Figure 9-7):

```
select * from Win32_OperatingSystem where Version like "6.1%"
```

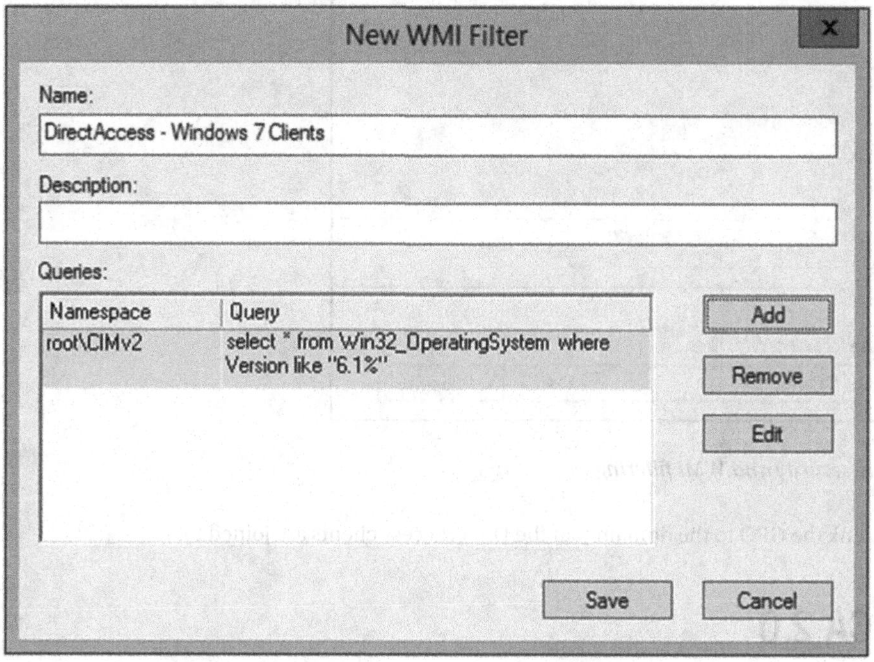

Figure 9-7. *Create a new WMI filter*

■ **Note**   A warning message may appear after creating the WMI filter stating that the namespace entered is not a valid namespace on the local computer or that you do not have access to this namespace on this computer. This warning message can be safely ignored.

Deploy Group Policy Object

In the GPMC, select the newly created GPO and click **Scope**. Under **Security Filtering** click **Add** and specify the DirectAccess client security group. Highlight **Authenticated Users** and click **Remove**. Finally, select the drop-down list under **WMI Filtering** and choose the WMI filter created previously (Figure 9-8).

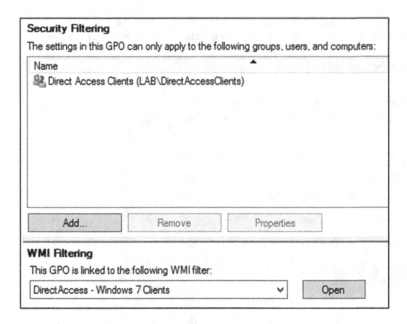

Figure 9-8. *Configure security and WMI filtering*

Once complete, link the GPO to the domain that the DirectAccess clients are joined to.

Installing DCA 2.0

On a 64-bit Windows 7 client, double-click **Microsoft_DirectAccess_Connectivity_Assistant_2_0_x64.msi**.
On a 32-bit Windows 7 client, double-click **Microsoft_DirectAccess_Connectivity_Assistant_2_0_x86.msi**.
When prompted to install the **Update for Windows (KB2666914)**, click **Yes** (Figure 9-9).

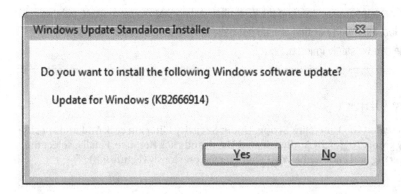

Figure 9-9. *Install update KB2666914*

Once the installation is complete, click **Restart Now** (Figure 9-10).

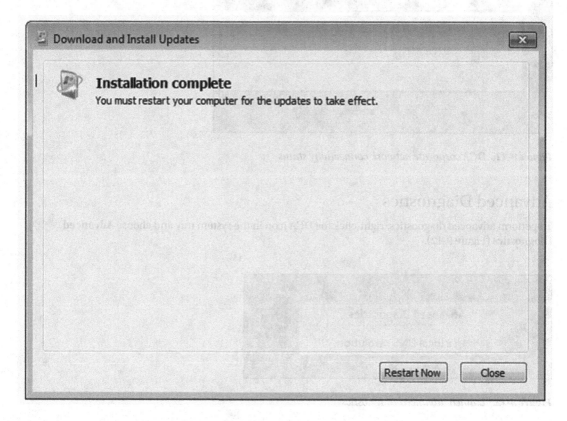

Figure 9-10. Restart is required after installing DCA

■ **Note**   Software deployment mechanisms such as Active Directory software installation policies, System Center Configuration Manager (SCCM), or any third-party software distribution solution can be used to automate the distribution of the DCA to Windows 7 clients.

DCA Operation

The following topics will describe the operation of the DCA on a Windows 7 client.

Connectivity Status

To view corporate network connectivity status, click the DCA icon in the system tray. When the client is connected to the corporate network, or if the client has successfully connected remotely via DirectAccess or VPN, the DCA will report that corporate network connectivity is working.

Figure 9-11. *DCA corporate network connectivity status*

Advanced Diagnostics

To perform advanced diagnostics, right-click the DCA icon in the system tray and choose **Advanced Diagnostics** (Figure 9-12).

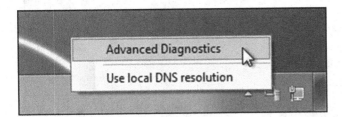

Figure 9-12. *Launch advanced diagnostics*

The DCA will automatically generate and collect diagnostic log data for review by an administrator. To view collected log data, click **Open logs directory** (Figure 9-13).

Figure 9-13. *Open the log file directory*

The DCA automatically generates an HTML report, which is also contained in the .cab file. The report includes connectivity status reports and diagnostic information collected from the client. If an admin script was configured, its output is recorded in a text file included here (Figure 9-14).

Figure 9-14. *DCA diagnostic log files*

Local DNS Resolution

To temporarily disconnect from DirectAccess and use local DNS resolution, right-click the DCA icon in the system tray and choose **Use local DNS resolution** (Figure 9-15).

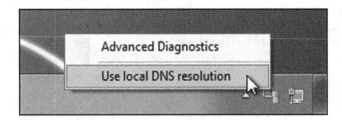

Figure 9-15. *Use local DNS resolution*

___

■ **Note**   Enabling local DNS resolution does not completely disable DirectAccess; it only disables the NRPT. The DirectAccess IPsec connections remain established, allowing for the full use of outbound management for DirectAccess clients even if the user has chosen to use local DNS resolution.

___

Summary

For the best experience, it is recommended that Windows 10 clients be used exclusively for DirectAccess. Windows 10 provides full support for all enterprise DirectAccess features, including automatic site selection and transparent failover in multisite deployments, IP-HTTPS IPv6 transition technology performance enhancements, and an integrated network connectivity status indicator.

Windows 7 clients can still be deployed with DirectAccess in Windows Server 2016, but they don't perform as well, fewer clients are supported concurrently, and in some scenarios they may require additional software (the DCA) to be deployed.

CHAPTER 10

Monitor and Report

Once DirectAccess is installed and configured, the Remote Access Management console can be used to monitor the health and status of the DirectAccess server and supporting infrastructure. If a problem is detected, its status will be indicated and helpful information for resolving the issue will be provided.

All DirectAccess connections, along with user information and details about internal resources accessed over the connection, can be logged. Log data can be stored in a local Windows Internal Database (WID), a local or remote Remote Access Dial-In User Service (RADIUS) server, or both. With logging configured, the Remote Access Management console can be used to view currently connected clients and to generate usage reports of historical user activity for compliance and auditing purposes.

System Monitoring

DirectAccess relies on supporting infrastructure services such as Active Directory, DNS, PKI, and others to provide remote access for clients. Issues or outages with any of these services can prevent access to internal resources via DirectAccess. DirectAccess constantly monitors the status and health of these dependent services with the Remote Access Management console to ensure they are accessible.

Dashboard

Select **Dashboard** in the Remote Access Management console to display an overview of the current configuration and operation status along with summary information for DirectAccess client connections (Figure 10-1).

© Richard M. Hicks 2016
R. M. Hicks, *Implementing DirectAccess with Windows Server 2016*, DOI 10.1007/978-1-4842-2059-7_10

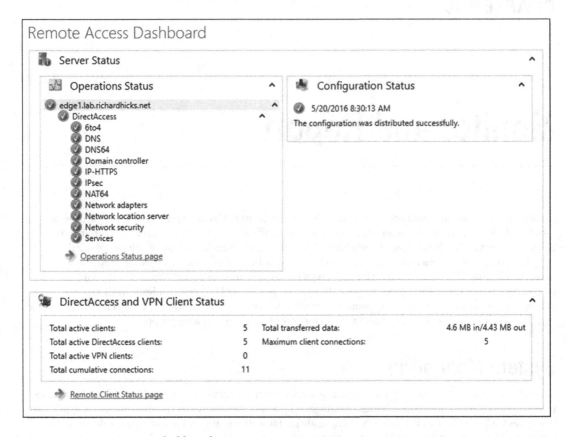

Figure 10-1. Remote access dashboard

■ **Note**   For load-balanced clusters, operations status information for all nodes in the cluster is displayed. For multisite deployments, the operations status summary information for all entry points is shown. Expanding the load-balanced cluster or entry point and selecting individual servers displays status information for the server selected.

Green checkmarks next to individual supporting services and technologies indicate they are online and healthy. These marks will change to a warning or error status for services that are degraded or unavailable. To view detailed information for any service, click the **Operations Status** page link or click **Operations Status** in the navigation tree (Figure 10-2) .

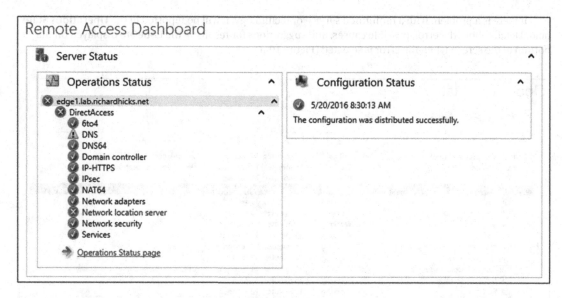

Figure 10-2. *Remote access dashboard displaying warning and error status*

Operations Status

Select **Operations Status** to view detailed information on the status and health of supporting services and technologies. Select an individual service to view information pertaining to its current state (Figure 10-3).

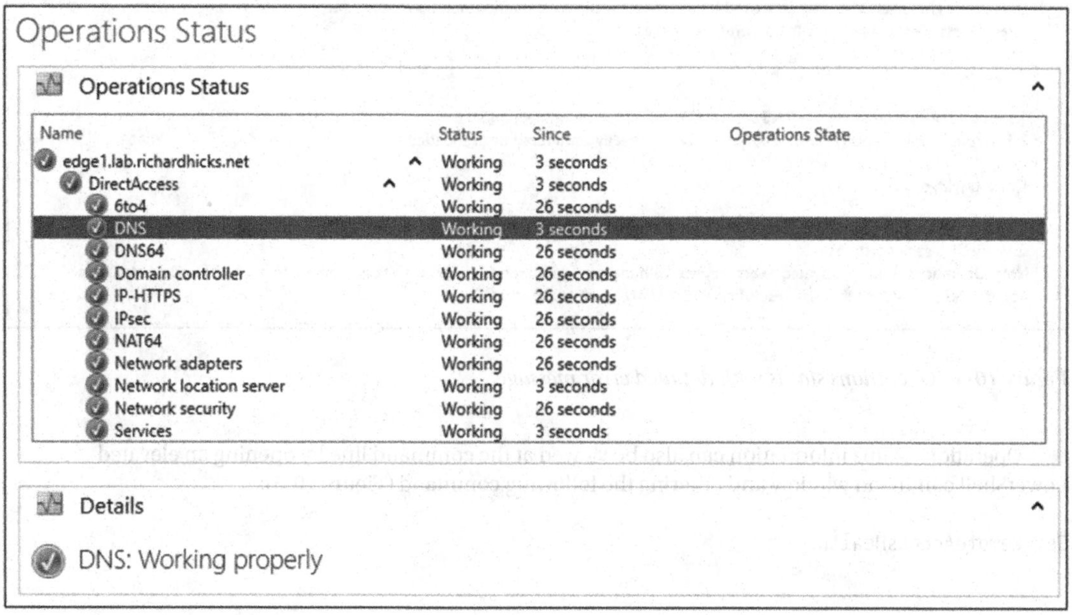

Figure 10-3. *Operations status details*

If there is a problem with a monitored service or technology, it will be reported in the **Operations State** field. Details about the error, possible causes, and suggestions for resolving the issue are displayed on the bottom of the screen when the error is selected (Figure 10-4).

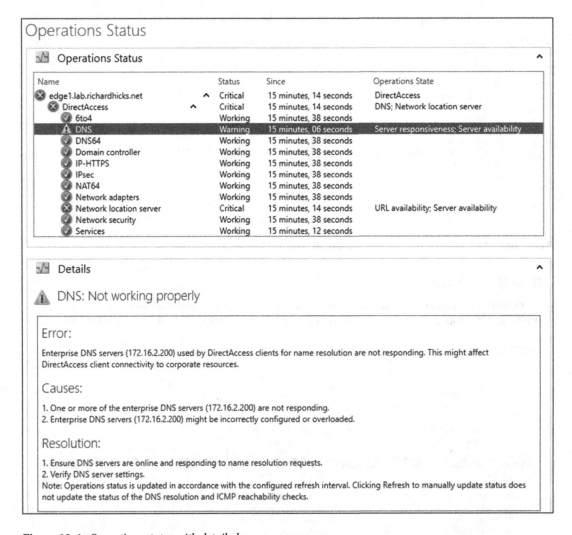

Figure 10-4. *Operations status with detailed error message*

Operations status information can also be viewed at the command line by opening an elevated PowerShell command window and entering the following command (Figure 10-5):

```
Get-RemoteAccessHealth
```

```
Administrator: Windows PowerShell                                          —    □    ×

PS C:\> Get-RemoteAccessHealth

Component              RemoteAccessServer    HealthState    TimeStamp              Id    OperationStatus
---------              ------------------    -----------    ---------              --    ---------------
Server                 localhost             OK             5/21/2016 2:37:49 PM
6to4                   localhost             OK             5/21/2016 2:37:26 PM
Vpn Addressing         localhost             Disabled       5/21/2016 2:37:26 PM
Network Security       localhost             OK             5/21/2016 2:37:26 PM
Dns                    localhost             OK             5/21/2016 2:37:49 PM
IP-Https               localhost             OK             5/21/2016 2:37:26 PM
Nat64                  localhost             OK             5/21/2016 2:37:26 PM
Dns64                  localhost             OK             5/21/2016 2:37:26 PM
IPsec                  localhost             OK             5/21/2016 2:37:26 PM
Kerberos               localhost             Disabled       5/21/2016 2:37:26 PM
Domain Controller      localhost             OK             5/21/2016 2:37:26 PM
Management Servers     localhost             Disabled       5/21/2016 2:37:26 PM
Network Location ...   localhost             OK             5/21/2016 2:37:49 PM
Otp                    localhost             Disabled       5/21/2016 2:37:26 PM
High Availability      localhost             Disabled       5/21/2016 2:37:26 PM
Isatap                 localhost             Disabled       5/21/2016 2:37:26 PM
Vpn Connectivity       localhost             Disabled       5/21/2016 2:37:26 PM
Teredo                 localhost             Disabled       5/21/2016 2:37:26 PM
Network Adapters       localhost             OK             5/21/2016 2:37:26 PM
Services               localhost             OK             5/21/2016 2:37:49 PM


PS C:\> _
```

Figure 10-5. *Get-RemoteAccessHealth PowerShell command*

User Monitoring

The visibility of current client connections and which internal resources they are accessing is crucial to supporting DirectAccess. By using the Remote Access Management console, the administrator can quickly view connection status and activity for DirectAccess clients.

Remote Access Client Status

Select **Remote Client Status** to view the status for connected DirectAccess clients. Selecting an individual connection displays details about the connection and resources accessed (Figure 10-6).

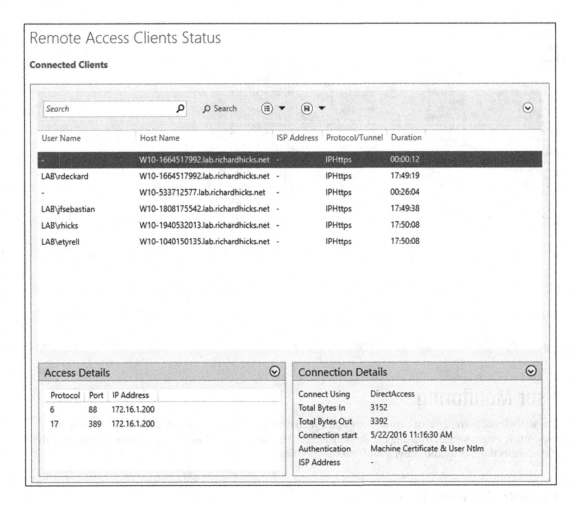

Figure 10-6. Remote access client status

▪ **Note** Some connections may not include username information. This is expected behavior that occurs when a DirectAccess client computer is connected but the user has not yet logged on. In addition, it is not uncommon to see multiple entries for the same computer. This can happen when a DirectAccess client drops its connection and reconnects—for example, when roaming between wireless access points.

Right-click on a column heading to include additional fields in the display (Figure 10-7).

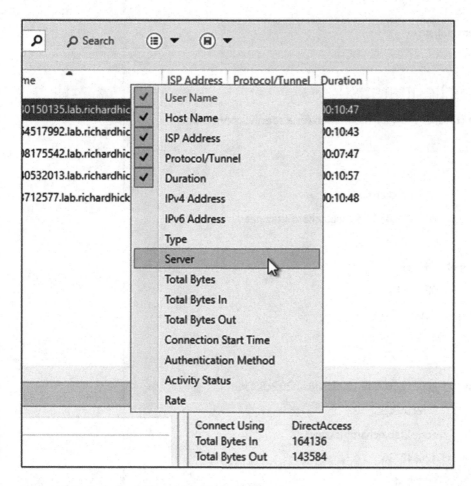

Figure 10-7. Include additional fields to be displayed

Right-click an individual connection and choose **Details** to view detailed information and statistics about the connection (Figure 10-8).

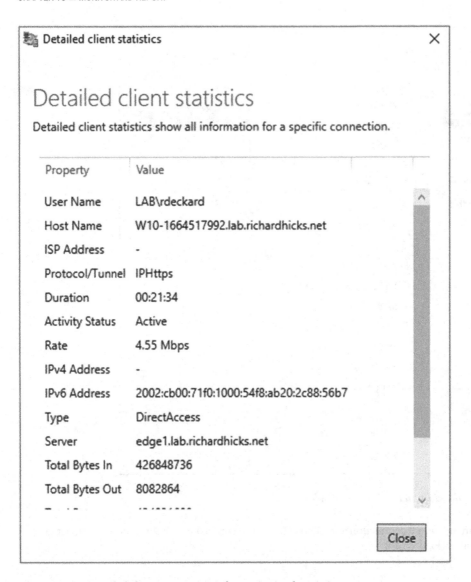

Figure 10-8. *Detailed client connection information and statistics*

■ **Note** The ISP address field is always blank when IP-HTTPS IPv6 transition technology is used to establish a DirectAccess connection.[1] This happens because the ISP address is derived from the IPv6 address used by the client to establish the IPsec security association with the DirectAccess server. For clients using the 6to4 or Teredo IPv6 transition technologies, their public IPv4 address is embedded in their IPv6 address. However, IP-HTTPS uses random IPv6 addresses, which prevents the DirectAccess server from collecting and displaying this information.

---

[1]It is possible to gain much more detailed information about the DirectAccess connection, including the ISP address for IP-HTTPS connections, using Windows component event logging. More details can be found here: https://blogs.
technet.microsoft.com/martin_j_solis/2015/03/20/additional-way-to-monitor-directaccess-machineuser-activity-on-windows-2012-and-2012r2-directaccess-with-component-event-logging/

Administrators can perform searches to narrow the list of displayed results. Enter text for which to search in the **Search** field and press Enter or click **Search** (Figure 10-9).

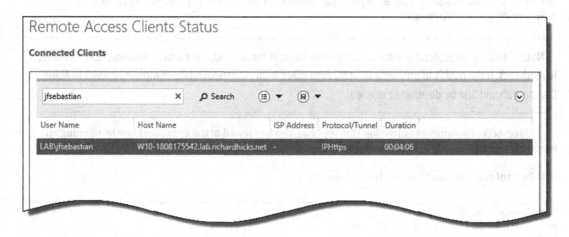

Figure 10-9. *Search connected clients*

Click the **Save** icon to save the search query for future use (Figure 10-10).

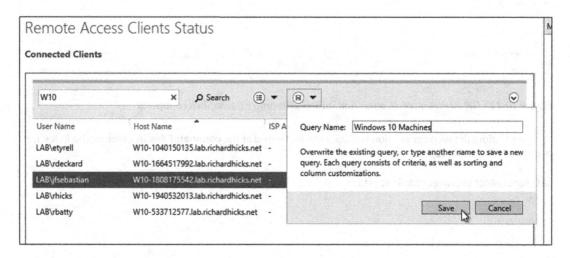

Figure 10-10. *Save a search query*

The Remote Access Management console does not allow the administrator to forcibly disconnect connected DirectAccess clients. To terminate a DirectAccess connection, open an elevated PowerShell command window and enter the following command:

```
Get-NetIPsecMainModeSA | Where-Object {$_.RemoteFirstId.Identity -like "*<computer_name>*"}
| Remove-NetIPsecMainModeSA
```

For example, to disconnect a computer named CLIENT1, the command would appear as follows:

```
Get-NetIPsecMainModeSA | Where-Object {$_.RemoteFirstId.Identity –like "*client1*"}
| Remove-NetIPsecMainModeSA
```

▪ **Note** When a DirectAccess IPsec security association is terminated, the client will automatically attempt to reconnect. If the goal is to prevent a DirectAccess client from reconnecting, its computer account in Active Directory should first be disabled or deleted.

DirectAccess summary connection statistics can also be viewed at the command line by opening an elevated PowerShell command window and entering the following command (Figure 10-11):

```
Get-RemoteAccessConnectionStatisticsSummary
```

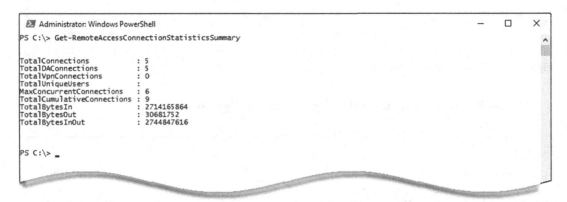

Figure 10-11. *Get-RemoteAccessConnectionStatisticsSummary PowerShell command*

In addition, detailed connection statistics can be viewed at the command line by entering the following command (Figure 10-12):

```
Get-RemoteAccessConnectionStatistics
```

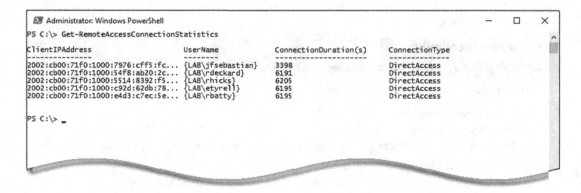

Figure 10-12. *Get-RemoteAccessConnectionStatistics PowerShell command*

Accounting

DirectAccess can be configured to store log data using either Inbox or RADIUS accounting methods. Inbox accounting uses a local Windows Internal Database (WID) on each DirectAccess server to store log data. RADIUS accounting sends log data to a local or remote RADIUS server for storage. Both accounting methods can be configured at the same time, if necessary.

■ **Note**   Inbox accounting must be configured in order to enable reporting functionality in the Remote Access Management console.

Inbox Accounting

Highlight **Reporting** in the Remote Access Management console and click **Configure Accounting**. Select the option to **Use inbox accounting**. Optionally, specify how long to store the account logs and click **Apply** (Figure 10-13).

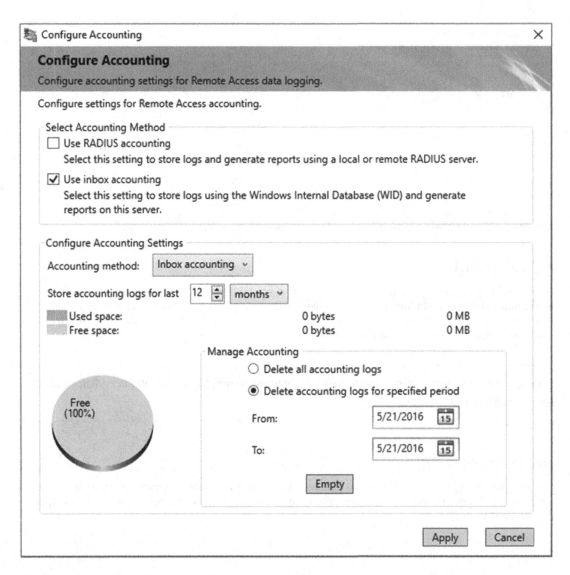

Figure 10-13. *Configure inbox accounting*

■ **Note**   After enabling inbox accounting, it is recommended that the database be optimized using guidance published by Microsoft, found here: `https://technet.microsoft.com/en-us/library/mt693376.aspx`.

RADIUS Accounting

Highlight **Reporting** in the Remote Access Management console and click **Configure Accounting**. If accounting is already configured, click **Configure Accounting** in the **Tasks** pane and select **Use RADIUS accounting**. Choose **RADIUS accounting** from the **Accounting Method** drop-down box, double-click the blank field, enter the RADIUS server name and shared secret, and click **Apply** (Figure 10-14).

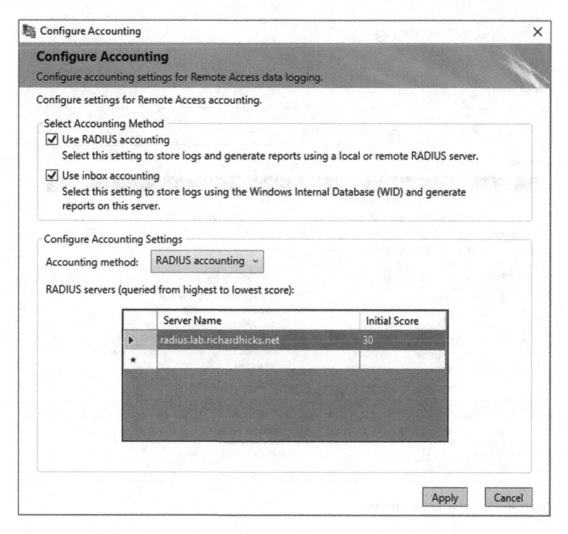

Figure 10-14. *Configure RADIUS accounting*

■ **Note** RADIUS server configuration and reporting options differ greatly by vendor and are outside the scope of this book. In addition, RADIUS accounting is limited and provides less detailed connection information than using Inbox accounting provides.

Reporting

To generate historical reports for DirectAccess connections, highlight **Reporting** in the Remote Access Management console, choose a **Start date** and **End date**, and click **Generate Report**. Select an entry for which to display access and connection details (Figure 10-15).

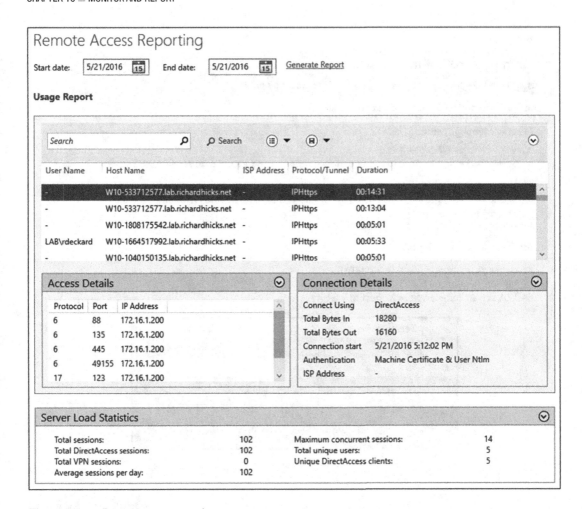

Figure 10-15. *Remote access reporting*

Right-click on a column heading to include additional fields in the display (Figure 10-16).

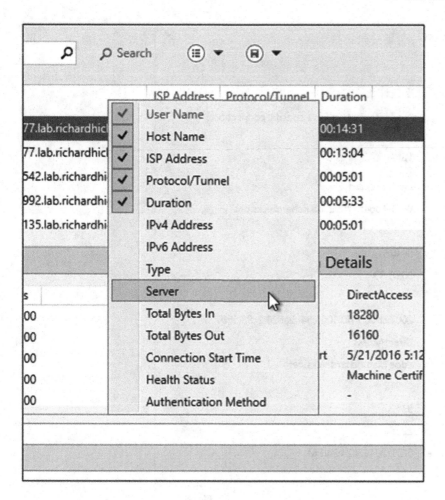

Figure 10-16. *Include additional fields to be displayed*

Double-click an entry to view additional detailed client statistics (Figure 10-17).

Figure 10-17. *Detailed client statistics*

Administrators can perform searches to narrow the list of displayed results. Enter text for which to search in the Search field and press Enter or click **Search** (Figure 10-18).

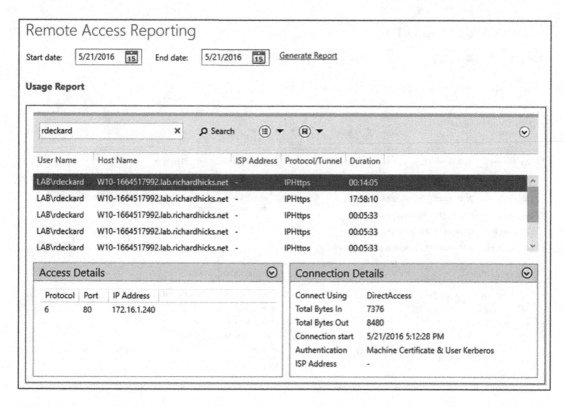

Figure 10-18. *Search the logged connections*

Click the **Save** icon to save the search query for future use (Figure 10-19).

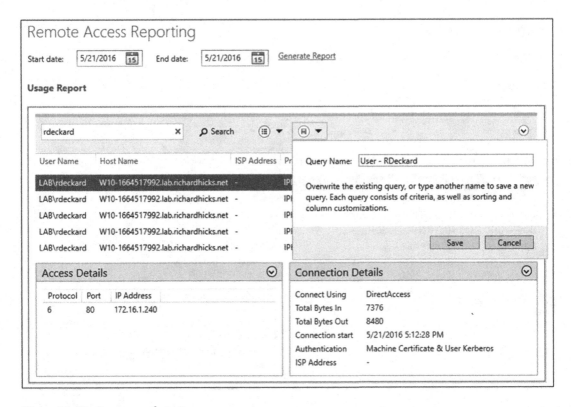

Figure 10-19. Save a search query

DirectAccess report details can also be viewed at the command line by opening an elevated PowerShell command window and entering the following command (Figure 10-20):

```
Get-RemoteAccessUserActivity -UserName <username> -StartDateTime <start date> -EndDateTime
<end date>
```

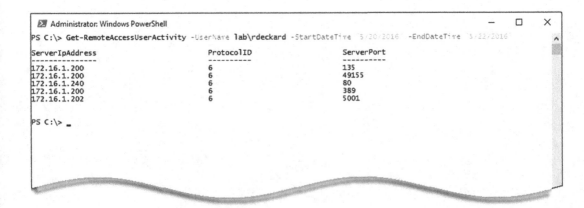

Figure 10-20. Get-RemoteAccessUserActivity PowerShell command

Summary

The DirectAccess Management Console can be used to monitor the health and status of DirectAccess and its various supporting infrastructure services. It can also be used to view near real-time DirectAccess connection statistics and user activity. DirectAccess accounting using inbox or RADIUS can be enabled to record connection and user activity, allowing for the generation of reports for compliance and auditing purposes.

CHAPTER 11

Troubleshoot

DirectAccess is a thing of beauty when it's working correctly. Typically, it *just works*, and there's little ongoing maintenance required once it is deployed. When it isn't working correctly, however, it can be quite frustrating. There are a lot of moving parts to DirectAccess, and knowing where to look first is often challenging.

DirectAccess is made up of Windows platform technologies, so many of the tools and procedures outlined in this chapter are likely to be familiar to the DirectAccess administrator. On the client side, Windows 8.x and Windows 10 make the troubleshooting effort easier with the native integration of many PowerShell commands to view DirectAccess settings and status information.

There are myriad factors that can prevent DirectAccess from working properly. By taking a systematic and methodical approach to the troubleshooting process, often the issue can be identified and resolved quickly.

It's important to understand that this chapter is not a comprehensive troubleshooting guide. It cannot cover all deployment options and every possible failure scenario. However, it will provide the administrator with details and information that can be applied to troubleshoot most common deployment scenarios. The tools and techniques described here can be used to troubleshoot more complex deployment scenarios when required.

DirectAccess Client Connection Process

The following outlines the process of a DirectAccess client making a successful connection to the DirectAccess server and accessing resources on the Internal network. Use this as a reference so as to understand where the connection process is failing and where it is best to focus troubleshooting efforts.

1. A DirectAccess client computer is added to a security group and receives DirectAccess client settings via group policy.

2. When the DirectAccess client is started, or after any network interface status change, the DirectAccess client enables the Public firewall profile and detects if it is inside or outside the network by attempting to contact the NLS.

3. If the DirectAccess client computer can successfully connect to the NLS (receives a 200 OK response to an HTTP GET, the certificate is valid, trusted, and the subject name matches), the client enables the Domain firewall profile, and no attempt to establish a DirectAccess connection is made.

4. If the DirectAccess client computer cannot successfully connect to the NLS, the Name Resolution Policy Table (NRPT) is activated and the client will attempt to establish a DirectAccess connection.

5. An IPv6 transition technology is selected, an entry point is selected, and a connection is made to the DirectAccess server.

6. The DirectAccess client attempts to connect to a domain controller to authenticate. Connection Security Rules (CSRs) in the Windows firewall are triggered, and IPsec security associations are established. In most deployment scenarios, there are two distinct connections made. The first is the infrastructure tunnel, authenticated using the computer certificate and its AD computer account (NTLM). The second is the user (intranet) tunnel, authenticated using the computer certificate and the user's AD account (Kerberos).

7. If strong user authentication is enabled, the user must supply those credentials after logging on to their device.

8. Once the user has successfully authenticated, they will have full access to the Internal network.

9. On Windows 8.x and Windows 10 clients, the client will attempt to resolve the name of the web-probe host URL and establish a connection. If successful, the connection status in the UI will indicate "Connected."

Server and Client Configuration

Before troubleshooting DirectAccess connectivity, the configuration of the DirectAccess server, client, and supporting infrastructure should be reviewed to ensure that all systems are capable of supporting DirectAccess communication.

DirectAccess Server

To support DirectAccess connectivity, the server must meet all installation prerequisites, be configured correctly, and have proper network connectivity both inbound and outbound.

Group Policy

DirectAccess server settings are applied via Active Directory Group Policy Objects (GPOs). Ensure that the DirectAccess Server Settings policy is applied to the DirectAccess server by opening an elevated PowerShell command window and entering **gpresult /r /scope:computer** (Figure 11-1).

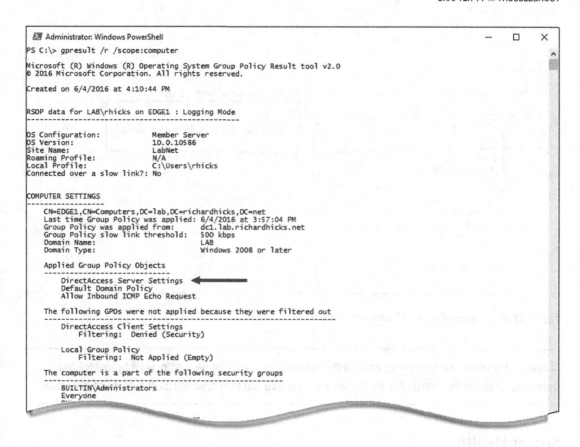

Figure 11-1. *Confirm DirectAccess Server GPO application*

In addition, verify that the server has received the latest GPOs by entering **gpupdate /force** in an elevated PowerShell command window. Once complete, open the Remote Access Management console and highlight **Dashboard**. The configuration status should have a green checkmark and indicate that the configuration was distributed successfully (Figure 11-2).

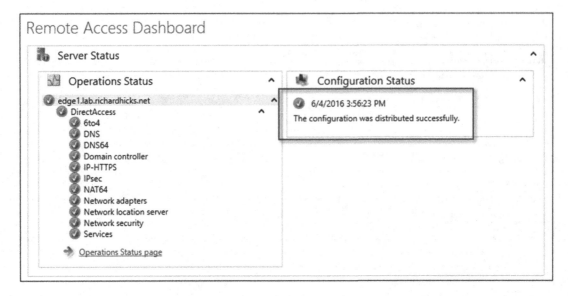

Figure 11-2. Configuration distributed successfully

■ **Note**   For multisite deployments, confirm the configuration status for each entry point by highlighting
Operations Status in the Remote Access Management console and then selecting each entry point individually.

Server Health

In the Remote Access Management console, highlight **Operations Status** and ensure that the DirectAccess
server and all supporting infrastructure services are healthy and operational (Figure 11-3). If any
components or services are unhealthy or unavailable, resolve them before continuing.

Operations Status

Operations Status			
Name	Status	Since	Operations State
edge1.lab.richardhicks.net	Working	21 minutes, 19 seconds	
DirectAccess	Working	21 minutes, 19 seconds	
6to4	Working	26 minutes, 19 seconds	
DNS	Working	21 minutes, 19 seconds	
DNS64	Working	26 minutes, 19 seconds	
Domain controller	Working	26 minutes, 19 seconds	
IP-HTTPS	Working	26 minutes, 19 seconds	
IPsec	Working	26 minutes, 19 seconds	
NAT64	Working	26 minutes, 19 seconds	
Network adapters	Working	26 minutes, 19 seconds	
Network location server	Working	21 minutes, 19 seconds	
Network security	Working	26 minutes, 19 seconds	
Services	Working	21 minutes, 19 seconds	

Figure 11-3. Verify DirectAccess operations status (GUI)

Optionally, the administrator can confirm DirectAccess health status by entering the following command in an elevated PowerShell command window (Figure 11-4):

```
Get-RemoteAccessHealth | Where-Object HealthState -NE Disabled | Format-Table -Autosize
```

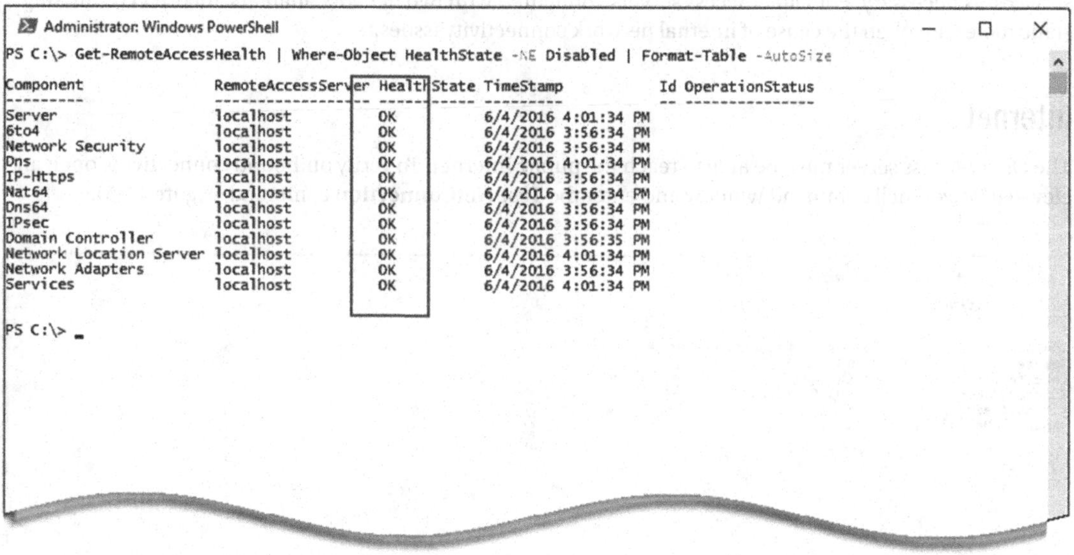

Figure 11-4. *Verify DirectAccess operations status (PowerShell)*

Network Connectivity

The DirectAccess server must have the correct Windows firewall profiles assigned to its network interfaces. In addition, it is crucial that the DirectAccess server have network connectivity both inbound and outbound to allow DirectAccess clients to connect to the DirectAccess server, and to allow clients to connect to internal resources.

Firewall Profiles

When the DirectAccess server is configured with two network adapters, ensure that the Internal network adapter has been assigned the Domain firewall profile, and that the External network adapter has been assigned the Public profile. This can be confirmed by opening an elevated PowerShell command window and entering the following command:

```
Get-NetConnectionProfile | Select-Object Name, NetworkCategory
```

Alternatively, the firewall profile can be found by opening an elevated command prompt window and entering the following command:

```
Netsh advfirewall show currentprofile
```

Internal

The DirectAccess server must be able to connect to all internal networks and services. This includes domain controllers, internal DNS servers, systems-management servers, and any servers that will be accessed by remote DirectAccess clients. Verify that the DirectAccess server can reach all remote internal subnets and services, as necessary. For DirectAccess servers configured with two network adapters, incorrect or missing static routes are often the cause of internal network connectivity issues.[1]

Internet

The DirectAccess server must be able to reach the public Internet. To verify outbound connectivity, open an elevated PowerShell command window and enter the **Test-NetConnection** command (Figure 11-5).

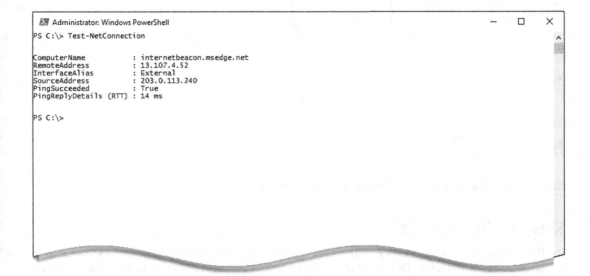

Figure 11-5. *Verify Internet connectivity using Test-NetConnection*

The DirectAccess server itself must also be reachable from the public Internet. First, confirm that the DirectAccess server's public hostname resolves to the correct IP address by using the **Resolve-DnsName** PowerShell command (Figure 11-6).

---

[1]https://directaccess.richardhicks.com/2013/06/19/network-interface-configuration-for-multihomed-windows-server-2012-directaccess-servers/

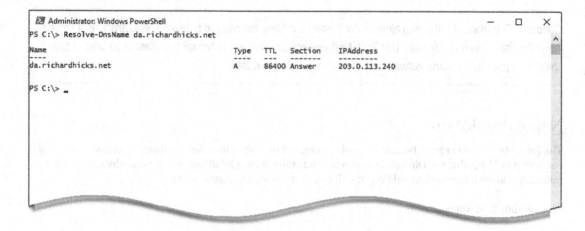

Figure 11-6. *Verify public hostname resoultion using the Resolve-DnsName PowerShell command*

If name resolution is working correctly, confirm that the DirectAccess server can accept incoming IP-HTTPS connections by entering the following PowerShell command on a Windows 8.x or Windows 10 client connected to the public Internet (Figure 11-7):

```
Test-NetConnection -Port 443 <FQDN>
```

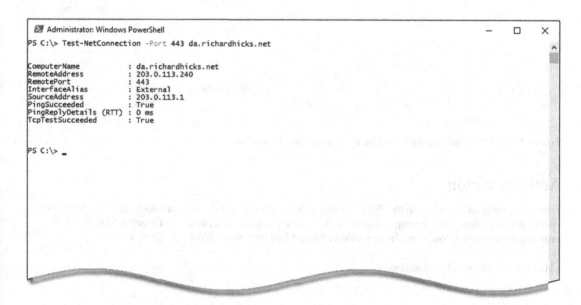

Figure 11-7. *Test IP-HTTPS connectivity using Test-NetConnection*

> ■ **Note** The use of ICMP (PING) alone is not always a reliable indicator of network connectivity, as it can be (and often is) blocked by firewalls. Use **Test-NetConnection -Port** or the Nmap[2] tool (described later in this chapter) to positively confirm network connectivity whenever possible.

Name Resolution

The DirectAccess server must be able to resolve internal hostnames in order to support DirectAccess connections. Verify that the DirectAccess server can resolve names in all internal domains by entering the following command in an elevated PowerShell command window (Figure 11-8):

```
Resolve-DnsName <domain>
```

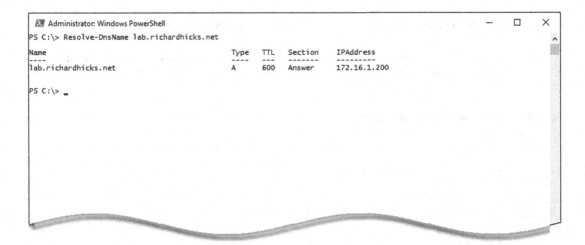

Figure 11-8. Verify internal name resolution using Resolve-DnsName

Authentication

Domain communication is vital for DirectAccess, as the machine and the user are both authenticated when connecting remotely. Ensure proper domain controller communication from the DirectAccess server by entering the following command in an elevated PowerShell command window (Figure 11-9):

```
nltest.exe /sc_verify:<domain>
```

---

[2]https://nmap.org/

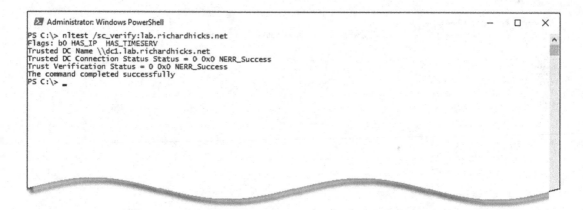

```
Administrator: Windows PowerShell                                    —    □    ×
PS C:\> nltest /sc_verify:lab.richardhicks.net
Flags: b0 HAS_IP  HAS_TIMESERV
Trusted DC Name \\dc1.lab.richardhicks.net
Trusted DC Connection Status Status = 0 0x0 NERR_Success
Trust Verification Status = 0 0x0 NERR_Success
The command completed successfully
PS C:\> _
```

Figure 11-9. Verfiy domain communication using nltest.exe

Certificates

DirectAccess uses an SSL certificate for the IP-HTTPS IPv6 transition technology and, optionally, a computer certificate for IPsec authentication and encryption.

SSL Certificate

Verify the SSL certificate is valid, trusted, and includes the Server Authentication Enhanced Key Usage (EKU). The certificate must be installed in the local computer certificate store and must include the private key. Also, the Subject field must match the public hostname defined in Step 2 of the Remote Access configuration setup on the DirectAccess server. When supporting Windows 7 clients, the Certificate Revocation List (CRL) must be publicly accessible.

Computer Certificate

For many deployment scenarios, the DirectAccess server must also have a computer certificate to support IPsec authentication and encryption. The certificate must be issued by a Public Key Infrastructure (PKI) with a minimum key length of 1024 bits. It must be signed using a minimum of Secure Hash Algorithm 1 (SHA1) and include the Client Authentication EKU. It must be valid (not expired), trusted, have a private key, and be installed in the local computer certificate store. The certificate must also share a common root Certification Authority (CA) with the DirectAccess clients.

IPv6

IPv6 must not be disabled on the DirectAccess server. This can be confirmed by checking the **HKLM\SYSTEM\ CurrentControlSet\Services\Tcpip6\Parameters\DisabledComponents** registry key. It should not exist. If it does, it must be set to 0. In addition, all IPv6 transition technologies on the DirectAccess server must be enabled.

Windows Firewall

The Windows firewall must be enabled for all profiles on the DirectAccess server. This can be verified by issuing the following command in an elevated PowerShell command window (Figure 11-10):

```
Get-NetFirewallProfile –PolicyStore ActiveStore | Format-Table Name, Enabled
```

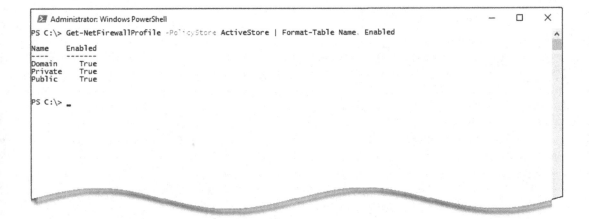

Figure 11-10. *Verify the Windows firewall is enabled for all profiles using the Get-NetFirewallProfile PowerShell command*

■ **Note** Third-party firewalls can be installed on the DirectAccess server, but the Windows firewall must not be disabled. In addition, the Windows firewall must be registered for CSRs. This can be verified by entering the **netsh advfirewall show global** command in an elevated command prompt window and confirming that the Windows firewall is listed for the **ConSecRuleCategory** category.

Services

The following services must be running on the DirectAccess server in order to support DirectAccess connections:

- IP Helper (IPHlpSvc)
- Windows Firewall (Mpssvc)
- Base Filtering Engine (BFE)
- IPsec Policy Agent (PolicyAgent)
- IKE and AuthIP IPsec Keying Modules (IKEEXT)
- KDC Proxy Server Services (KPSSVC)[3]
- RemoteAccess Management Services (RaMgmtSvc)

These services can be viewed by using the Services management console (services.msc) or by using the **Get-Service** PowerShell command.

---

[3]This service is only required when the option to enable Windows 7 client computers to connect via DirectAccess is not selected.

Unsupported Configurations

There are a number of unsupported DirectAccess configurations that may also prevent DirectAccess from working correctly. When troubleshooting, it is recommended to consult Microsoft's DirectAccess Unsupported Configurations guide.[4]

DirectAccess Client

To support DirectAccess connectivity, the client must meet installation prerequisites, be configured correctly, and have proper network connectivity both inbound and outbound.

Operating System SKU

DirectAccess is only supported with the following Windows client operating systems:[5]

- Windows 10 Enterprise

- Windows 10 Education

- Windows 7 Enterprise

- Windows 7 Ultimate

DirectAccess will not function on any version of the Home or Professional editions. To confirm the client operating system version, open the **Control Panel** and navigate to **System and Security** and then **System** (Figure 11-11).

---

[4]https://technet.microsoft.com/en-us/library/dn464274(v=ws.11).aspx.
[5]Although not commonly used as client operating systems, the Windows Server 2008 R2, Windows Server 2012, Windows Server 2012 R2, and Windows Server 2016 server operating systems are also supported DirectAccess clients.

Figure 11-11. *Confirm supported Windows SKU*

Alternatively, the **systeminfo.exe** utility can be used to view the client operating system version (Figure 11-12).

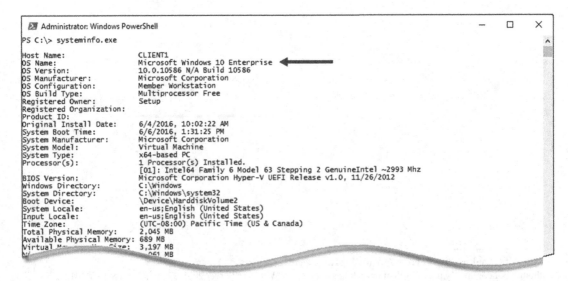

Figure 11-12. *Confirm supported Windows SKU*

Group Policy

DirectAccess server settings are applied via Active Directory Group Policy Objects (GPOs). Ensure that the server settings policy is applied to the DirectAccess server by entering **gpresult /r /scope:computer** in an elevated PowerShell command window (Figure 11-13):

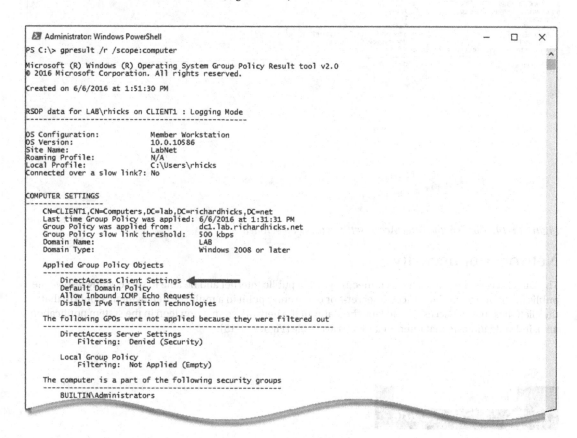

Figure 11-13. Confirm the DirectAccess client GPO application

Additionally, the **Get-DAClientExperienceConfiguration** PowerShell command can be used to confirm that the client has received the DirectAccess settings via the group policy and that the IPv6 addresses listed for the **IPsecTunnelEndpoints** match the IPv6 addresses on the DirectAccess server (Figure 11-14).

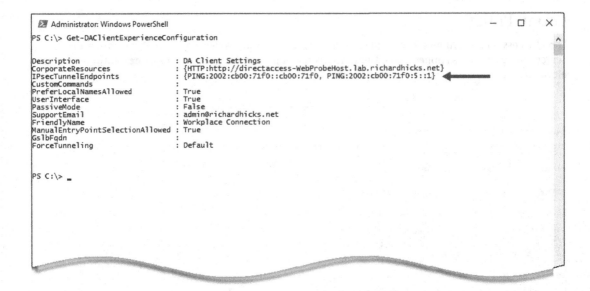

Figure 11-14. Confirm the DirectAccess settings using PowerShell

Network Connectivity

The DirectAccess client must have connectivity to the public Internet and be able to successfully resolve the public hostname of the DirectAccess server—or of the entry point in a multisite deployment. Confirm that the client has Internet access by viewing the status of the network connection icon in the system notification area. It should indicate that Internet access is available (Figure 11-15).

Figure 11-15. Confirm Internet access

Alternatively, the **Test-NetConnection** and **Resolve-DnsName** PowerShell commands can be used to confirm that the client has an active Internet connection and that it can successfully resolve public hostnames.

Domain Connectivity

The DirectAccess client must have a valid computer account in Active Directory. Ensure proper domain controller communication from the DirectAccess client by entering **nltest.exe /sc_verify:<domain>** in an elevated command prompt window when the client is on the Internal network.

Certificates

For some deployment scenarios, the DirectAccess client must also have a computer certificate to support IPsec authentication and encryption. The certificate must be issued by a PKI with a minimum key length of 1024 bits. It must be signed using a minimum of SHA1 and include the Client Authentication EKU. It must be valid (not expired), trusted, have a private key, and be installed in the local computer certificate store. The certificate must also share a common root CA with the DirectAccess server.

IPv6

IPv6 must not be disabled on the DirectAccess client. This can be confirmed by checking the **HKLM\ SYSTEM\CurrentControlSet\Services\Tcpip6\Parameters\DisabledComponents** registry key. It should not exist. If it does, it must be set to 0.

IPv6 Transition Technologies

DirectAccess clients are commonly on the public IPv4 Internet and must use an IPv6 transition technology to establish a connection to the DirectAccess server. Not all IPv6 transition technologies are required to be enabled. The following sections provide details for ensuring they are configured correctly where enabled.

6to4

To view 6to4 configuration and state information, use the **Get-Net6to4Configuration** PowerShell command, or **netsh interface 6to4 show interface** or **show state**. If the 6to4 IPv6 transition technology is enabled, enter **ipconfig** in a command prompt window and confirm that a Global Unicast Address[6] (GUA) is assigned to the 6to4 tunnel adapter (Figure 11-16).

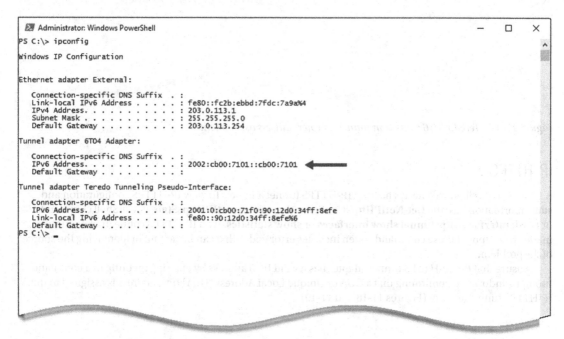

Figure 11-16. 6to4 IPv6 transition tunnel adapter address assignment

---

[6]https://technet.microsoft.com/en-us/library/cc759208(v=ws.10).aspx

Teredo

To view Teredo configuration and state information, use the **Get-NetTeredoConfiguration** or **Get-NetTeredoState** PowerShell commands, or **netsh interface teredo show state**. If the Teredo IPv6 transition technology is supported, enter **ipconfig** in a command prompt window and confirm that a GUA IPv6 address is assigned to the Teredo tunnel adapter (Figure 11-17).

```
Administrator: Windows PowerShell                                    —    □    ×
PS C:\> ipconfig

Windows IP Configuration

Ethernet adapter External:

   Connection-specific DNS Suffix  . :
   Link-local IPv6 Address . . . . . : fe80::fc2b:ebbd:7fdc:7a9a%4
   IPv4 Address. . . . . . . . . . . : 203.0.113.1
   Subnet Mask . . . . . . . . . . . : 255.255.255.0
   Default Gateway . . . . . . . . . : 203.0.113.254

Tunnel adapter 6TO4 Adapter:

   Connection-specific DNS Suffix  . :
   IPv6 Address. . . . . . . . . . . : 2002:cb00:7101::cb00:7101
   Default Gateway . . . . . . . . . :

Tunnel adapter Teredo Tunneling Pseudo-Interface:

   Connection-specific DNS Suffix  . :
   IPv6 Address. . . . . . . . . . . : 2001:0:cb00:71f0:90:12d0:34ff:8efe  ◄——
   Link-local IPv6 Address . . . . . : fe80::90:12d0:34ff:8efe%6
   Default Gateway . . . . . . . . . :
PS C:\> _
```

Figure 11-17. *Teredo IPv6 transition tunnel adapter address assignment*

IP-HTTPS

A DirectAccess client will always have an IP-HTTPS tunnel adapter. To view IP-HTTPS configuration and state information, use the **Get-NetIPHttpsConfiguration** or **Get-NetIPHttpsState** PowerShell commands, or **netsh interface httpstunnel show interfaces** or **show statistics**. If an IP-HTTPS connection cannot be made, the output of these commands often includes error codes that can be helpful in identifying the source of the problem.

Ensure that the IP-HTTPS tunnel adapter has a valid IPv6 address by entering **ipconfig** in a command prompt window and confirming that a GUA or Unique Local Address (ULA) IPv6 address is assigned to the IP-HTTPS tunnel adapter (Figures 11-18 and 11-19).

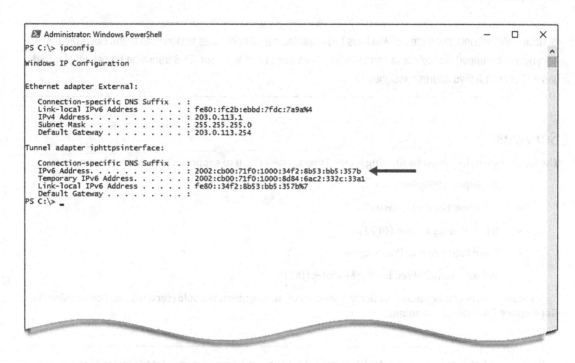

Figure 11-18. *IP-HTTPS tunnel adapter with GUA IPv6 address*

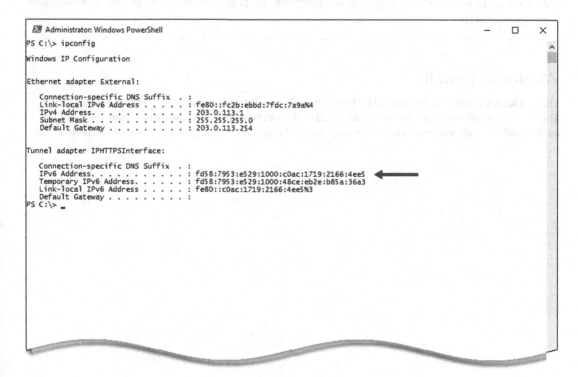

Figure 11-19. *IP-HTTPS tunnel adapter with ULA IPv6 address*

■ **Note**   All network interfaces in Windows have link-local IPv6 addresses assigned to them. However, this is not enough to support DirectAccess connectivity. There must be at least one IPv6 transition tunnel adapter that has a GUA or ULA IPv6 address assigned to it.

Services

The following services must be running on the DirectAccess client to support a DirectAccess connection:

- IP Helper (IPHlpSvc)

- Windows Firewall (Mpssvc)

- Base Filtering Engine (BFE)

- IPsec Policy Agent (PolicyAgent)

- IKE and AuthIP IPsec Keying Modules (IKEEXT)

These services can be viewed by using the Services management console (services.msc) or by using the **Get-Service** PowerShell command.

■ **Note**   The Network Connectivity Assistant (Ncasvc) must also be running in order to provide DirectAccess connection-status information in the GUI and via PowerShell, and to support smart card and one-time password (OTP) authentication.

Windows Firewall

The Windows firewall must be enabled for both the Public and Private profiles on the DirectAccess client. This can be verified by issuing the **Get-NetFirewallProfile –PolicyStore ActiveStore** command or the **netsh advfirewall show all** command and confirming that the Public and Private profiles are enabled (Figure 11-20).

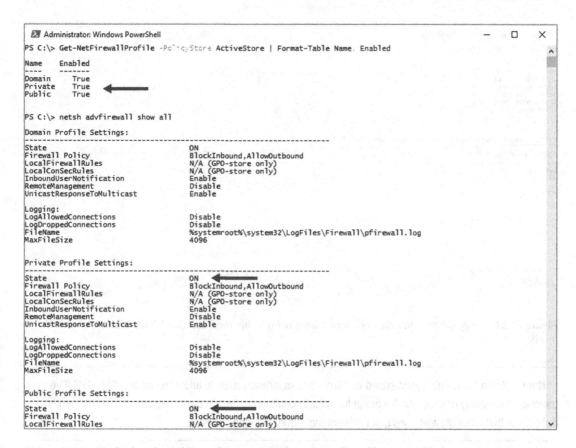

Figure 11-20. *Verfiy that the Public and Private Windows firewall profiles are enabled*

DirectAccess connections can only be established if the *current* network connection is using either the Public or Private profile. To view the Windows firewall profile assigned to the current network connection, use the **Get-NetConnectionProfile** PowerShell command or the **netsh advfirewall monitor show currentprofile** command to ensure that either the Public or Private profile is active (Figure 11-21).

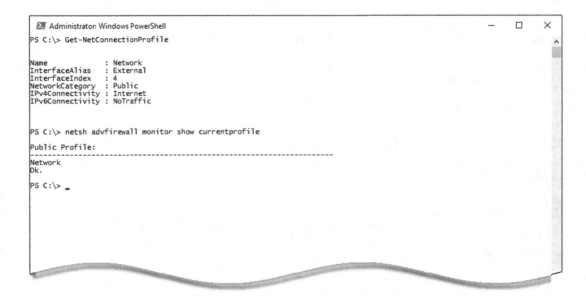

Figure 11-21. Verify the current network connection is using either the Public or Private Windows firewall profile

---

■ **Note** When the client is provisioned for DirectAccess, firewall rules to allow Teredo and IP-HTTPS IPv6 transition technology communication are automatically configured. Ensure these rules are not subsequently disabled or that other firewall rules don't prevent them from working correctly.

Connectivity Troubleshooting

When a DirectAccess client can't establish a connection or access internal resources remotely, the following steps can help you identify the root cause.

Connection Security Rules

If the DirectAccess server has received the DirectAccess Client Settings group policy, it should be configured with Connection Security Rules (CSRs) that establish IPsec Security Associations (SAs) between the client and server. Ensure that these rules are in place by opening the Windows firewall with Advanced Security (WFAS) management console (wf.msc) and highlighting **Connection Security Rules** (Figure 11-22).

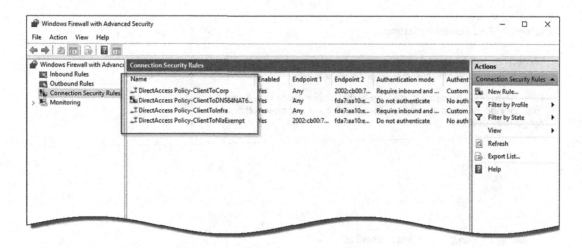

Figure 11-22. *Connection security rules in the Windows firewall*

Double-click the **DirectAccess Policy-ClientToInfra** CSR, select the **Advanced** tab, and then click **Customize** in the IPsec tunneling section. Confirm that the remote tunnel endpoint IPv6 address is correct and assigned to the DirectAccess server (Figure 11-23) .

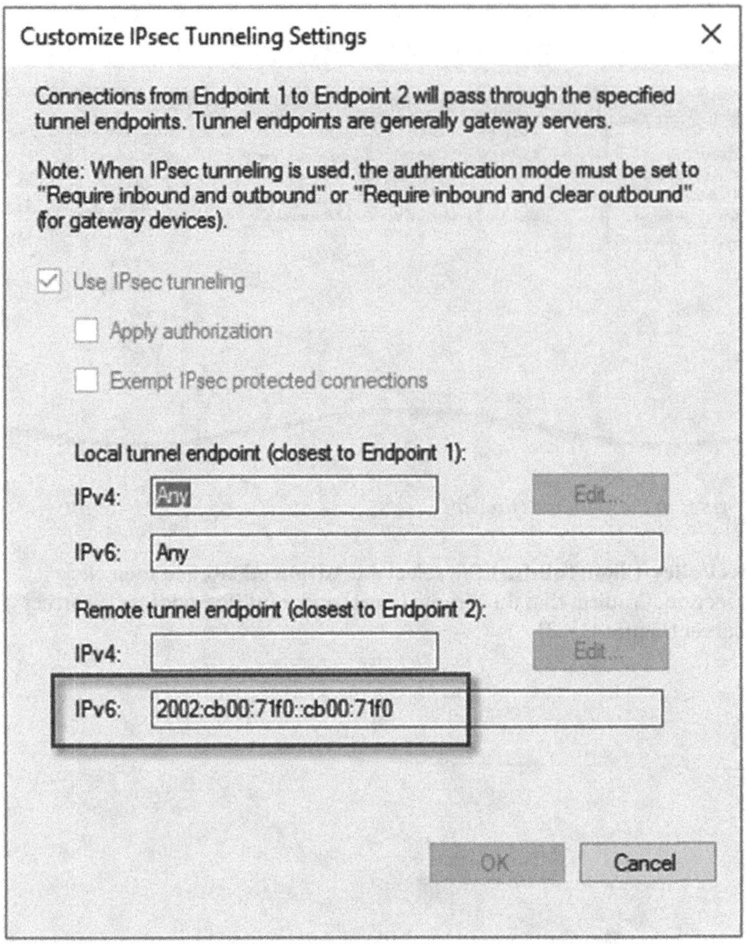

Figure 11-23. *Identify remote tunnel endpoint IPv6 address*

Repeat these steps on the **DirectAccess Policy-ClientToCorp** CSR.

Ping Tunnel Endpoints

Attempt to ping the DirectAccess IPsec tunnel endpoint addresses from a DirectAccess client. In addition to the method described previously, the IPsec tunnel endpoint addresses can be found in Windows 8.x and Windows 10 using the **Get-DAClientExperienceConfiguration** PowerShell command (Figure 11-24).

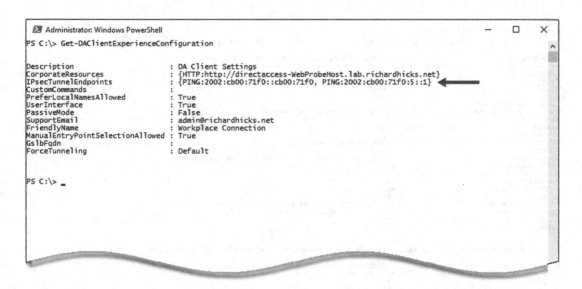

Figure 11-24. Identify IPsec tunnel endpoint IPv6 addresses (Windows 8.x/10)

In Windows 7, enter **netsh advfirewall consec show rule name="DirectAccess Policy-ClientToCorp" type=dynamic** and **netsh advfirewall consec show rule name="DirectAccess Policy-ClientToInfra" type=dynamic** and then ping the **RemoteTunnelEndpoint** IPv6 addresses (Figure 11-25).

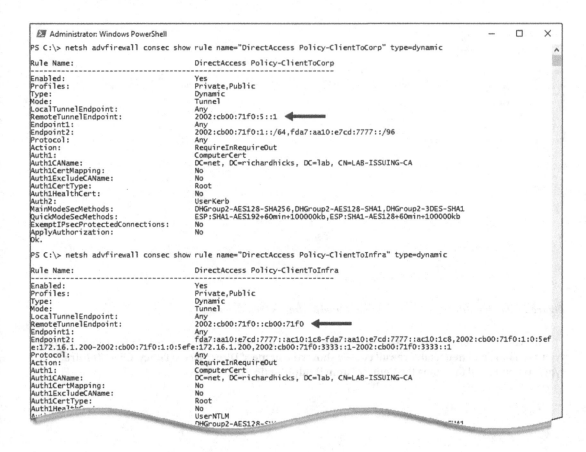

Figure 11-25. Identify IPsec tunnel endpoint IPv6 addresses (Windows 7)

■ **Note**   If the tunnel endpoint IPv6 addresses do not respond to ping requests, ensure that the Windows firewall on the DirectAccess server is configured to allow inbound ICMPv6 echo requests.

If the IPsec tunnel endpoint addresses are correct and cannot be reached, investigate issues related to the IPv6 transition technology as outlined previously in this chapter.

Ping Internal Servers

Attempt to ping an internal server by its hostname. The name should resolve to an IPv6 address and respond accordingly (Figure 11-26).

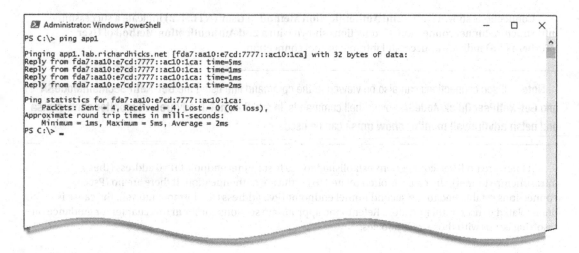

Figure 11-26. Ping internal server by hostname

If it does not respond to the ping, ensure that the internal server is configured to allow inbound ICMPv4 echo requests. If it does not resolve to an IPv6 address, verify IPsec connection establishment and name resolution.

IPsec Connections

To view current IPsec connections, open the WFAS management console, expand **Monitoring**, and then expand **Security Associations** and highlight **Main Mode** (Figure 11-27).

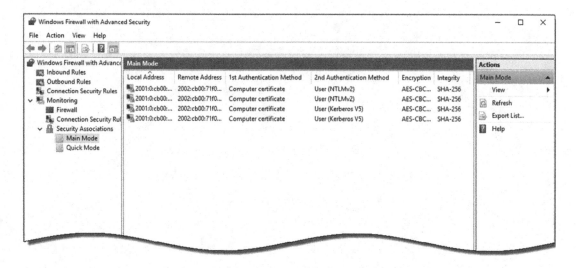

Figure 11-27. View IPsec security associations

Connections shown with a **2nd Authentication Method** of **User (NTLMv2)** indicate a successful infrastructure tunnel connection. Connections shown with a **2nd Authentication Method** of **User (Kerberos V5)** indicate a successful intranet tunnel connection.

■ **Note** IPsec connections can also be viewed at the command line using the **Get-NetIPSecMainModeSA** and **Get-NetIPsecQuickModeSA** PowerShell commands. In addition, **netsh advfirewall monitor show mmsa** and **netsh advfirewall monitor show qmsa** can be used.

If there are no IPsec connections established to the first tunnel endpoint IPv6 address (the infrastructure tunnel), the cause is often related to certificate authentication. If there are no IPsec connections established to the second tunnel endpoint IPv6 address (the intranet tunnel), the cause is often related to user authentication. Refer to the appropriate sections earlier in this chapter for guidance on resolving issues with those technologies.

Name Resolution

If name resolution is not working, the DirectAccess client will fail to authenticate and will not be able to access internal resources. DirectAccess uses the Name Resolution Policy Table (NRPT) to ensure that only name-resolution requests for the Internal namespace are sent to the DNS64 service running on the DirectAccess server. Ensure that the NRPT is configured correctly and that only namespaces on the Internal network are defined in the NRPT.

In Windows 8.x and Windows 10, the NRPT can be viewed by entering **Get-DnsClientNrptPolicy** in an elevated PowerShell command window (Figure 11-28).

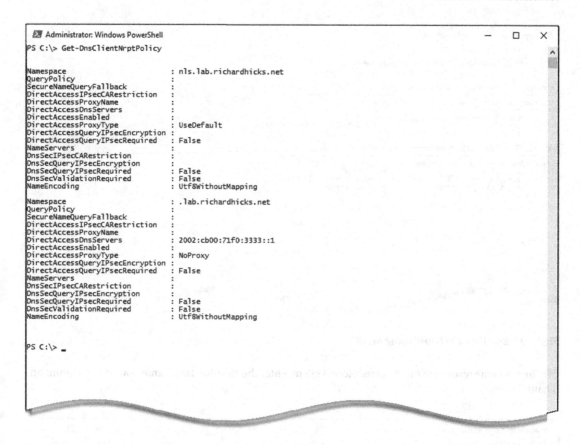

Figure 11-28. *View the NRPT using PowerShell*

In Windows 7, the NRPT can be viewed by entering **netsh namespace show effectivepolicy** in an elevated PowerShell command window (Figure 11-29) .

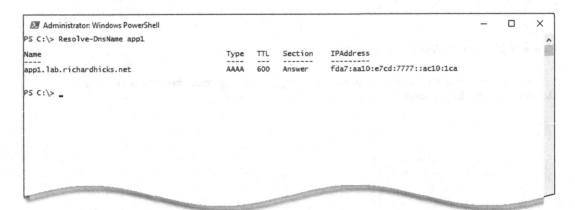

```
Administrator: Windows PowerShell                                    —   □   ×
PS C:\> netsh namespace show effectivepolicy

DNS Effective Name Resolution Policy Table Settings


Settings for nls.lab.richardhicks.net
-----------------------------------------------------------------
DirectAccess (Certification Authority)  :
DirectAccess (IPsec)                    : disabled
DirectAccess (DNS Servers)              :
DirectAccess (Proxy Settings)           : Use default browser settings


Settings for .lab.richardhicks.net
-----------------------------------------------------------------
DirectAccess (Certification Authority)  :
DirectAccess (IPsec)                    : disabled
DirectAccess (DNS Servers)              : 2002:cb00:71f0:3333::1
DirectAccess (Proxy Settings)           : Bypass proxy


PS C:\> _
```

Figure 11-29. *View the NRPT using Netsh*

To test name resolution on the DirectAccess client, enter the **Resolve-DNSName** PowerShell command (Figure 11-30).

```
Administrator: Windows PowerShell                                    —   □   ×
PS C:\> Resolve-DnsName app1

Name                        Type  TTL   Section   IPAddress
----                        ----  ---   -------   ---------
app1.lab.richardhicks.net   AAAA  600   Answer    fda7:aa10:e7cd:7777::ac10:1ca

PS C:\> _
```

Figure 11-30. *Testing name resolution using the Resolve-DNSName PowerShell command*

The Windows nslookup.exe utility will not work by default, because it is not NRPT-aware and will send all name-resolution requests to the DNS servers configured on the network adapter. However, nslookup will work by providing the address of the DNS server (the DNS64 service) to be used for the query (Figure 11-31).

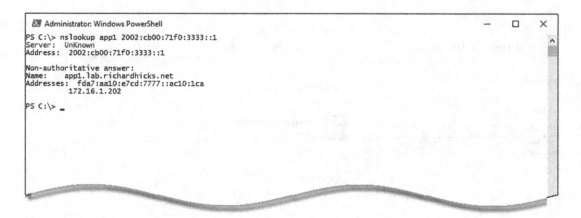

Figure 11-31. Testing name resolution using the nslookup command

Helpful Tools and Commands

The following is a list of helpful tools and commands that can make DirectAccess connectivity troubleshooting easier.

DirectAccess Connection Status

The DirectAccess connection status can be viewed in the Windows 8.x and Windows 10 user interface. Click the network connection icon in the system notification area and then click **Workplace Connection**. Here, the current DirectAccess connection status will be displayed. If additional action is required or the connection failed, it will be indicated here (Figure 11-32).

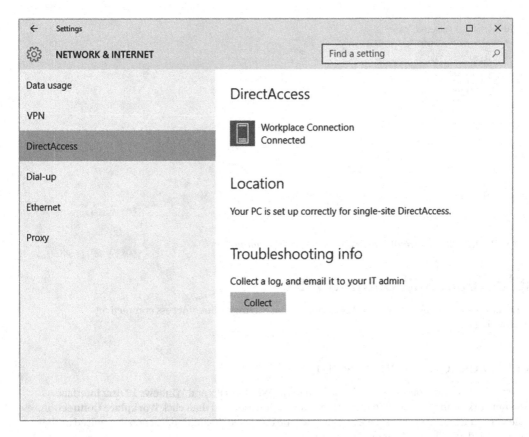

Figure 11-32. *DirectAccess connection status*

■ **Note** It is possible that a DirectAccess connection can be established successfully while the status indicator still indicates a "Connecting" status. This can happen when the web-probe host URL is not reachable from the DirectAccess client. The web-probe host URL is defined in Step 1 of the Remote Access configuration setup. Ensure that this URL can be resolved correctly and that it is reachable over the DirectAccess connection. When an external load balancer is used, additional configuration on the load balancer is required if the web-probe host is hosted on the DirectAccess servers.[7]

Alternatively, DirectAccess connection status can be viewed using the **Get-DAConnectionStatus** PowerShell command. A successful connection will show the status as **Connected Remotely**. If the client cannot establish a connection, it will provide additional information about the failure.

Detailed logging and configuration information can also be gathered by clicking **Collect** in the Troubleshooting info section.

---

[7]https://directaccess.richardhicks.com/2014/08/12/directaccess-clients-in-connecting-state-when-using-external-load-balancer/

■ **Note** To generate diagnostic logs on the DirectAccess client, a help desk email address must be specified in Step 1 of the Remote Access configuration setup. In addition, an email program must also be installed and configured on the client.

DirectAccess Connectivity Assistant

The DirectAccess Connectivity Assistant (DCA) v2.0 is an optional component that can be installed on Windows 7 clients to provide a visual indicator of DirectAccess connectivity status. It can also be used to automate the collection of diagnostic logging information. Configuration of the DCA is covered in Chapter 9, "Supporting Windows 7 Clients."

IPsec Auditing

Enabling IPsec auditing can help you identify issues related to authentication for DirectAccess connections. To enable IPsec auditing, enter the following commands in an elevated command prompt window on the DirectAccess client:

- auditpol.exe /set /subcategory:"IPsec Main Mode" /success:enable /failure:enable

- auditpol.exe /set /subcategory:"IPsec Quick Mode" /success:enable /failure:enable

- auditpol.exe /set /subcategory:"IPsec Extended Mode" /success:enable / failure:enable

After enabling IPsec auditing, restart the client computer and attempt to connect to resources on the Internal network. If unsuccessful, search the security event logs for event IDs between 4600 and 5500 for details about IPsec authentication and connection establishment.

Firewall Logging

The Windows firewall may be blocking connections inbound or outbound on the DirectAccess client. Disabling the firewall is not an option, as it is required for DirectAccess connectivity. Enabling firewall logging allows the administrator to see if any traffic is being denied. To enable firewall logging, enter the following commands in an elevated PowerShell command window:

```
Set-NetFirewallProfile -All -LogFileName c:\firewalllog.txt -LogMaxSizeKilobytes 32767
-LogAllowed True -LogBlocked True
```

Alternatively, firewall logging can be enabled by entering the following commands in an elevated command prompt window:

```
netsh advfirewall set allprofiles logging filename c:\firewalllog.txt
netsh advfirewall set allprofiles logging maxfilesize 32767
netsh advfirewall set allprofiles logging allowedconnections enable
netsh advfirewall set allprofiles logging droppedconnections enable
```

■ **Note** There is a known issue with Windows 8.1 and Windows Server 2012 R2, where enabling firewall logging can cause the firewall service to freeze and crash.[8] Before enabling firewall logging on these operating systems, ensure that the May 2016 update rollup for Windows 8.1 and Windows Server 2012 R2 (KB3156418) has been installed.[9]

Message Analyzer

The Microsoft Message Analyzer[10] is helpful for troubleshooting application connectivity over DirectAccess. The Message Analyzer allows the administrator to view network traffic *inside* the IPsec tunnels. After installation, run the Message Analyzer as an administrator. Click **Favorite Sessions** and choose **Loopback and Unencrypted IPSEC**. Attempt to connect to the internal resource and stop the trace when complete. Once finished, network trace information from inside the IPsec tunnel will be visible (Figure 11-33).

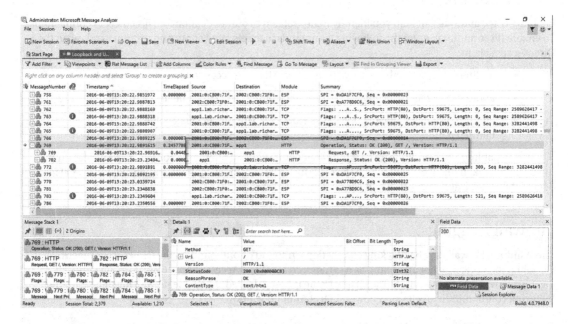

Figure 11-33. *Viewing network commmunciation inside the DirectAccess IPsec tunnels using Message Analyzer*

Common things to look for when troubleshooting application connectivity over DirectAccess are calls being made by the application directly to IPv4 addresses or name-resolution request failures.

---

[8]https://support.microsoft.com/en-us/kb/3155768
[9]https://support.microsoft.com/en-us/kb/3156418
[10]https://www.microsoft.com/en-us/download/details.aspx?id=44226

Nmap

The Network Mapper[11] (Nmap) tool can be helpful when validating the network communication path between the DirectAccess client and server. A discovery script[12] is also available that allows the administrator to query the DirectAccess server to ensure that the IP-HTTPS listener is responding (Figure 11-34).

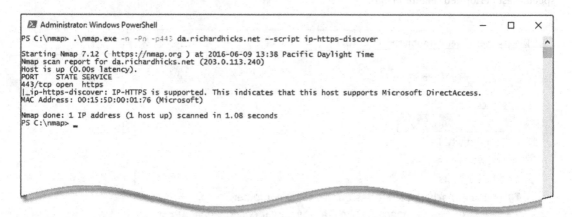

```
Administrator: Windows PowerShell                                       —    □    ×
PS C:\nmap> .\nmap.exe -n -Pn -p443 da.richardhicks.net --script ip-https-discover

Starting Nmap 7.12 ( https://nmap.org ) at 2016-06-09 13:38 Pacific Daylight Time
Nmap scan report for da.richardhicks.net (203.0.113.240)
Host is up (0.00s latency).
PORT    STATE SERVICE
443/tcp open  https
|_ip-https-discover: IP-HTTPS is supported. This indicates that this host supports Microsoft DirectAccess.
MAC Address: 00:15:5D:00:01:76 (Microsoft)

Nmap done: 1 IP address (1 host up) scanned in 1.08 seconds
PS C:\nmap> _
```

Figure 11-34. *Testing DirectAccess IP-HTTPS connectivity using Nmap*

Tracing

Tracing can be performed to gather low-level information about the DirectAccess connection. It also includes detailed information about the DirectAccess configuration and environment that can be used in additional investigations by the administrator or a Microsoft support engineer. To enable tracing, enter the following commands in an elevated command prompt window:

```
netsh trace start scenario=directaccess report=yes capture=yes  tracefile=c:\datrace.etl
netsh wfp capture start file=c:\wfpcap.cab
Get-NetAdapter | Restart-NetAdapter
```

■ **Note**   On Windows 7 clients, disable and enable the network adapter in the GUI to force the client to restart the DirectAccess connection.

Reproduce the issue by attempting to connect to an internal resource. After attempting to connect, stop the capture and trace by entering the following commands:

```
netsh wfp capture stop
netsh trace stop
```

---

[11]https://nmap.org/
[12]https://directaccess.richardhicks.com/2015/11/30/directaccess-ip-https-discovery-script-for-nmap/

DirectAccess Client Troubleshooting Tool

The Windows DirectAccess Client Troubleshooting Tool[13] is a utility from Microsoft that automates the testing and evaluation of the DirectAccess connection. After downloading the tool, click **Run Tests** to begin. After the tests have been completed, click on a test to show detailed results and information about the specific test performed (Figure 11-35).

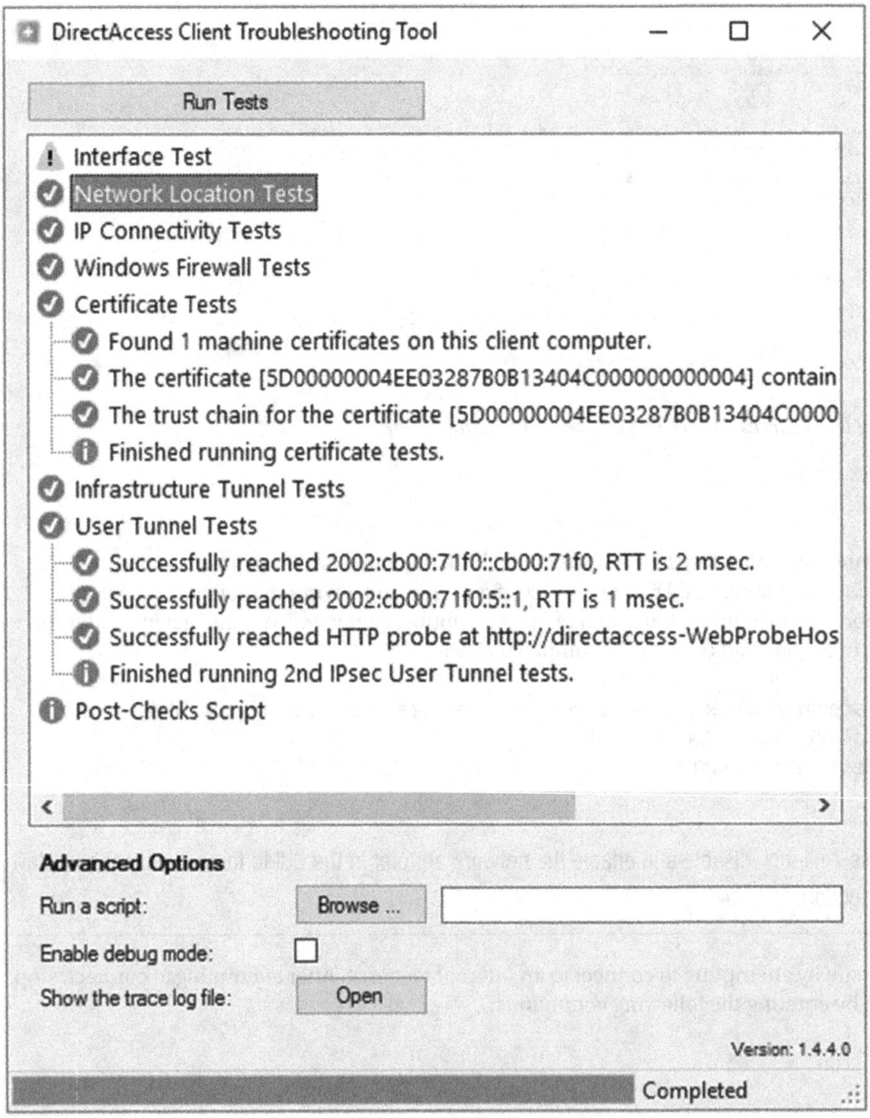

Figure 11-35. *DirectAccess client connectivity troubleshooting tool*

---

[13]https://www.microsoft.com/en-us/download/details.aspx?id=41938

Additionally, highly detailed information about the tests being performed and their results, along with client configuration information, is available by viewing the trace log file generated by the tool.

Summary

To effectively troubleshoot DirectAccess connectivity issues, it is essential to have a fundamental understanding of how DirectAccess works correctly. At its core, DirectAccess connectivity is nothing more than IPsec tunnels established by the client and server. DirectAccess client and server settings, distributed through the Active Directory Group Policy, configure the client and server to support secure, authenticated, and encrypted communication over the public Internet.

When troubleshooting DirectAccess connectivity, remain objective and focus on the basics. Start at the beginning and take it one step at a time. Don't be overwhelmed by the complexity of DirectAccess. By following the guidance in this chapter, the DirectAccess administrator should be able to resolve many of the most common issues that might prevent DirectAccess from working correctly.

CHAPTER 12

■ ■ ■

Migrate to Windows Server 2016 DirectAccess

For organizations that have previously deployed DirectAccess using Windows Server 2008 R2, Forefront Unified Access Gateway (UAG) 2010, Windows Server 2012, or Windows Server 2012 R2, migrating to DirectAccess in Windows Server 2016 can be accomplished in one of two ways.

If DirectAccess is deployed with Windows Server 2012 or 2012 R2, it is possible to perform an in-place upgrade of the operating system to Windows Server 2016. However, this is not generally recommended, as experience has shown limited success using this approach. A safer and much less disruptive way to upgrade is to create a parallel deployment of DirectAccess using Windows Server 2016 and then migrate users to the new infrastructure.

If DirectAccess is deployed with Windows Server 2008 R2 or UAG 2010, an in-place upgrade is not supported. In these scenarios, implementing DirectAccess using a parallel deployment and migrating users to the new infrastructure is the only available migration path.

Requirements

Much of the existing DirectAccess supporting infrastructure can be reused when configuring a parallel deployment of DirectAccess using Windows Server 2016. Services such as Active Directory, Public Key Infrastructure (PKI), and the Network Location Server (NLS) can be used by both implementations at the same time without conflict. However, a parallel deployment will require the following unique components.

IP Addresses

It probably goes without saying, but the new DirectAccess servers will require unique IP addresses. This includes public IP addresses assigned to the DirectAccess server, or to the edge firewall for perimeter/DMZ deployments.

Public Hostname

The public hostname for the new DirectAccess deployment must be unique. It must also have a corresponding entry in the public DNS, and an SSL certificate with a matching subject name must be used. Multi-SAN SSL certificates are not supported,[1] so a unique certificate will be required. Alternatively, a wildcard certificate can be used.

---

[1]https://directaccess.richardhicks.com/2016/03/28/directaccess-and-multi-san-ssl-certificates-for-ip-https/

© Richard M. Hicks 2016

R. M. Hicks, *Implementing DirectAccess with Windows Server 2016*, DOI 10.1007/978-1-4842-2059-7_12

Security Groups

Unique security groups for the new deployment must be configured. Once configured, DirectAccess clients from the original deployment will be moved to these new security groups, enabling them to receive settings for the new deployment and connect to the new infrastructure.

Group Policy Objects

Distinct Active Directory Group Policy Objects (GPOs) are required for the new deployment. These new GPOs will be applied to the security groups created previously. If the DirectAccess Connectivity Assistant (DCA) v2.0 has been deployed for Windows 7 clients, a new DCA GPO must be created for the new deployment.

Configuration

Prepare the first DirectAccess server for the new Windows Server 2016 deployment as outlined in Chapter 3. During the configuration, be sure to specify a unique security group when prompted by the Remote Access Setup Wizard (Figure 12-1).

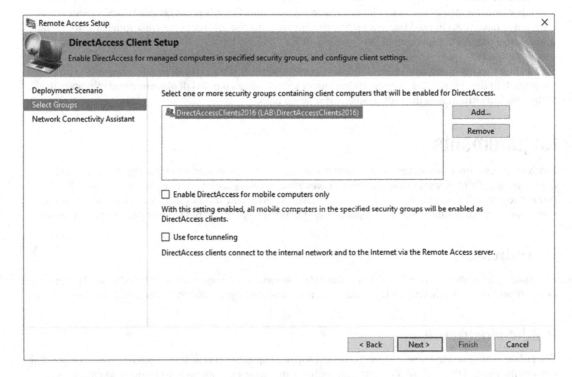

Figure 12-1. Select a unique Active Directory security group

Enter the unique public hostname for the new deployment (Figure 12-2).

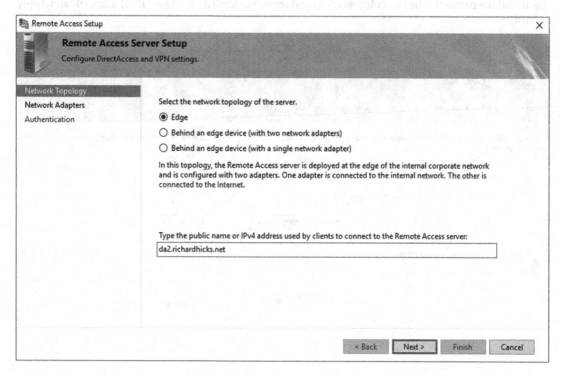

Figure 12-2. Enter the unique public hostname

Before applying the changes, review the configuration settings. Click **Change** next to **GPO settings** to specify unique names for the DirectAccess client and server settings GPOs (Figure 12-3). Click **OK** and **Apply** to finish.

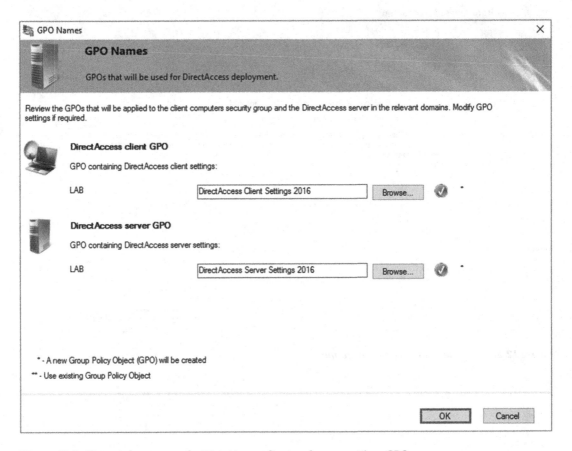

Figure 12-3. *Enter unique names for DirectAccess client and server settings GPOs*

Client Migration

Once a new, parallel deployment of DirectAccess is in place, migrating existing clients from a previous version of DirectAccess to Windows Server 2016 only requires moving their AD computer account from their original DirectAccess security group to the security group designated for them for the new deployment. Once a DirectAccess client restarts, it will receive the DirectAccess client settings for the new deployment and automatically establish a connection to the new infrastructure. This also applies to DirectAccess clients that are currently outside the network.

■ **Note**   Use caution to ensure that clients belong to only one DirectAccess client settings security group.

For testing purposes, it is possible to force a DirectAccess client to update its group membership status and apply new group policy settings without restarting. To accomplish this, open an elevated PowerShell command window and enter the following commands:

```
klist -lh 0 -li 0x3e7 purge
gpupdate /force
```

■ **Note**   When performing these steps on a remotely connected DirectAccess client, it may be necessary to restart the network connection. Either disable and re-enable the network interface in the GUI, or enter the following command in an elevated PowerShell command window:

Get-NetAdapter | Restart-NetAdapter

Additional Use Cases

Creating a parallel deployment of DirectAccess is not only useful for migrating from previous versions of DirectAccess, but is also beneficial in the following scenarios.

QA and Testing

Having a parallel deployment to perform configuration testing and quality assurance can often be helpful. The QA/Test deployment can be used to validate configuration changes and verify updates without potential negative impact on the production environment.

Delegated Administration

DirectAccess lacks support for delegated administration. For organizations that are geographically dispersed, or that have multiple business units that operate autonomously, it may be beneficial to deploy multiple instances of DirectAccess and assign unique administrators to each deployment instead of enabling multisite.

Configuration Changes

Some configuration changes can be disruptive to remote DirectAccess clients. For example, making changes to PKI or enabling multisite can potentially cut off access for DirectAccess clients outside the network, requiring them to physically come back to the office or connect remotely using client-based VPN to update their group policy. Implementing a parallel deployment and migrating users over can reduce the impact and prevent service disruption for existing remote clients.

Unique Client Requirements

There are a few important DirectAccess settings that are global in scope and apply to all provisioned DirectAccess clients. For example, enforcing strong user authentication using smart cards or one-time passwords (OTP) usually applies to all clients. If the requirement for smart card authentication applies only to a subset of users, implementing a separate DirectAccess deployment will be required.

Summary

Deploying DirectAccess with Windows Server 2016 in parallel with a previous version of DirectAccess can greatly ease the pain of performing an in-place upgrade, while at the same time allowing for a measured and controlled rollout for existing DirectAccess clients.

In addition, having multiple individual DirectAccess deployments provides greater deployment flexibility for organizations with unique requirements based on geography or business units.

CHAPTER 13

Managing Out

One of the key differentiators of DirectAccess compared to traditional, client-based VPN is that the DirectAccess connection is bidirectional. Not only can remote users seamlessly access applications and data on the corporate network from anywhere, but IT administrators can also initiate outbound network connections to connected DirectAccess clients to perform remote administration, wherever they are, and even if a user is not logged on.

From a client perspective, DirectAccess is an IPv6-only solution. The DirectAccess client communicates with the DirectAccess server using IPv6 exclusively. Conversely, if an IT administrator on the internal network wants to connect to a remote DirectAccess client, the internal machine must also use IPv6.

IPv6

IPv6 must be used to support outbound connections to DirectAccess clients from internal management systems; for example, from a management workstation or server. Microsoft's formal guidance for outbound management with DirectAccess is to deploy IPv6 on the internal network natively. Unfortunately, that is easier said than done. Deploying IPv6 is non-trivial, and is a task that should not be taken lightly. Since most organizations do not have IPv6 deployed, an IPv6 transition technology can be used to enable managing out.

ISATAP

The Intrasite Automatic Tunnel Addressing Protocol (ISATAP)[1] is an IPv6 transition technology that allows IPv6 communication over an IPv4 network. Unlike 6to4, Teredo, and IP-HTTPS, which are used by the DirectAccess *client* to tunnel IPv6 traffic over the IPv4 Internet, ISATAP is used by systems on the internal network to initiate communication outbound to connected DirectAccess clients.

Supportability

Outbound management using the DirectAccess server as the ISATAP router is only supported for single-server DirectAccess deployments.[2] Using ISATAP on the DirectAccess server is not supported when load balancing (NLB or external) is enabled or multisite is configured. For these deployment scenarios, an external ISATAP router must be configured.

---

[1]http://www.ietf.org/rfc/rfc5214.txt
[2]https://technet.microsoft.com/en-us/library/dn464274(v=ws.11).aspx#bkmk_isa

© Richard M. Hicks 2016   237
R. M. Hicks, *Implementing DirectAccess with Windows Server 2016*, DOI 10.1007/978-1-4842-2059-7_13

ISATAP Router

The ISATAP router is automatically installed and configured when DirectAccess is enabled. No additional configuration is required by the administrator to enable managing out on the DirectAccess server.

■ **Note** If there is a firewall between the DirectAccess server and the internal network, it must be configured to allow inbound and outbound IP protocol 41 in order for ISATAP to work correctly.

ISATAP Client

To enable outbound management using ISATAP, a client machine (workstation or server) must be configured to use the DirectAccess server as its ISATAP router. This is accomplished in one of several ways.

Manual Configuration

A workstation or server can be manually configured to use the DirectAccess server as its ISATAP router by using PowerShell. Open an elevated PowerShell command window and enter the following commands:

```
Set-NetISATAPConfiguration -State Enabled
Set-NetISATAPConfiguration -Router <DirectAccess server IPv4 address or hostanme>
```

Alternatively, ISATAP can be configured manually by opening an elevated command prompt window and entering the following commands:

```
Netsh interface isatap set state enabled
Netsh interface isatap set router <DirectAccess server IPv4 address or hostname>
```

■ **Note** The drawback to using this method is that manual configuration is error prone and does not scale well. However, it can be effective for initial testing, or if only a small number of management workstations and/or servers require outbound management functionality.

DNS

All supported versions of Windows, in addition to many other operating systems, will automatically enable and configure an ISATAP tunnel adapter after successfully resolving the hostname **ISATAP** to an IPv4 address. The quick and simple way to do this for DirectAccess is to add an A Host record in the internal DNS called ISATAP that resolves to the IPv4 address of the Internal network interface of the DirectAccess server (Figure 13-1).

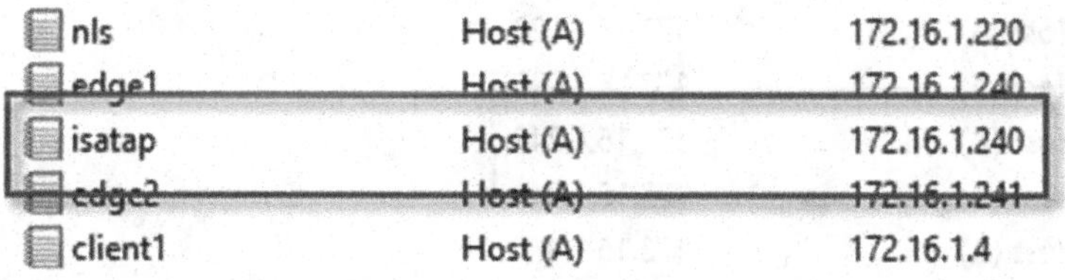

nls	Host (A)	172.16.1.220
edge1	Host (A)	172.16.1.240
isatap	Host (A)	172.16.1.240
edge2	Host (A)	172.16.1.241
client1	Host (A)	172.16.1.4

Figure 13-1. ISATAP DNS entry

For security reasons, most DNS servers will not respond to queries for ISATAP by default. On Windows DNS servers, for example, ISATAP is included in the DNS Global Query Block list.[3] To configure a Windows DNS server to respond to queries for ISATAP, open an elevated PowerShell command window and enter the following command:

```
Set-DnsServerGlobalQueryBlockList -List wpad
```

Confirm that ISATAP has been removed from the Global Query Block List by entering the following PowerShell command:

```
Get-DnsServerGlobalQueryBlockList
```

Alternatively, the Global Query Block List can be updated by opening an elevated command prompt window and entering the following command:

```
dnscmd.exe /config /globalqueryblocklist wpad
```

The Global Query Block List can be viewed by entering the following command:

```
dnscmd.exe /info /globalqueryblocklist
```

■ **Note**   The drawback to using this method is that every workstation and server in the enterprise that successfully resolves ISATAP to an IPv4 address will have an ISATAP tunnel adapter. This is often unnecessary and can produce unexpected results.

Group Policy

For many organizations, outbound management is required only for a few specific machines, commonly administrator workstations and systems-management servers. An Active Directory Group Policy Object (GPO) can be used to restrict the deployment of ISATAP settings to only those machines that specifically require manage-out functionality.

To do this, create a unique entry in DNS (*not* called ISATAP) that resolves to the internal IPv4 address of the DirectAccess server (Figure 13-2).

---

[3]https://technet.microsoft.com/en-us/library/cc794902(v=ws.10).aspx

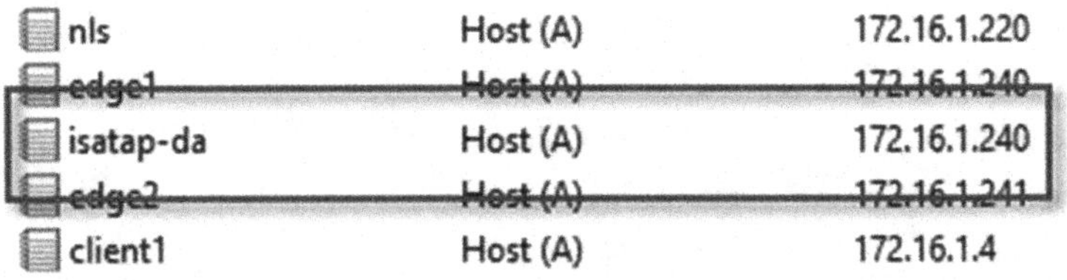

nls	Host (A)	172.16.1.220
~~edge1~~	~~Host (A)~~	~~172.16.1.240~~
isatap-da	Host (A)	172.16.1.240
~~edge2~~	~~Host (A)~~	~~172.16.1.241~~
client1	Host (A)	172.16.1.4

Figure 13-2. *Custom ISATAP DNS entry*

Open the Group Policy Management console, then right-click **Group Policy Objects** and choose **New**. Enter a descriptive name for the new GPO. Right-click the newly created GPO and choose **Edit**. Expand **Computer Configuration**, **Policies**, **Administrative Templates**, **Network**, and **TCP/IP Settings**. Highlight **IPv6 Transition Technologies** and double-click **Set ISATAP Router Name**. Choose **Enabled** and enter the unique DNS name created previously, then click **Next Setting** (Figure 13-3) .

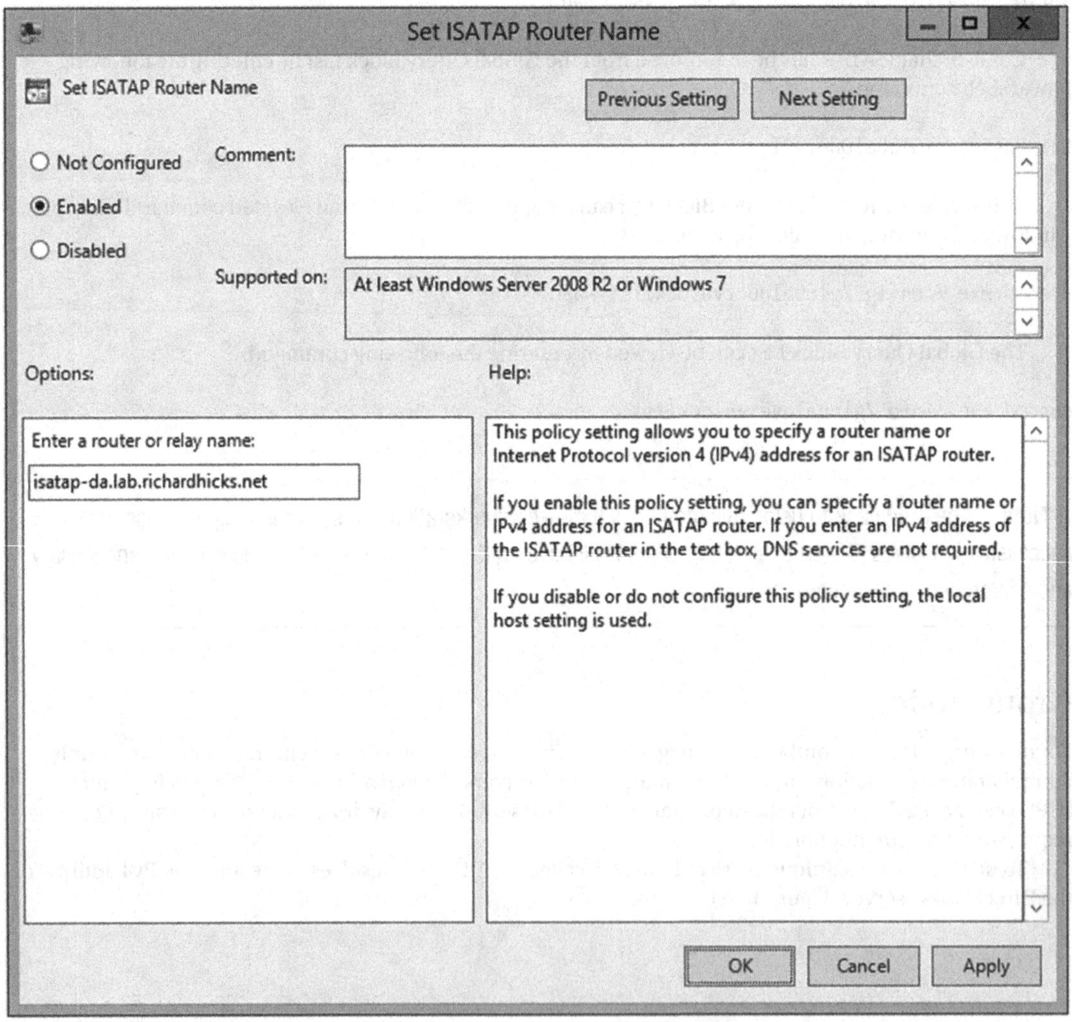

Figure 13-3. *Set theISATAP router name*

Choose **Enabled**, then select **Enabled State** from the drop-down list and click **OK** (Figure 13-4).

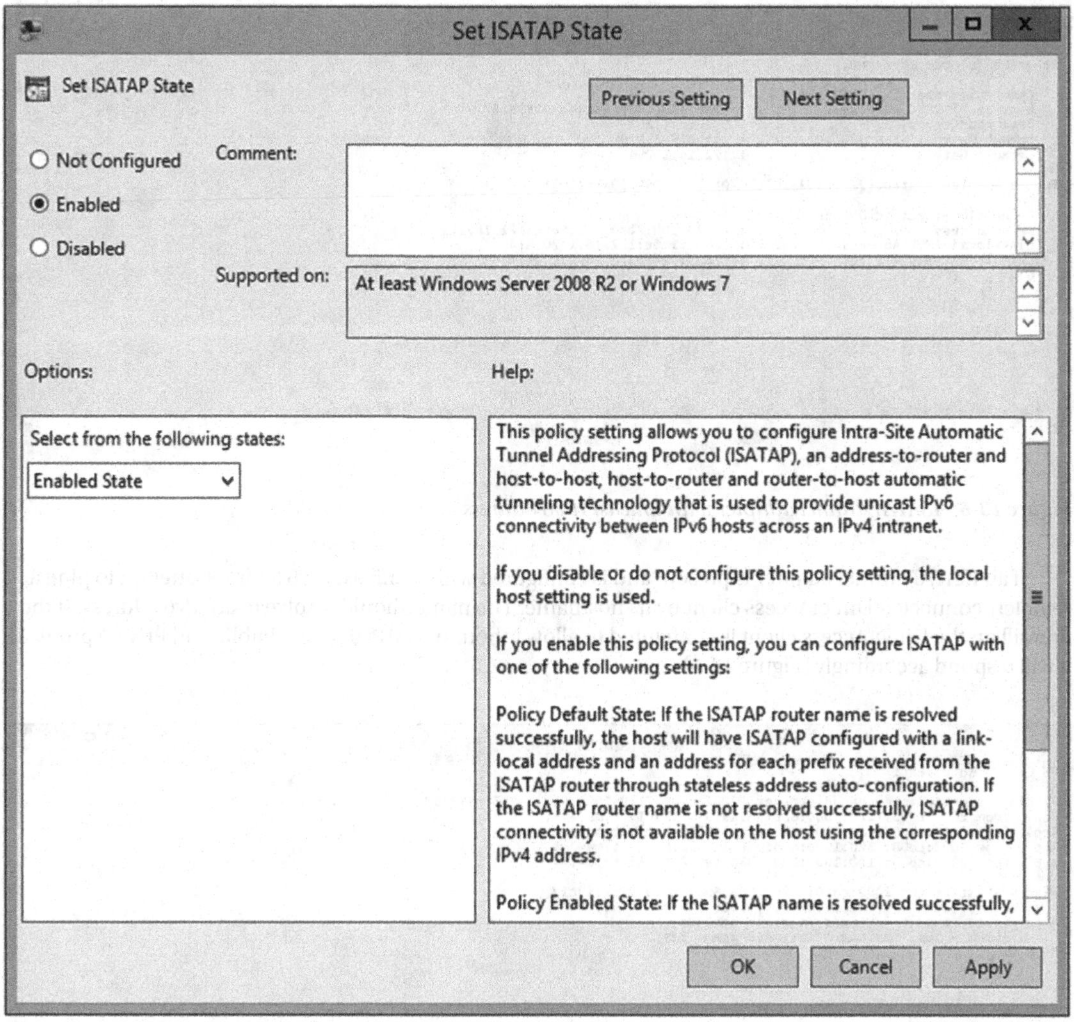

Figure 13-4. Set the ISATAP state

Link the GPO to an Organizational Unit (OU) that contains the workstations and servers that will require DirectAccess managing out. Alternatively, security filtering can be used to restrict the application of the GPO to individual machines or a security group that includes those machines, as required.

Connectivity Testing

Confirm that the management system configured to use ISATAP has an ISATAP tunnel adapter with a unicast IPv6 address assigned to it (Figure 13-5).

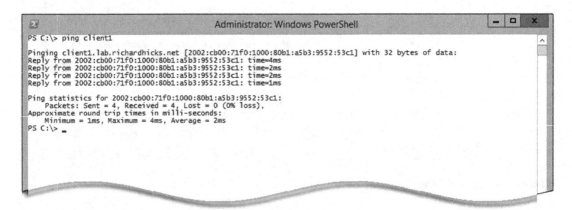

```
Administrator: Windows PowerShell                                        _  □  X

PS C:\> ipconfig

Windows IP Configuration

Ethernet adapter Ethernet:

   Connection-specific DNS Suffix  . :
   Link-local IPv6 Address . . . . . : fe80::68a5:bfce:c44a:9183%12
   IPv4 Address. . . . . . . . . . . : 172.16.1.202
   Subnet Mask . . . . . . . . . . . : 255.255.255.0
   Default Gateway . . . . . . . . . : 172.16.1.254

Tunnel adapter isatap.{2ED5E832-30FC-4F0A-B547-29F9E94B521D}:

   Connection-specific DNS Suffix  . :
   IPv6 Address. . . . . . . . . . . : 2002:cb00:71f0:1:0:5efe:172.16.1.202
   Link-local IPv6 Address . . . . . : fe80::5efe:172.16.1.202%14
   Default Gateway . . . . . . . . . : fe80::5efe:172.16.1.240%14
PS C:\> _
```

Figure 13-5. ISATAP tunnel adapter with unicast IPv6 address

If an ISATAP tunnel adapter is present and is configured with a unicast IPv6 address, attempt to ping a remotely connected DirectAccess client by its hostname. The name should resolve to an IPv6 address. If the firewall on the DirectAccess client is configured to allow inbound ICMPv6 on the Public and Private profiles, it will respond accordingly (Figure 13-6).

```
Administrator: Windows PowerShell                                        _  □  X

PS C:\> ping client1

Pinging client1.lab.richardhicks.net [2002:cb00:71f0:1000:80b1:a5b3:9552:53c1] with 32 bytes of data:
Reply from 2002:cb00:71f0:1000:80b1:a5b3:9552:53c1: time=4ms
Reply from 2002:cb00:71f0:1000:80b1:a5b3:9552:53c1: time=2ms
Reply from 2002:cb00:71f0:1000:80b1:a5b3:9552:53c1: time=2ms
Reply from 2002:cb00:71f0:1000:80b1:a5b3:9552:53c1: time=1ms

Ping statistics for 2002:cb00:71f0:1000:80b1:a5b3:9552:53c1:
    Packets: Sent = 4, Received = 4, Lost = 0 (0% loss),
Approximate round trip times in milli-seconds:
    Minimum = 1ms, Maximum = 4ms, Average = 2ms
PS C:\> _
```

Figure 13-6. Ping a remotely connected DirectAccess client by name

---

■ **Note** If the management workstation is unable to resolve the DirectAccess client's hostname to an IPv6 address, ensure that the client has successfully registered its IPv6 address in the internal DNS.

Remote Management

Once a management system has been configured to use ISATAP, it can be used to fully manage remotely connected DirectAccess clients. For example, on a management workstation or server, an administrator can initiate a Remote Desktop Protocol (RDP) session to a DirectAccess client, or use any number of popular management tools and techniques, such as Windows Remote Assistance, System Center Configuration Manager (SCCM) Remote Control, VNC, TeamViewer, PowerShell Remoting, and much more. In addition, file shares are accessible, and native Windows system-management tools like the Computer Management console and Performance Monitor function properly as well[4] (assuming client firewall policy allows it; see later in this chapter for more details).

DirectAccess Management Computers

A user must be logged on to the DirectAccess client for an ISATAP-enabled management system to establish a connection. The management system must be added to the DirectAccess management servers list to allow it to connect to DirectAccess clients where the user has not yet logged on.

Open the Remote Access Management console, highlight **DirectAccess and VPN**, then go to **Step 3** and click **Edit**. Click **Management** and then double-click a blank field. Enter the Fully-Qualified Domain Name (FQDN) of the management workstation or server. Click **OK** and then **Finish** (Figure 13-7).

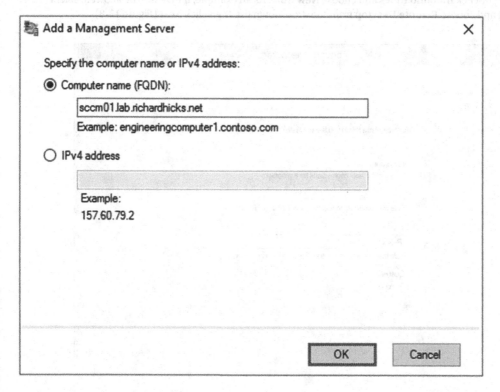

Figure 13-7. *Add a management server*

Alternatively, a system can be added to the management servers list by opening an elevated PowerShell command window and enter the following command:

```
Add-DAMgmtServer -MgmtServer [management server FQDN]
```

Windows Firewall

DirectAccess clients that are outside of the network have either the Public or Private Windows firewall profile enabled. These profiles are more restrictive than the Domain profile and often prevent remote-management tools from working correctly. To resolve this, a GPO will be created to configure the Windows firewall on DirectAccess clients to securely allow remote communication only from the DirectAccess management workstations and servers on the internal network.

GPO

Open the Group Policy Management console, right-click **Group Policy Objects**, and choose **New**. Enter a descriptive name for the new GPO and click **OK**. Right-click the new GPO and choose **Edit**. Expand **Computer Configuration**, **Policies**, **Windows Settings**, **Security Settings**, and **Windows Firewall with Advanced Security**. Right-click **Inbound Rules** and choose **New Rule**. As an example, if RDP is to be allowed, select **Predefined** and choose **Remote Desktop** from the drop-down list, then click **Next** (Figure 13-8).

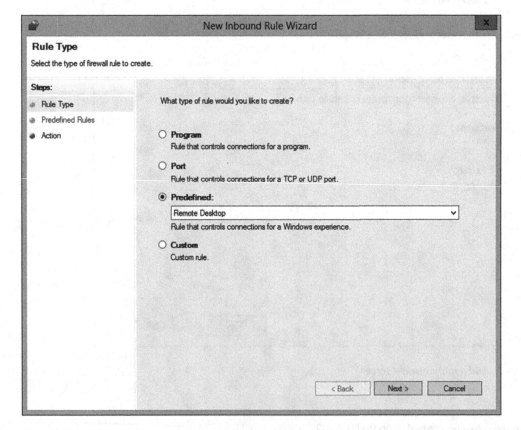

Figure 13-8. *Choose the predefined Remote Desktop rule*

Select the **Remote Desktop - User Mode (TCP-In)** rule and click **Next** (Figure 13-9).

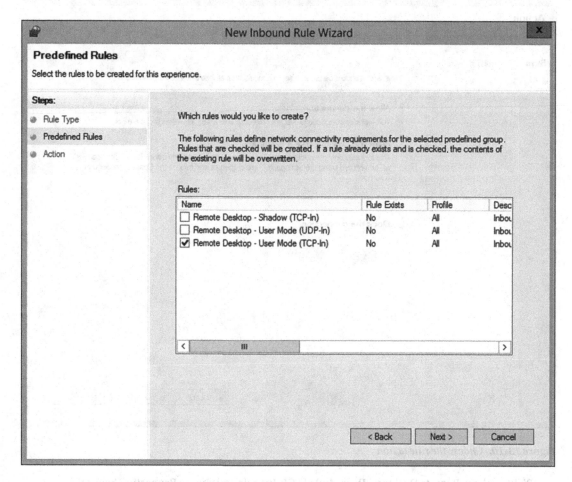

Figure 13-9. *Choose the firewall rules to create*

Choose **Allow the connection** and click **Finish** (Figure 13-10).

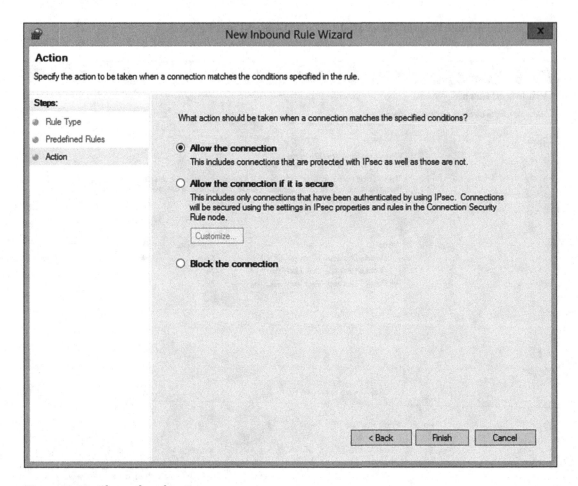

Figure 13-10. *Choose the rule action*

Right-click the **Remote Desktop - User Mode (TCP-In)** rule and choose **Properties**. Select the **Advanced** tab and then uncheck **Domain** (Figure 13-11).

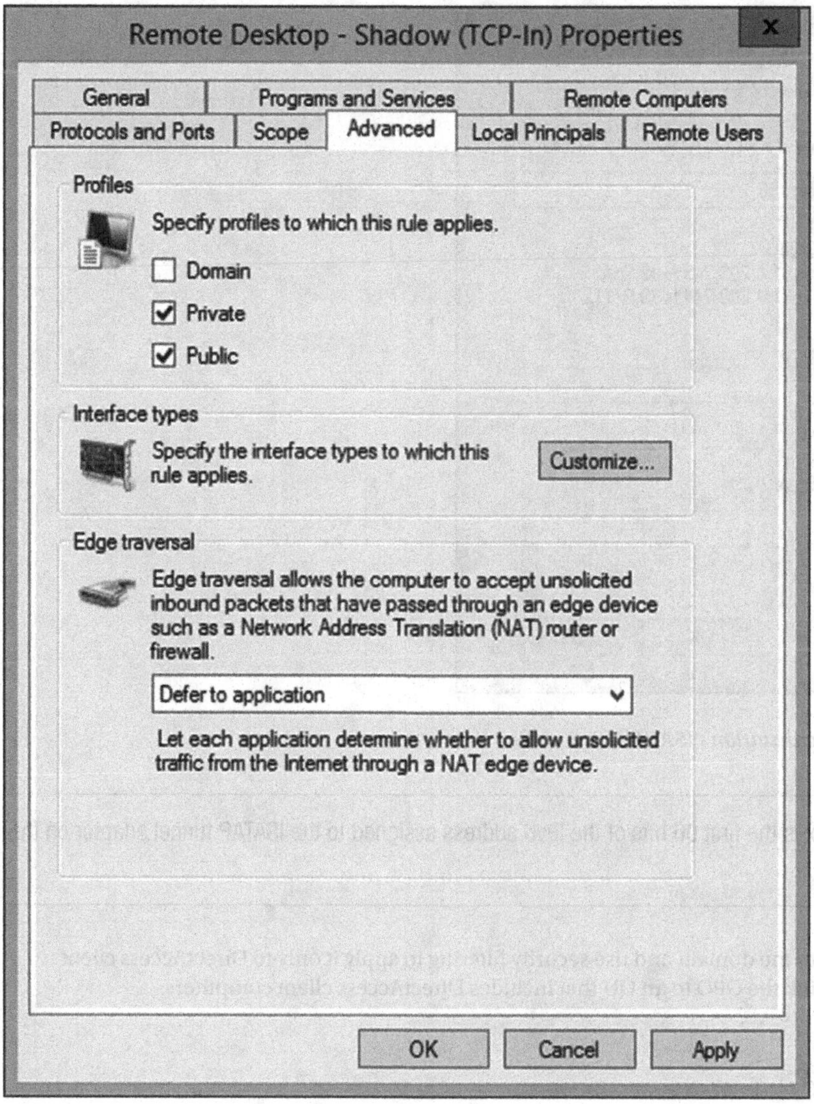

Figure 13-11. Uncheck the Domain profile

Select the **Scope** tab and select **These IP addresses**. Click **Add** and enter the organization's ISATAP IPv6 prefix, then click **OK** twice (Figure 13-12).

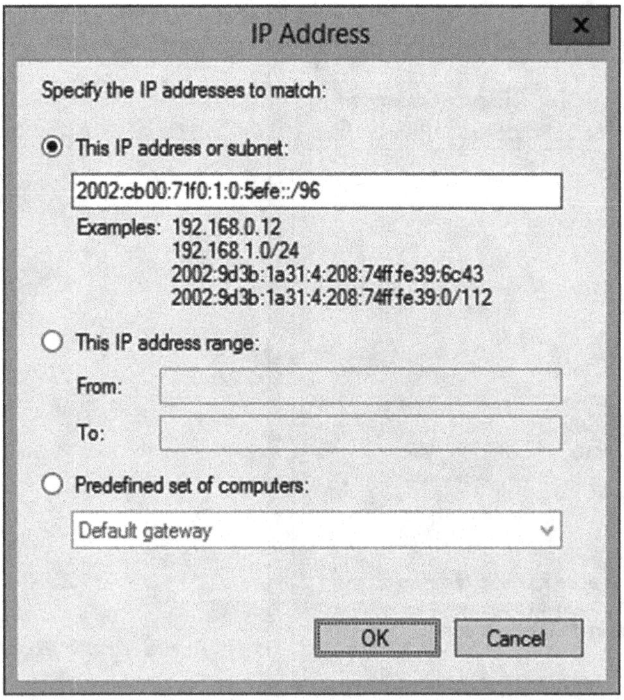

Figure 13-12. *Enter the organziation's ISATAP IPv6 prefix*

■ **Note** The ISATAP prefix is the first 96 bits of the IPv6 address assigned to the ISATAP tunnel adapter on the DirectAccess server.

Finally, link this GPO to the domain and use security filtering to apply it only to DirectAccess client computers. Alternatively, link the GPO to an OU that includes DirectAccess client computers.

Additional Services

The steps outlined previously to allow RDP can also be used to deploy additional firewall rules for other management services. Common WFAS rules to allow remote systems management for DirectAccess clients using popular Windows management tools include the following:

- COM+ Network Access (DCOM-In)

- COM+ Remote Administration (DCOM-In)

- File and Printer Sharing (Echo Request - ICMPv6-In)

- File and Printer Sharing (SMB-In)

- Performance Logs and Alerts (DCOM-In)

- Performance Logs and Alerts (TCP-In)

- Remote Desktop - User Mode (TCP-In)

- Remote Event Log Management (NP-In)

- Remote Event Log Management (RPC)

- Remote Event Log Management (RPC-EPMAP)

- Remote Scheduled Tasks Management (RPC)

- Remote Scheduled Tasks Management (RPC-EPMAP)

- Remote Service Management (NP-In)

- Remote Service Management (RPC)

- Remote Service Management (RPC-EPMAP)

- Remote Volume Management - Virtual Disk Service (RPC)

- Remote Volume Management - Virtual Disk Service Loader (RPC)

- Remote Volume Management (RPC-EPMAP)

- Windows Firewall Remote Management (RPC)

- Windows Firewall Remote Management (RPC-EPMAP)

- Windows Remote Management (HTTP-In)

Summary

Configuring DirectAccess for managing out allows administrators to realize the full potential of the DirectAccess solution. Using the same familiar administration tools and procedures, remote DirectAccess clients can be managed easily and effectively regardless of where they are. Managing out enables compelling uses cases, such as remote help desk support, proactive software and configuration installation, proactive vulnerability scans, and much more.

The best way to take advantage of DirectAccess' managing-out capabilities is to deploy IPv6 on the corporate network. If IPv6 is not yet deployed, the ISATAP IPv6 transition technology can be used in the interim.

APPENDIX A

■■■

DirectAccess with Native IPv6

Throughout this book, the configuration of DirectAccess assumes that IPv6 is not natively deployed on the internal network. This is the most common deployment scenario at the time of this writing.

Configuring DirectAccess differs only slightly when IPv6 is deployed natively on the internal network. The Remote Access Setup Wizard automatically detects when IPv6 is in use on the internal network and presents some additional dialog boxes during configuration.

There are some changes that must be made to internal IPv6 network routing to support DirectAccess client connections. There are also important implications for the use of IPv6 transition technologies when IPv6 has been deployed on the intranet.

A big advantage of having IPv6 deployed natively on the internal network is that managing out is fully supported in all deployment scenarios without requiring an IPv6 transition technology.

IPv6 Readiness

It is recommended that DirectAccess be installed and configured after IPv6 has been deployed on the internal network. If DirectAccess is installed and configured in an IPv4-only network, and later IPv6 is deployed, DirectAccess will continue to work without issue using IPv4. However, to enable DirectAccess clients to connect to corporate resources using their native internal IPv6 address, the configuration must be removed and reinstalled, or a parallel deployment must be configured and clients be migrated to the new deployment.

If IPv6 is not yet deployed on the internal network, but the organization has already obtained IPv6 addressing, IPv6 addresses can be assigned to the DirectAccess server prior to configuration in preparation for the eventual deployment of IPv6 internally. This will eliminate the need to rebuild the environment after IPv6 is deployed.

In this scenario, DNS64 must be configured to use IPv4 only after the initial configuration is complete. Open an elevated PowerShell command window on the DirectAccess server and enter the following command:

```
Set-NetDNSTransitionConfiguration -OnlySendAQuery $True
```

After IPv6 has been deployed on the internal network, the DirectAccess server can be configured to return native IPv6 addresses for internal resources by entering the following PowerShell command:

```
Set-NetDNSTransitionConfiguration -OnlySendAQuery $False
```

© Richard M. Hicks 2016
R. M. Hicks, *Implementing DirectAccess with Windows Server 2016*, DOI 10.1007/978-1-4842-2059-7_14

Remote Access Setup Wizard

On **Step 2** of the Remote Access Setup Wizard, the user interface (UI) will automatically select IPv6 addresses assigned to the Internal and External network adapters (Figure A-1).

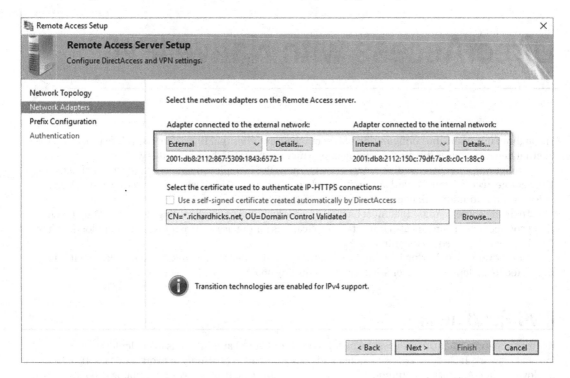

Figure A-1. *Network adapter selection with native IPv6*

The Remote Access Setup Wizard automatically supplies the **Internal network IPv6 prefix** and the **IPv6 prefix assigned to DirectAccess client computers** based on the IPv6 address assigned to the Internal network interface of the DirectAccess server. The UI assumes a standard /48 IPv6 site prefix. In addition, the IPv6 prefix assigned to clients is designated from this same /48 prefix. These details can be updated if they do not accurately reflect internal IPv6 network prefix assignments (Figure A-2).

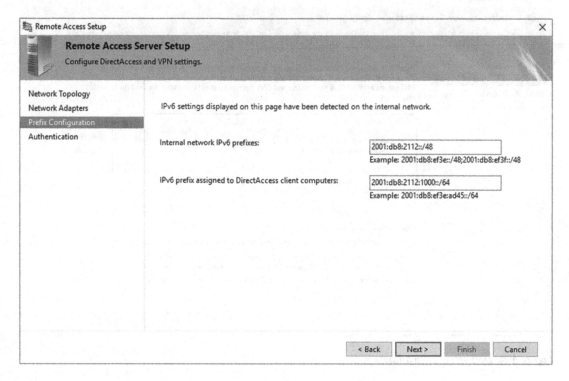

Figure A-2. *Automatically detected IPv6 network prefixes*

When configuring DNS, the DNS server address for the Internal namespace will not be the familiar DNS64 IPv6 address ending in 3333::1. Instead, it will be the native IPv6 address assigned to the Internal network interface of the DirectAccess server (Figure A-3).

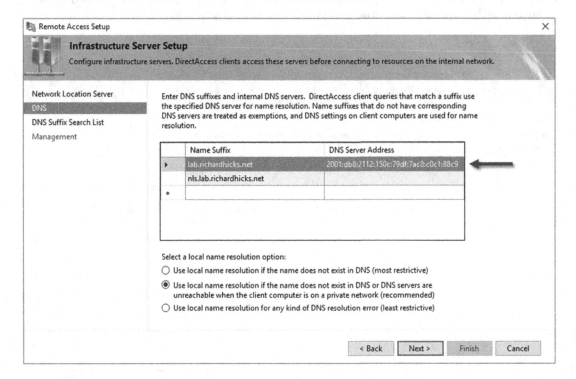

Figure A-3. *DNS server IPv6 address*

Load Balancing

The default IPv6 prefix length for DirectAccess clients using the IP-HTTPS IPv6 transition technology is /64. When enabling load balancing, the administrator may encounter an error message stating **The length of the prefix used to assign IPv6 addresses to DirectAccess clients connecting over IP-HTTPS should be 59 bits** (Figure A-4).

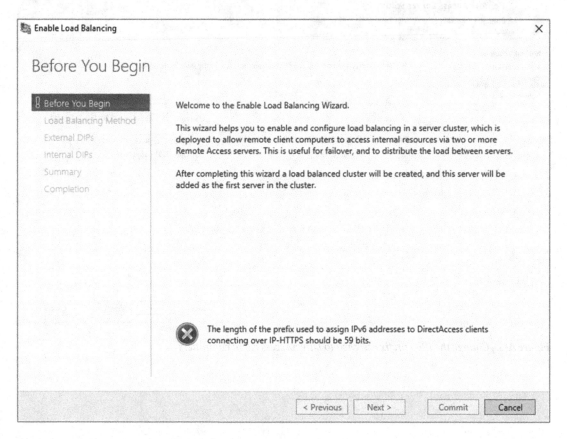

Figure A-4. IP-HTTPS IPv6 prefix-length error message

To resolve this issue, click **Edit** on **Step 2** in the Remote Access Management console, select **Prefix Configuration**, change the IPv6 prefix assigned to DirectAccess client computers to **/59**, and click **Next**, **Finish** twice, and then **Apply** (Figure A-5).

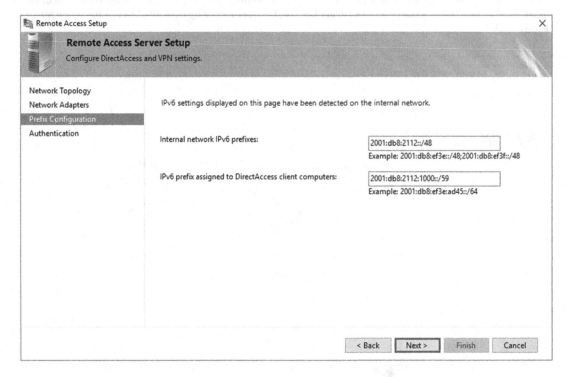

Figure A-5. *Change the IPv6 prefix assigned to DirectAccess client computers*

Once the IP-HTTPS IPv6 prefix has been changed, enable load balancing as outlined in Chapter 6, "Configure DirectAccess Load Balancing." When IPv6 is deployed natively, the UI will prompt the administrator for new dedicated external IPv4 and IPv6 addresses (Figure A-6).

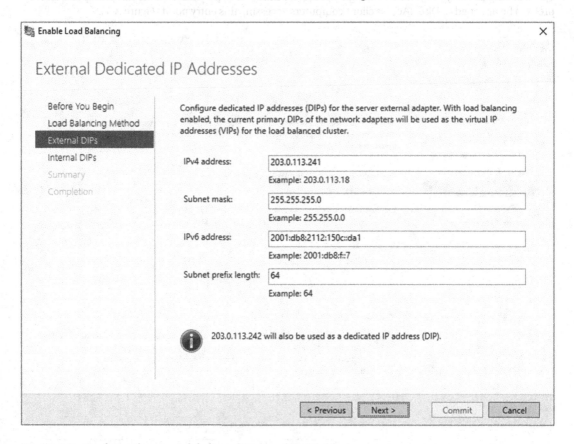

Figure A-6. *Configure the external dedicated IPv4 and IPv6 addresses*

■ **Note**   It is not necessary to change the internal IPv6 address of the DirectAccess server when enabling load balancing. Only the dedicated IPv4 address will be changed.

Multisite

When adding an entry point to an existing DirectAccess multisite deployment, the UI will prompt for an IPv6 prefix to be assigned to DirectAccess client computers accessing this entry point (Figure A-7).

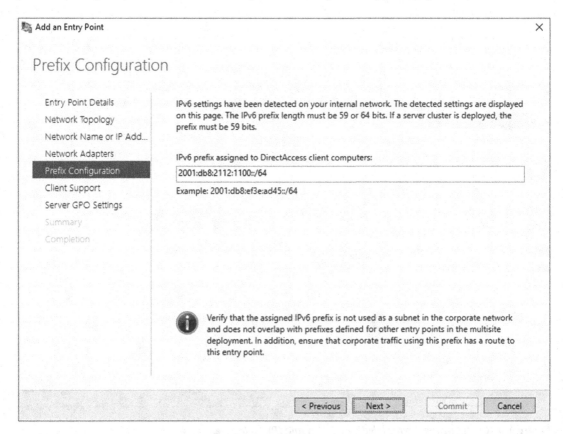

Figure A-7. *Multisite entry point IPv6 prefix assignment for DirectAccess client computers*

Network Prefix Routing

The IPv6 network routing tables on the internal network must be configured to allow remote DirectAccess client connectivity. Routes must be created to forward packets that are destined for any DirectAccess client IPv6 network prefixes to the Internal network interface of the DirectAccess server. The IPv6 prefix used by remote DirectAccess clients is determined by the IPv6 transition technology used to connect to the DirectAccess server.

6to4

The use of the 6to4 IPv6 transition technology should be avoided in all DirectAccess deployments, as there are potential configuration and stability issues associated with its use.[1] However, if 6to4 is used by DirectAccess clients, the **2002::/16** IPv6 prefix[2] must be routed to the Internal network interface of the DirectAccess server.

■ **Note**   Remote clients can only access the internal network using 6to4 when DirectAccess is deployed in a single-server, single-site configuration. 6to4 should not be used by DirectAccess clients when load balancing is configured or multisite is enabled.

Teredo

Teredo addresses are derived from the **2001::/32** prefix, with the next 32 bits representing the DirectAccess server's primary external IPv4 address.[3] For example, a client connecting to a DirectAccess server with a primary IPv4 address of **203.0.113.240** will use a Teredo IPv6 prefix of **2001:0:cb00:71f0::/64**. This IPv6 prefix must be routed to the Internal network interface of the DirectAccess server.

■ **Note**   Remote clients can only access the internal network using Teredo when DirectAccess is deployed in a single server and single or multisite configuration. Teredo should not be used by DirectAccess clients when load balancing is configured, either in single or multisite deployments, unless an external load balancer capable of monitoring DirectAccess connection flows is implemented.

IP-HTTPS

IP-HTTPS addresses are derived from the IPv6 prefix that is defined during DirectAccess server configuration (Figure A-2). This prefix must be routed to the Internal network interface of the DirectAccess server.

---

[1]https://directaccess.richardhicks.com/2015/02/02/disable-6to4-ipv6-transition-protocol-for-directaccess-clients/
[2]https://en.wikipedia.org/wiki/6to4#Address_block_allocation
[3]https://en.wikipedia.org/wiki/Teredo_tunneling#IPv6_addressing

When load balancing is enabled, a /59 IPv6 prefix derived from the original /48 site prefix is designated for the cluster. Each cluster member then uses a /64 prefix for DirectAccess client address assignment. The individual /64 IPv6 prefixes for each DirectAccess server in the cluster must be routed to their corresponding Internal network interfaces. The /59 entry-point prefix can be found by highlighting DirectAccess and VPN in the Remote Access Management console and highlighting an individual entry point (Figure A-8).

Figure A-8. IPv6 prefix assigned to clients connecting over IP-HTTPS HTTPS

Native IPv6 HTTPS

When the DirectAccess server is configured with a Global Unicast Address (GUA) IPv6 address assigned to its External interface and it is accessed by a DirectAccess client that also has a GUA IPv6 address, the client will not be able to establish a remote connection to internal resources unless the DirectAccess server is configured as the IPv6 default gateway on the internal network.

▪ **Note** Configuring the DirectAccess server as the IPv6 default gateway for the internal network is not an ideal solution in most cases. For this reason, it is recommended that the DirectAccess server not be configured with a GUA IPv6 address on its External network interface.

Managing Out

Managing out is supported in all deployment scenarios, including load-balanced and multisite configurations, without the need for a transition technology when IPv6 is natively deployed on the internal network. Managing out using native IPv6 requires the configuration of network prefix routing as described previously in this chapter.

Summary

DirectAccess implementations where IPv6 is natively deployed on the internal network are not yet common. However, there are only a few subtle differences when configuring DirectAccess when IPv6 is in use. When IPv6 is deployed on the intranet, careful attention must be paid to the internal IPv6 routing infrastructure to ensure that all IPv6 packets destined for DirectAccess client networks are forwarded to the appropriate DirectAccess server as necessary.

In addition, having IPv6 deployed natively allows for full support of outbound management capabilities in all DirectAccess deployment scenarios, including load-balanced and multisite configurations.

APPENDIX B

■■■

DirectAccess and Force Tunneling

DirectAccess clients use split tunneling in the default configuration, enabling them to access the Internet directly while at the same time being connected to the corporate network. This configuration is efficient, but it introduces some potential security risks that can be mitigated by enabling force tunneling.

How It Works

With force tunneling enabled, the Name Resolution Policy Table (NRPT) is configured to send DNS requests for all namespaces to the DNS64 service on the DirectAccess server. This differs fundamentally from split tunneling, where the NRPT is configured to only send DNS requests for the Internal namespace to the DNS64 service.

When configured, the end result is that all network access for connected DirectAccess clients is sent over the DirectAccess connection, including requests for both internal and public resources.

Use Cases

Force tunneling is often enabled to address the following security challenges.

Web-Browsing Policy

The most common use case for enabling force tunneling is to enforce access-control policies for web browsing on connected DirectAccess clients. This ensures that DirectAccess clients are protected from accessing non-approved websites regardless of whether they are inside or outside the network.

Network Bridging

Commonly, force tunneling is enabled to prevent packets from being routed from the Internet through the DirectAccess client to the corporate network. This is more of a perceived risk than an actual one. Unlike traditional client-based VPN, DirectAccess IPsec connections use AuthIP, so each packet transmitted over the DirectAccess connection is authenticated. Even if it were somehow possible to bridge the Internet and DirectAccess connections, these packets would be dropped because they are not properly authenticated.

Prerequisites

An internal web proxy server must be deployed to support force tunneling for DirectAccess clients. In addition, IP-HTTPS is the only supported IPv6 transition technology in this scenario. It is recommended that all other IPv6 transition technologies be disabled on the client.[1]

Enable Force Tunneling

To enable force tunneling, open the Remote Access Management console, highlight **DirectAccess and VPN**, and then click **Edit** on **Step 1**. Click **Select Groups** and select the option to **Use force tunneling**. Click **Next** and then click **Finish** twice (Figure B-1).

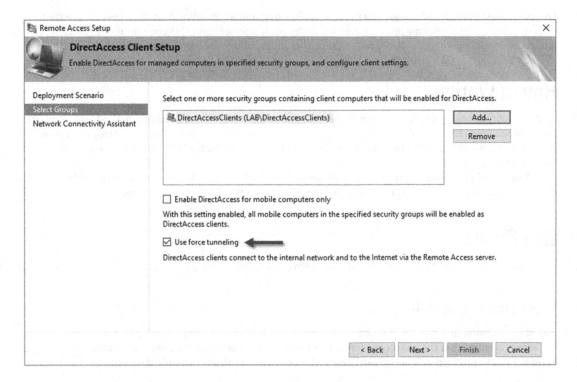

Figure B-1. *Enable force tunneling*

[1]https://directaccess.richardhicks.com/2013/08/27/disabling-unused-ipv6-transition-technologies-for-directaccess-clients/

Alternatively, force tunneling can be enabled by opening an elevated PowerShell command window on the DirectAccess server and entering the following command:

```
Set-DAClient -ForceTunnel Enabled
```

Name Resolution Policy Table

Enabling force tunneling automatically configures the NRPT to direct name-resolution requests for all namespaces to the DNS64 service running on the DirectAccess server. The DirectAccess server's public hostname and the Network Location Server (NLS) are automatically excluded (Figure B-2).

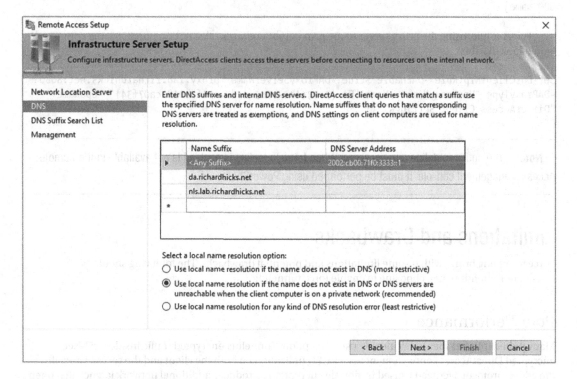

Figure B-2. Force tunneling DNS server configuration

Define Corporate Proxy

To define a proxy server to be used by DirectAccess clients, open an elevated PowerShell command window on the DirectAccess server and enter the following command:

```
Get-DnsClientNrptRule -GpoName [DirectAccess client settings GPO name]
```

When using the default name of the DirectAccess client settings GPO created when installing DirectAccess, the command would look like this:

```
Get-DnsClientNrptRule -GpoName "DirectAccess Client Settings" | Where-Object Namespace -eq "." |
Select-Object Name
```

Note the name of the NRPT rule for the namespace "." in the output of the previous command. Enter it along with the name and port of the proxy server in the following PowerShell command:

```
Set-DnsClientNrptRule -DAEnable $True -DAProxyServerName [proxy server name:port]
-DAProxyType "UseProxyName" -Name [NRPT rule name] -GpoName [DirectAccess client settings
GPO name]
```

For example, using the proxy server name proxy.lab.richardhicks.net on port 8080, the command would look like this:

```
Set-DnsClientNrptRule -DAEnable $true -DAProxyServerName "proxy.lab.richardhicks.net:8080"
-DAProxyType "UseProxyName" -Name "DA-{3ee344b4-b7c3-4cd7-a91f-b0182ca07f34}" -GpoName
"DirectAccess Client Settings"
```

■ **Note**   The option to define a proxy server when force tunneling is enabled is not available in the Remote Access Management console. It must be performed using PowerShell.

Limitations and Drawbacks

Force tunneling brings with it some limitations and potential drawbacks. The following should be considered carefully when choosing to enable force tunneling.

Poor Performance

Many public Internet sites today already use encryption. Tunneling encrypted traffic inside the IPsec-encrypted DirectAccess connection increases CPU utilization on both the client and the server. Crucially, the added protocol overhead caused by double encryption introduces additional network latency that often results in a degraded user experience.

This becomes exponentially worse when supporting Windows 7 DirectAccess clients that are connecting with the IP-HTTPS IPv6 transition technology. Windows 7 clients use only encrypted cipher suites when establishing an IP-HTTPS transition tunnel, resulting in *triple* encryption when accessing encrypted resources on the Internet.

Reduced Scalability

Force tunneling increases CPU utilization on the DirectAccess server. In addition, the amount of network traffic processed by the DirectAccess server negatively impacts scalability, resulting in far fewer concurrent connections being supported by a single server.

Web-Browsing Experience

Much of the content accessed on the Internet today is served via Content Delivery Networks (CDNs), which are geographically distributed to ensure content is delivered from locations nearest to the client. Force tunneling can disrupt proper CDN functionality, as Internet requests will appear to come from the location of the proxy server, not the actual location of the DirectAccess client. Content may be served from suboptimal locations, resulting in further degraded performance. Further, geography-specific content (for example, local news or weather, or time-zone-specific information) may not be delivered correctly.

In addition, DirectAccess clients communicate with the DirectAccess server using IPv6 exclusively. Requests for any Internet resources by an IPv4 address will fail.

Force Tunneling and OTP

Force tunneling prevents the operation of one-time password (OTP) strong user authentication. These two configurations are mutually exclusive and cannot be enabled at the same time.

All or Nothing

Enabling force tunneling is an all or nothing choice. There are no supported options for whitelisting specific websites to be excluded from the force-tunneling requirement. When this option is selected, all client traffic is forced back over the DirectAccess connection. This is especially challenging for Voice over IP (VoIP) software such as Skype for Business (SFB). The added latency introduced often degrades call and video quality for remote users.

Summary

Force tunneling can be enabled for DirectAccess clients in order to address some of the security challenges imposed by split tunneling. However, there are some serious limitations and potentially negative side effects to implementing this change.

A more effective alternative to enabling force tunneling is to use the remote filtering capabilities of an existing on-premise firewall or web proxy server. Also, there are some excellent web-based security solutions for controlling Internet access for DirectAccess clients. Leveraging these will provide additional security for remote clients, while at the same time reducing the demands on the DirectAccess infrastructure. It will also provide a much better overall user experience for clients accessing Internet resources when connected via DirectAccess.

APPENDIX C

■ ■ ■

DirectAccess Security Hardening

The DirectAccess server is an access gateway by which remote users can access resources on the internal network. As such, it makes an appealing target for attackers. It is vital that the DirectAccess server is properly secured to ensure that it is not compromised.

In addition to common security implementation best practices, careful attention should be given to some of the default settings for the IP-HTTPS IPv6 transition technology, the SSL/TLS configuration, and the Windows firewall. Service hardening and attack-surface reduction can also be performed to further improve overall system security.

Security Best Practices

The DirectAccess server should be configured using industry standard security best practices,[1] which include removing or disabling any unneeded roles or features and disabling unused services. In addition, following security administration best practices and securing administrative workstations[2] is encouraged.

IP-HTTPS Preauthentication

When a client establishes a connection to the DirectAccess server using the IPv6 transition technology, the client authenticates the server, but the server does not authenticate the client. This is by design, as the transition tunnel was never meant to be a security enforcement point. That job is capably left to IPsec.

The default configuration for IP-HTTPS leaves open the potential for an unauthorized client to establish an IP-HTTPS connection to the DirectAccess server, allowing it to obtain an IPv6 address using the standard IPv6 Neighbor Discovery[3] process. This exposes the server and clients to possible IPv6 denial-of-service (DoS) attacks.[4]

Enabling IP-HTTPS preauthentication can mitigate this risk. The most effective way to do this is with an application delivery controller (ADC)[5,6]. If a suitable ADC is not available, IP-HTTPS preauthentication can be enabled on the IP-HTTPS listener itself.

---

[1]https://technet.microsoft.com/en-us/library/dd277328.aspx
[2]https://blogs.technet.microsoft.com/askpfeplat/2016/03/14/secure-administrative-workstations/
[3]https://en.wikipedia.org/wiki/Neighbor_Discovery_Protocol
[4]https://www.ernw.de/download/newsletter/ERNW_Newsletter_53_MS_DA_Security_Assessment_Signed.pdf
[5]https://directaccess.richardhicks.com/2016/05/10/directaccess-ip-https-preauthentication-using-citrix-netscaler/
[6]https://directaccess.richardhicks.com/2016/05/23/directaccess-ip-https-preauthentication-using-f5-big-ip/

R. M. Hicks, *Implementing DirectAccess with Windows Server 2016*, DOI 10.1007/978-1-4842-2059-7_16

To enable IP-HTTPS preauthentication, open an elevated PowerShell command window on the DirectAccess server and enter the following command:

```
netsh http show sslcert
```

Note the certificate hash of the SSL certificate assigned to the IP-HTTPS listener and provide it when entering the following commands:

```
netsh http delete sslcert ipport=0.0.0.0:443
netsh http add sslcert ipport=0.0.0.0:443 certhash=[certificate_hash] appid={5d8e2743-ef20-
4d38-8751-7e400f200e65} clientcertnegotiation=enable dsmapperusage=enable
```

■ **Note**   The previous steps must be performed on each DirectAccess server in load-balanced or multisite deployments.

Once IP-HTTPS preauthentication is enabled, only clients with a certificate issued by the internal PKI will be able to establish an IP-HTTPS connection to the DirectAccess server.

■ **Note**   Using IP-HTTPS preauthentication requires the deployment of computer certificates to all DirectAccess clients. However, certificate authentication for IPsec is optional. Preauthentication can still be performed in scenarios where the Kerberos Proxy is used.

Windows Firewall

For edge-facing and perimeter/DMZ deployments, where the DirectAccess server is configured with two network interfaces, configuration of the Windows firewall is crucial. Performing a port scan of the DirectAccess server's External network interface in the default configuration commonly indicates critical Transmission Control Protocol (TCP) ports left open and exposed to the Internet, including Remote Procedure Call (RPC - TCP port 135) and Server Message Block (SMB - TCP port 445) (Figure C-1) .

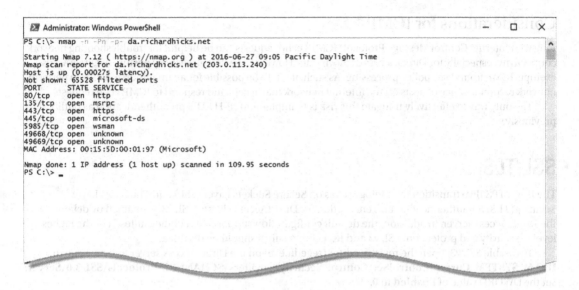

```
Administrator: Windows PowerShell                                    —   □   ×
PS C:\> nmap -n -Pn -p- da.richardhicks.net

Starting Nmap 7.12 ( https://nmap.org ) at 2016-06-27 09:05 Pacific Daylight Time
Nmap scan report for da.richardhicks.net (203.0.113.240)
Host is up (0.00027s latency).
Not shown: 65528 filtered ports
PORT       STATE SERVICE
80/tcp     open  http
135/tcp    open  msrpc
443/tcp    open  https
445/tcp    open  microsoft-ds
5985/tcp   open  wsman
49668/tcp  open  unknown
49669/tcp  open  unknown
MAC Address: 00:15:5D:00:01:97 (Microsoft)

Nmap done: 1 IP address (1 host up) scanned in 109.95 seconds
PS C:\> _
```

Figure C-1. *DirectAccess server external network port scan*

To remediate this exposure, remove the Public firewall profile from all firewall rules in the following firewall groups:

- Remote Access

- File and Printer Sharing

- Windows Remote Management

- World Wide Web Services (HTTP)

- Secure World Wide Web Services (HTTPS)

Alternatively, open an elevated PowerShell command window on the DirectAccess server and enter the following commands:

```
Set-NetFirewallRule -DisplayGroup "Remote Access" -Profile Public -Enabled False
Set-NetFirewallRule -DisplayGroup "File and Printer Sharing" -Profile Public -Enabled False
Set-NetFirewallRule -DisplayGroup "Windows Remote Management" -Profile Public -Enabled False
Set-NetFirewallRule -DisplayGroup "World Wide Web Services (HTTP)" -Profile Public -Enabled
False
Set-NetFirewallRule -DisplayGroup "Secure World Wide Web Services (HTTPS)" -Profile Public
-Enabled False
```

■ **Note**   These steps must be performed on each DirectAccess server in load-balanced or multisite deployments.

Considerations for ICMP

Ping with Internet Control Message Protocol (ICMP) echo requests can be helpful for troubleshooting network connectivity, especially for DirectAccess deployments. However, the default security posture of DirectAccess exempts ICMP from IPsec policy processing. As such, it might be possible for an unauthorized user to perform network reconnaissance of hosts on the internal network that accept and respond to ICMP echo requests.

The only way to effectively mitigate this risk is to implement IP-HTTPS preauthentication as outlined previously.

SSL/TLS

The IP-HTTPS IPv6 transition technology relies on Secure Sockets Layer (SSL) and Transport Layer Security (TLS) for authentication and encryption for DirectAccess clients. SSL v3[7] is enabled by default on the DirectAccess server. In addition, the default configuration supports RC4 cipher suites.[8] For the highest level of security and protection, SSL v3 and RC4 cipher suites should be disabled.

To disable SSL v3, open the registry editor (regedit.exe) on the DirectAccess server and navigate to **HKLM\SYSTEM\CurrentControlSet\Control\SecurityProviders\SCHANNEL\Protocols\SSL 3.0\Server**; set the DWORD value of **Enabled** to **0**.

■ **Note**   Create this registry key and value if it does not already exist.

To disable support for SSL and TLS cipher suites that use RC4, navigate to **HKLM\SYSTEM\ CurrentControlSet\Control\SecurityProviders\SCHANNEL\Ciphers** and set the DWORD value of **Enabled** to **0** in each of the following registry keys:

- RC 128/128
- RC4 40/128
- RC4 56/128

The following is a script to disable SSL v3 and RC4 cipher suites. Open an elevated PowerShell command window on the DirectAccess server and enter the following commands:

```
# // Disable SSL v3
New-Item -Path "HKLM:\SYSTEM\CurrentControlSet\Control\SecurityProviders\SCHANNEL\Protocols\
SSL 3.0\Server" -Force

New-ItemProperty -Path "HKLM:\SYSTEM\CurrentControlSet\Control\SecurityProviders\SCHANNEL\
Protocols\SSL 3.0\Server" -PropertyType dword -Value 0 -Name Enabled

# // Disable RC4 Cipher Suites
$writable = $true
$key = (get-item HKLM:\SYSTEM\CurrentControlSet\Control\SecurityProviders\SCHANNEL\).
OpenSubKey("Ciphers", $writable).CreateSubKey("RC4 128/128")
$key.SetValue("Enabled", "0", "DWORD")
```

---

[7]https://blog.qualys.com/ssllabs/2014/10/15/ssl-3-is-dead-killed-by-the-poodle-attack
[8]https://blog.qualys.com/ssllabs/2013/03/19/rc4-in-tls-is-broken-now-what

```
$key = (get-item HKLM:\SYSTEM\CurrentControlSet\Control\SecurityProviders\SCHANNEL\).
OpenSubKey("Ciphers", $writable).CreateSubKey("RC4 56/128")
$key.SetValue("Enabled", "0", "DWORD")

$key = (get-item HKLM:\SYSTEM\CurrentControlSet\Control\SecurityProviders\SCHANNEL\).
OpenSubKey("Ciphers", $writable).CreateSubKey("RC4 40/128")
$key.SetValue("Enabled", "0", "DWORD")
```

■ **Note**   Repeat these steps on each DirectAccess server in the load-balanced cluster and/or multisite deployment.

Null Cipher Suites

DirectAccess includes support for null-encrypted cipher suites. They are used by Windows 8.x and Windows 10 clients when using the IP-HTTPS IPv6 transition technology to connect to the DirectAccess server. The use of null-encrypted cipher suites is an important scalability and performance feature. It prevents the needless double encryption of DirectAccess communication.

Disabling support for null cipher suites should be avoided, as this provides no additional security benefits. Unlike SSL/TLS-based VPN or a web server, the DirectAccess workload is unique in that the payload is already encrypted. Encrypting it again serves no purpose. Removing support for null-encrypted cipher suites only reduces the overall scalability and performance of the solution.

Server Core

To provide the highest level of security for the DirectAccess server, it is recommended that the Server Core deployment mode be used. Server Core is a refactored installation option for Windows Server 2016 that does not include a graphical user interface (UI) or any Windows Shell components. Not only does this configuration drastically reduce the attack surface of the server, but it also reduces servicing requirements and disk space usage and speeds up system start-up times.

When a server is deployed using Server Core, it must be managed exclusively from the command line. Often it is easier to perform the initial installation, configuration, and testing with the full GUI installed. Once DirectAccess has been configured and tested, then the GUI can be removed prior to placing the server into production.

To convert a full GUI installation to Server Core, open an elevated PowerShell command window on the DirectAccess server and enter the following command:

```
Uninstall-WindowsFeature Server-Gui-Mgmt-Infra
```

Once complete, the server can only be managed locally via the command line using PowerShell, netsh. exe, or native operating system commands.

To manage the DirectAccess server remotely using either PowerShell or the Remote Access Management console, install the Remote Access Management Tools role on another Windows Server 2016 or 2012 R2 server by opening an elevated PowerShell command window and entering the following command:

```
Install-WindowsFeature RSAT-RemoteAccess -IncludeAllSubFeature
```

■ **Note** The DirectAccess server can be managed from a Windows 10 workstation by installing the Remote Server Administration Tools (RSAT), found here: `https://www.microsoft.com/en-us/download/details.aspx?id=45520`

Minimal Server Interface

An alternative to using Server Core is to configure the Minimal Server Interface. This is an installation mode that provides some of the benefits of Server Core but retains some of the familiar GUI management tools, such as the Remote Access Management console. To convert a full GUI installation to the Minimal Server Interface, open an elevated PowerShell command window on the DirectAccess server and enter the following command:

```
Uninstall-WindowsFeature Server-Gui-Shell
```

Summary

DirectAccess is a secure remote-access solution out of the box, but it can benefit from some additional security-hardening steps to further ensure the highest level of protection.

The default security posture can be improved by performing IP-HTTPS preauthentication and making some adjustments to the Windows firewall. The SSL/TLS configuration can be altered to mitigate potential security challenges, and the attack surface can be reduced significantly with the use of the Server Core configuration.

Index

R. M. Hicks, *Implementing DirectAccess with Windows Server 2016*, DOI 10.1007/978-1-4842-2059-7

■ T

■ U

■ V

■ W, X, Y, Z

Get the eBook for only $5!

Why limit yourself?

Now you can take the weightless companion with you wherever you go and access your content on your PC, phone, tablet, or reader.

Since you've purchased this print book, we're happy to offer you the eBook in all 3 formats for just $5.

Convenient and fully searchable, the PDF version enables you to easily find and copy code—or perform examples by quickly toggling between instructions and applications. The MOBI format is ideal for your Kindle, while the ePUB can be utilized on a variety of mobile devices.

To learn more, go to www.apress.com/companion or contact support@apress.com.

Printed in the United States
By Bookmasters

Printed in the United States
By Bookmasters